Wildflowers of Eastern America

A Chanticleer Press Edition

Wildflowers of Eastern America

John E. Klimas and James A. Cunningham

Galahad Books, New York

This edition published in the United States of America in 1981 by:
Galahad Books
95 Madison Avenue
New York, New York 10016
By arrangement with Alfred A. Knopf, Inc., New York.
First published in the United States by Alfred A. Knopf, Inc. in 1974.

Prepared and produced by Chanticleer Press, Inc., New York

Library of Congress Catalog Card Number: 81-81103
ISBN: 0-88365-556-X
Printed in the United States of America.

To our wives, Toni Klimas and Nancy Cunningham, for their encouragement, patience, and, most of all, understanding while this book was being written.

Contents

Preface

Preparation of this book involved the efforts of a number of people who deserve our gratitude.

The authors owe many thanks to the photographers who submitted the hundreds of transparencies from which the final selections that appear in this book were made.

Delwood J. Carr, superintendent of the Buckley Wildlife Sanctuary in Kentucky, was most gracious in letting us use many of his original wildfood recipes.

Larry Pardue, Plant Information Director at the New York Botanical Garden, reviewed the manuscript and made many helpful suggestions.

Rachel Speiser, former illustrator for the New York Botanical Garden, supplied the drawings of flower parts and types of leaves.

Milton Rugoff of Chanticleer Press contributed many useful editorial comments.

Finally, we especially acknowledge Celeste Targum of Chanticleer Press who worked closely with us during all phases in the preparation of the book—prodding us, encouraging us, coping with our frustrations and finally pulling the whole thing together.

JOHN E. KLIMAS
JAMES A. CUNNINGHAM

Fairfield, Connecticut

Introduction

In the eastern United States, wildflowers form a colorful part of our natural surroundings for at least six months of the year. When we hike or walk in the country we find them along stream banks, in meadows, and in the shadowy silence of the forest. In the city they spring up in parks, vacant lots and even in the city dump. When we drive, we see them lining highways and rural roads or growing in waste places besides railroad tracks. Wherever they appear they add freshness and beauty. That is why identifying such flowers has always fascinated many people. This book covers the most common and most widespread wild flowering plants in the eastern part of the United States, from Maine to North Carolina and westward to the Mississippi River. It does not cover those wildflowers of the Southeast, especially in Florida and the Gulf states. It contains over 300 color photographs and 365 descriptions of herbaceous wild flowering plants that because of color, size or abundance are most conspicuous and that the amateur naturalist or casual hiker is most likely to see. In addition to those fully described here, 180 similar species are mentioned and should prove easy to identify.

It would of course have been impossible in a single volume of convenient size to cover all of the more than 3000 species of herbaceous wild flowering plants found in the eastern United States. The selection we have made is based on the questions and reactions of participants in the wildflower walks and lectures we have given over the years. We have also included some localized plants of special interest and a few woody plants that are often mistaken for herbaceous. Since this book was written to make the study of wildflowers not only interesting but easy, we have often disregarded subtle identifying characteristics in favor of more obvious ones, but not, we trust, at the expense of botanical accuracy.

Learning to identify wildflowers is only half the pleasure of studying them. Most flowers have a story to tell about the origins of their scientific or common names, their uses as food and in folk medicine. To help readers get to know flowers as more than just a combination of petals, sepals, pistils and stamens, we have added notes on old flower customs, curious uses among the Indians and early settlers, and sundry legends and folktales.

What Is a Wildflower?

Any flowering plant that can grow and reproduce unattended by man may be considered a wildflower; that is not to say that it was not once cultivated by man. In fact, man introduced many of our common wildflowers either accidentally or by design. The seeds of some were brought in by animals, perhaps caught in their fur or imbedded in the mud in their hooves. Shipments of food seeds from Europe as well as dried plant fiber used as packing materials also contained flower seeds. Many early settlers brought with them the seeds of cultivated European flowers to plant in their gardens and some of these flowers eventually escaped cultivation and became part of our natural landscape. Other seeds were brought in by physicians who used parts of plants in medicines and lotions. Even today some of the newer species of cultivated plants are escaping from gardens, establishing themselves locally, and are thus on the way to becoming "wildflowers."

When and Where To Look for Wildflowers

In the spring one searches for wildflowers in the woods. Since most of these early-blooming plants grow from bulbs or tubers, they do not need to wait for the germination of seeds. They are, moreover, given an early start by the heat generated in the natural mulch of fallen leaves. Most of these flowers are short-lived and by the end of May or early June the trees have developed their foliage. Only a relatively few shade-tolerant plants will flower in the woods. By that time, meadows and open woods have started to bloom. Some of these plants continue to bloom until the fall, but others pass quickly. They are replaced by late-blooming species in late summer and early fall. Most of the plants found in woods and undisturbed fields are native; naturalized aliens rarely compete successfully with the "natives" in their natural habitat and are usually found in the disturbed soils along highways, in vacant lots and neglected gardens, or along railroad beds.

Names of Wildflowers

Man started classifying all living things thousands of years ago but the systematic arrangement we use today was begun in the mid-18th century by the great Swedish botanist, Linnaeus. He suggested that the scientific name of any living thing should consist of two words, usually in scientific Latin form. The second word is the species, which is a group of plants that are alike except for individual variation. The first word is the genus, which is a group of species that have many characteristics in common and are therefore closely related. For example, most clovers are of the genus *Trifolium* but there are many species of clover within the genus. Genera which have broad characteristics in common are grouped into families. The general characteristics of families of plants whose members are included are covered elsewhere in this book.

Although learning the scientific Latin names of flowers may seem formidable to the novice, these names can be very informative. Thus, the species name *stellata* indicates that the flower is star-shaped, and *hirsuta* indicates that the plant is hairy. When Linnaeus was classifying the plants of the New World he was sent samples from early settlements by pioneer botanists and this is reflected in species names such as *virginiana*, *canadensis*, or *americanum*. Many of these botanists were immortalized by Linnaeus when he Latinized their names into a genus or species, such as the genus *Claytonia*, which honors John Clayton, an early American botanist.

The common names of wildflowers may seem easier to learn than their scientific names, but some wildflowers have never been given a common name and others have more than one. The common names, moreover, may vary from region to region. However, such names have their place. Often steeped in lore, they lend a special association to a flower. Whenever possible, we have therefore explained the origin of these names.

Folklore and Uses

Among the lore of flowers is their use in various religious ceremonies. *Verbena* was used by ancient Greeks in all their sacred rites, and the plant still retains some of its aura of magic and mystery. Some tribal medicine men and early doctors experimented with various plants and by a process of trial and error (sometimes fatal) found quite a few that were useful. Many practiced their healing art according to the "doctrine of signatures." This superstition held that each medicinal plant had an outward sign or "signature" that revealed its specific use. Thus, medicines and potions prepared from plants having heart-shaped leaves were utilized to treat heart disease. The shape of the leaf of *Hepatica* (from Latin *hepaticus*, meaning "pertaining to the liver") was thought to resemble the three-lobed human liver. Hence, it was used by herb doctors to treat liver ailments. The milky juice of the milkweed was taken as a "signature" that the plant could insure the flow of milk in nursing mothers. Because *Saxifraga* forces its way through crevices on rocky cliffs (the name combines two Latin words meaning "stone-breaker"), herb doctors believed that its roots could be used as a medicine to break up kidney stones and gallstones. Because the foul odor and color of the Red Trillium (*Trillium erectum*) was thought to resemble rotted flesh, the plant was used as a treatment for gangrene. This belief in "like cures like" was even carried to the extreme of "irritant-needs-a-counterirritant": to relieve the pain of rheumatism, Stinging Nettle (*Urtica dioica*) was rubbed on the affected joint. Undoubtedly the pain caused by the nettle made the victim forget about the rheumatism!

One question often asked is whether there is any scientific justification for such medicinal uses. The answer is that chemical analysis of some herbs has shown that they contain ingredients that definitely have medicinal value. For example, Yarrow (*Achillea millefolium*), which was applied to wounds to stop bleeding, contains a blood-clotting substance. But in the majority of cases the plant was nothing more than a placebo—the equivalent of the sugar-coated pill which, when prescribed by a doctor in whom a patient has faith, can sometimes work wonders.

Wild flowering plants also had other uses. *Sanguinaria*, the Bloodroot, contains a bright red sap that was used by the Indians for dyeing garments and basketwork and by pioneers' children for coloring Easter eggs. The purple berries of Pokeweed (*Phytolacca americana*) were not only used as a source of dye but the juice from the crushed berries was added to cheap whiskey by Pennsylvania farmers in Colonial times to simulate a "port wine."

Wild flowering plants also provided food for many peoples. American Indians ate the roots and berries of the Jack-in-the-Pulpit (*Arisaema* spp.), the tuber of Dwarf Ginseng (*Panax trifolius*), and the Cucumber Root (*Medeola virginiana*). The Lewis and Clark expedition used the underwater stem of the Arrowhead (*Sagittaria* spp.) as the main source of starch in their diet. The tuber of the Groundnut (*Apios americana*), which could be sliced and cooked like potatoes, was said to have sustained the Pilgrims during their first hard winter in New England.

How To Use This Book

The color illustrations are coordinated with the species descriptions in the text. Each illustration bears the same number as its text description. In the simplified keys the same number again precedes the name of the flower.

Some species are described in the text but are not illustrated and are therefore not numbered. They appear in the text among similar species that are illustrated.

Identification by Color and Season

All the flowers included in this book have been grouped according to color because that is the most obvious characteristic to the amateur naturalist. Five color groups are used: White-Green (including cream); Red-Pink (including rose); Yellow-Orange (including salmon); Blue-Violet (including lavender and violet); and Brown (including various shades of purple-brown, orange-brown and coral). Since one color sometimes shades into another, and the reader's interpretation of a color may also differ from that of the authors, the reader may have to search through a second color group to identify a flower. Where several color variants occur within a species, the color most often encountered is illustrated; the other colors of the flower are noted in the text.

Within the color groupings, flowers have been arranged roughly in the order of their blooming season. Thus an early-blooming flower will be shown in the first part of a color section, while summer or fall flowers are shown later in these sections. Finally, within each seasonal group the flowers are arranged according to general visual similarities: spiked flowers with spiked flowers, bell-shaped flowers with bell-shaped flowers, and so forth.

Because of the large number of species in some genera, a particular species may not be illustrated but another species may be shown; this will often prove helpful in making an identification. Once you have found the photograph of a flower resembling the one you are trying to identify, check your identification with the description in the text.

Using the Simplified Keys

Another way to identify a flowering plant is through the basic structure of the flower and the shape and arrangement of the leaves. These characteristics are used in the Simplified Keys that precede the text for the section on each color.

For example, if the flower you wish to identify is **White**, blooms in the **Spring**, is **Irregular** and has **Basal, Dissected** leaves, the key identifies it as Dutchman's Breeches (25) or Squirrel Corn. You should then turn to the descriptions of these two species in order to distinguish between the two and for additional information.

Descriptions of Species

The following data are included in each species description:

1. *Common name.* If a plant has a common name, it heads the description. The names used are those that seem to be most common.

2. *Scientific name.* The authority for the names used is the 8th Edition of *Gray's Manual of Botany* by Merritt L. Fernald.

3. *Flowers on Protected List.* The names of flowers that are relatively rare or in danger of becoming so due to overpicking are marked with the symbol †. These flowers are on the conservation lists of the Garden Club of America and the New England Wild Flower Society, Inc..

4. *Family.* Both common and scientific names are given for each flower. The various families of plants are described in a special section. Once you recognize a plant as belonging to a particular family, this information can help you narrow down your search without the use of the other keys.

5. *Plant Height.* The height of the plant (given in both the English and metric systems) is often important in identifying it. Depending upon the environmental conditions, it may be somewhat taller or shorter than the average.

6. *Flower.* a. Size (an important detail, especially since it is sometimes difficult to judge the size of a flower from a photograph); b. Structure (arrangement of the various flower parts); c. Arrangement of the flowers on the stem.

7. *Leaves.* a. Shape; b. Shape of leaf margin; c. Arrangement of leaves on stem.

8. *In Bloom.* The time of flowering. If a plant grows throughout the entire area, the early blooming period applies to those growing in the southern part of our area and the later blooming period applies to those growing at higher elevations or in more northerly regions.

9. *Habitat-Range.* Most plants grow only in a particular habitat. However, some plants "never read the book" and may grow in what appears to be a hostile environment. Environmental conditions also determine the range and distribution of many flowering plants. Therefore, knowledge of the range can also be of aid in identification.

10. *General Information.* The description of each flower includes other distinguishing features of the plant, color variations, characteristics of its fruit, folklore, and short descriptions of similar species or plants similar in appearance.

Further Aids to Identification

Flowers (see drawings following Introduction).

The flower is the reproductive part of the plant; it yields the seeds that can produce new plants. Its color, odor, nectar and pollen attract insects that insure its fertilization. The stem on which a flower grows is known as a *pedicel.* A flower consists of a base or *receptacle* to which other parts are attached. On the outside there are generally two sets of *perianth* parts arranged in whorls; the outer one, composed of sepals, is the *calyx*; the inner one, composed of *petals*, is the *corolla.* Both calyx and corolla may be similar and petal-like, as in most lilies. However, in many flowering plants they are different, with the calyx usually green and the petals of some other color. The perianth gives shape to the flower; and although flowers vary greatly in form, we have placed each flower in one of four groups — *regular, irregular, composite* and *indistinguishable. Regular* flowers have their petals and/or sepals arranged, like the spokes of a wheel, symmetrically around the center. They may even form a cup or bell, but the arrangement will still be symmetrical. The petals and/or sepals of *irregular* flowers are not uniform in shape or size. They are grouped to form upper and lower "lips" which may be lobed or divided in various ways. Familiar examples of these kinds of flowers are orchids and snapdragons. A *composite* is not a single flower but consists of a central cluster of tiny regular flowers forming a disk surrounded by a circle of tiny irregular flowers with corollas that appear to be petals. A daisy is a familar example of a composite. *Indistinguishable* flowers have either no recognizable petals or sepals or these parts are too small to be seen clearly without a magnifying glass. The form of such flowers is too difficult to be analyzed by anyone but a botanist.

Usually arising from the center of a flower is a *pistil* (or *pistils*), each consisting of a basal, bulbous *ovary*, a filamentous *style* which terminates in a *stigma*, an organ receptive to pollen. After pollination, the pollen grain forms a tube which passes down the center of the style and enters the ovary, where fertilization takes place. Surrounding the pistil are the *stamens*, each consisting of an elongated *filament* on the end of which is an *anther*, which produces pollen.

Flowers may be *terminal*, that is occurring singly at the end of a stem, or they may be *axillary*, that is emerging from the angle formed at the point where the leaf joins the stem. Flowers often occur in clusters or *inflorescences*, which vary in arrangement and have been given various names. A *raceme* is composed of a long axis on which flowers with pedicels or stems are distributed. A *spike* is similar, but the flowers lack pedicels. A *corymb* is like a raceme, with pedicels of different length, those of the lower flowers being much longer than the upper which results in a round or flat-topped cluster. A *panicle* is a compound inflorescence that may consist of a cluster of racemes, spikes, or corymbs. An *umbel* is a flat-topped cluster of flowers the pedicels of which originate at the same point on the stem. A *cyme* is an inflorescence in which the terminal bud is the first to open. It differs from the raceme, spike, corymb and panicle, in that the lowest buds open first and the terminal buds continue to grow for an indefinite period. *Leaves* (see drawings following Introduction).

Leaves are the most conspicuous parts of most plants and their shape and arrangement on the stem provide important clues to identification. They are separated into *simple* and *compound* types. A simple leaf is undivided; a compound leaf is divided into sections called *leaflets*. If the leaflets radiate from the end of the leaf stem, known as a *petiole*, it is *palmate*, that is, shaped like a hand with extended fingers. If they are arranged along either side of the main axis, the leaf is *pinnate*, or feather-shaped. The leaflets of a pinnate leaf may in turn be divided into secondary leaflets, forming a *bipinnate* leaf. If even further subdivisions occur, the leaf is *dissected*.

Leaves have many different shapes apart from being simple or compound. They may be *linear* or grasslike, *ovate* (egg-shaped), *cordate* (heart-shaped), *sagittate* (arrow-shaped), *spatulate* (spoon-shaped), *lanceolate* (lance-shaped), *reniform* (kidney-shaped). The margins of the leaf may be *entire* (smooth), *undulate* (wavy), *lobed* (with deep, rounded indentations) or *toothed* (with small or large sawtooth edges).

Most leaves are attached to a stem or branch by a petiole, but if this is absent the leaf is said to be sessile. In some plants, especially herbs, the leaves all arise at ground level and are therefore *basal*. If these are arranged in a circle or whorl, they form a *basal rosette*. When the leaves, which often differ in size, shape, and texture from the other leaves of a plant, are directly beneath a flower or cluster of flowers, they are called *bracts*. Leaves may be *opposite* each other on a stem, or *alternate*. *Clasping* describes a leaf that wholly or partly surrounds its stem.

Parts of a Flower

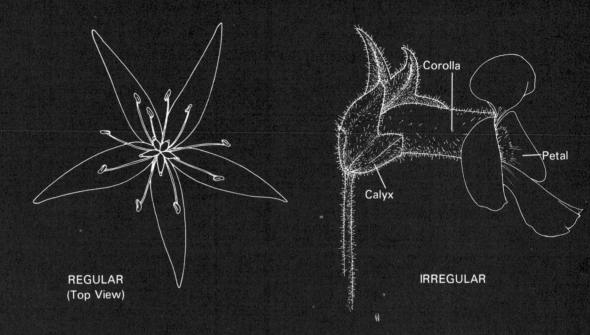

REGULAR
(Top View)

Corolla

Petal

Calyx

IRREGULAR

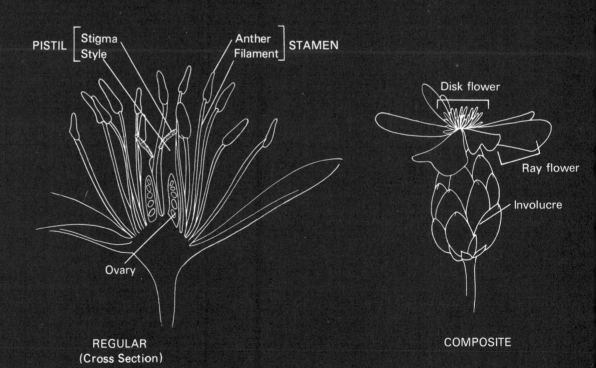

PISTIL [Stigma
Style

Anther
Filament] STAMEN

Ovary

REGULAR
(Cross Section)

Disk flower

Ray flower

Involucre

COMPOSITE

Flower Clusters

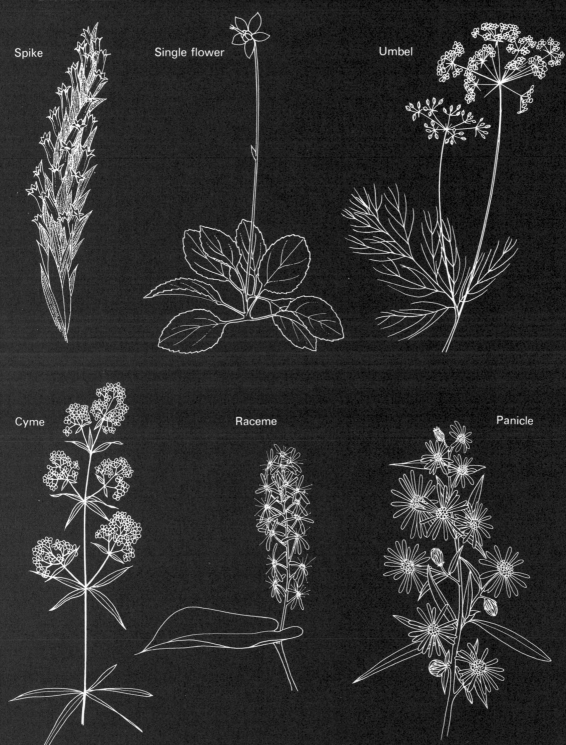

Spike

Single flower

Umbel

Cyme

Raceme

Panicle

Types of Leaves

SIMPLE

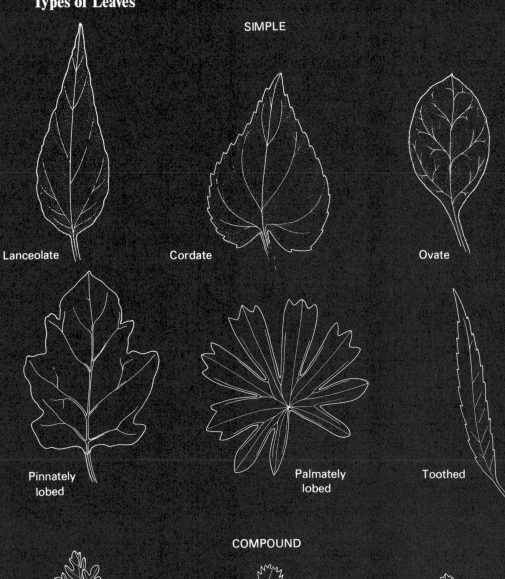

Lanceolate

Cordate

Ovate

Pinnately lobed

Palmately lobed

Toothed

COMPOUND

Dissected

Pinnate

Palmate

Arrangement of Leaves on Stem

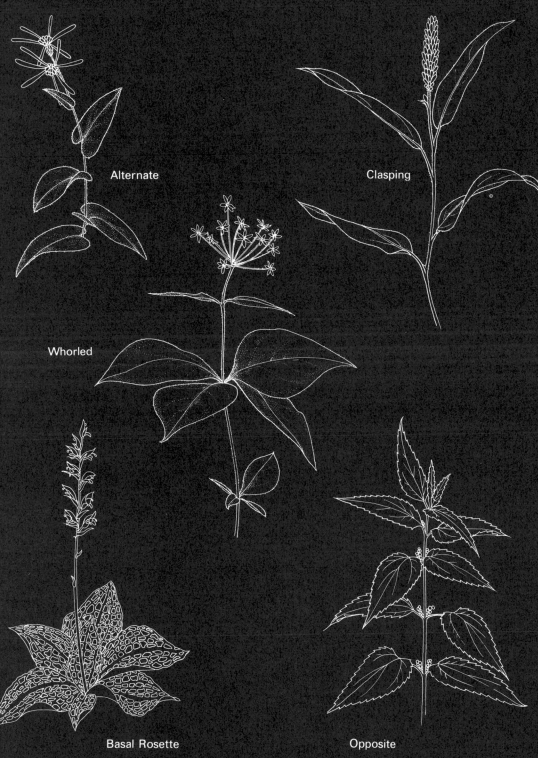

Alternate

Clasping

Whorled

Basal Rosette

Opposite

Glossary

Achene. A small, seedlike fruit containing one seed.

Alternate leaves. Arising singly from the stem, not in pairs.

Anther. The upper portion of a stamen, containing pollen grains.

Axil. The angle between the upper side of a leaf and the stem from which it rises.

Banner. Uppermost petal in a pea flower.

Basal leaves. Leaves at the base of the stem.

Berry. A fleshy fruit developed from a single ovary.

Bipinnate leaf. A compound leaf whose leaflets are divided into secondary leaflets.

Bracts. Modified leaves, usually situated at the base of a flower or inflorescence.

Bulb. A short underground stem, bearing fleshy food-storing scale leaves.

Calyx. Collective term for the leaflike sepals of a flower, usually green.

Campanulate. Bell-shaped.

Capsule. A dry fruit that splits open along several lines.

Cauline. Of or growing on a stem.

Clasping. A description of a leaf that wholly or partly surrounds its stem or petiole.

Claw. Narrowed base of a petal.

Composite flower. A central cluster of tiny regular flowers forming a disk surrounded by a circle of tiny irregular flowers with corollas that appear to be petals.

Compound leaf. A leaf divided into smaller leaflets.

Cordate. Heart-shaped.

Corm. A short, thickened underground stem, upright in position.

Corolla. Collectively, the petals of a flower.

Corymb. A form of inflorescence in which the lower pedicels or stems are longer, so that the flowers form a flat-topped or convex cluster.

Cross-pollination. The transfer of pollen from the anther of one plant to the stigma of a flower of another plant.

Cuneate leaf. Triangular and tapering to a point at the base.

Cyme. A type of inflorescence in which a terminal flower develops first, followed by secondary, tertiary, and other axes. The result is a flat or convex cluster.

Dioecious. Bearing male and female flowers on different plants of the same species.

Disc flower. The tubular flowers that compose the central part of a head of flowers in most Compositae.

Dissected leaf. Deeply cut into numerous segments.

Elliptic. Having the form of an ellipse.

Embryo. The small plant within the seed.

Entire leaf margin. Without divisions or teeth.

Exserted. Extending beyond, such as stamens protruding from a corolla.

Fascicle. A small bundle or cluster of fibers,leaves or flowers.

Filament. A thread; the stalk supporting an anther of a stamen.

Fimbriate. Fringed.

Glabrous. Bald.

Gland. A small secreting structure usually producing oil or nectar.

Glandular. Bearing glands that produce a sticky liquid.

Glaucous. A whitish powdery coating on the surface of leaves or fruit.

Head. A crowded cluster of sessile or nearly sessile flowers.

Herb. A nonwoody plant; usually remaining soft and succulent.

Indistinguishable flower. Lacking recognizable petals or sepals or with petals or sepals too small to be easily identified.

Inflorescence. A flower cluster; flowers collectively.

Involucre. A circle of bracts around a flower or flower cluster.

Irregular flower. With petals and/or sepals that are not uniform in shape but are usually grouped to form upper and lower "lips" that may be lobed

Keel. A ridge or rib; in a pea flower, the two lowest petals united along their lower margins.

Lanceolate leaf. Lance-shaped; much longer than wide; the widest portion below the middle.

Leaflet. One of the parts of a compound leaf.

Linear leaf. Long and narrow, with the margins essentially parallel.

Lobed. Indented at the margins not more than half way to the center.

Monoecious. Having both staminate and pistillate flowers borne on the same plant.

Node. The region of the stem where leaves or branches are attached.

Oblanceolate leaf. Shaped like a lance head; broadest toward the apex.

Obovate leaf. Egg-shaped, with narrow end at the base.

Opposite leaves. Leaves occurring in pairs at a node.

Ovary. The swollen basal portion of a pistil, within which seeds develop.

Ovate leaf. Egg-shaped, with broader end at the base.

Ovule. The immature seed in the ovary.

Palmate. With 3 or more divisions or lobes like outspread fingers of the hand.

Panicle. A compound raceme; elongated diversely branching flower cluster.

Pappus. A feathery tuft of bristles on certain fruits, as on the seeds of the dandelion.

Pedicel. The stalk of a flower.

Peduncle. A flower stalk or stem.

Perianth. The calyx or corolla or both.

Petal. A structural unit of a corolla; usually brightly colored.

Petiole. The stalklike portion of a leaf; attaches leaf to stem.

Pinnate leaf. A compound leaf with the leaflets arranged along the sides of a common petiole; literally like a feather.

Pistil. The female organ of a flower, typically consisting of a stigma, a tubular style, and an ovary at the base.

Pistillate flower. A flower with one or more pistils but no functional stamens.

Pod. Any dry fruit that opens on maturing.

Pollen. Spores produced in the anthers.

Pollination. The transfer of pollen from the anther to the stigma of the same or another flower.

Pubescent. Covered with hairs.

Raceme. An elongate, unbranched inflorescence in which the individual flowers are borne on pedicels along a stalk.

Ray flower. The flowers that encircle the disc flowers in some members of the daisy family.

Receptacle. End of the pedicel on which the flower parts are borne.

Regular flower. With petals and/or sepals arranged symmetrically around the center, like the spokes of a wheel.

Reniform. Kidney-shaped.

Rhizome. A horizontal underground stem, often enlarged by food storage; distinguished from roots by the presence of nodes.

Rootstock. Another term for rhizome.

Rosette. A circular cluster of leaves; usually basal.

Runner. A stem that grows horizontally over the surface of the soil, often developing new plants at the nodes or tip.

Sagittate. Arrow-shaped.

Saprophyte. A plant living on dead organic matter and lacking chlorophyll.

Scape. A leafless flower-bearing stem.

Sepal. A division of the calyx.

Serrated leaf. Having sharp teeth along the margin, resembling a saw.

Sessile. Without a stalk.

Sessile leaf. One lacking a petiole and with the blade attached directly.

Shrub. A branching woody plant.

Simple leaf. A leaf that consists of an undivided blade.

Spadix. A club-shaped spike of tiny flowers, usually enclosed in a spathe.

Spathe. A bract or pair of bracts, often large, enclosing an inflorescence.

Spatulate leaf. Shaped like a spatula; having a broad rounded end and a narrow base.

Species (abbreviation of plural, spp.). A fundamental category of taxonomic classification, ranking after a genus.

Spike. An elongated flower cluster with sessile or nearly sessile flowers.

Spur. A slender, usually hollow projection from some part of a flower.

Stamen. The male organ of a flower; composed of a filament topped with a pollen-producing anther; there are usually several in each flower.

Staminate flower. Bearing anthers and usually without pistils.

Standard. The upper petal or banner of a pea flower; also an iris petal.

Stigma. The tip of the pistil; it receives the pollen grains.

Stipules. Small leaflike appendages on either side of some petioles.

Style. The narrow part of the pistil, usually connecting ovary and stigma.

Succulent. A plant with fleshy, water-storing stems or leaves.

Tap root. A stout vertical root.

Tendril. A slender coiling modified leaf or stem that aids in the support of climbing plants.

Toothed leaf margin. With a sawtooth edge.

Umbel. A flower cluster in which the flower stalks arise from the same point, like the ribs of an umbrella.

Undulate. Having a wavy outer edge.

Whorled leaves. A circle of three or more leaves, branches, or pedicels at a node.

Wing. In plants, a projecting membrane found on margins of a seed, leaf, or leaf stalk; lateral petal of a pea flower.

Flower
Descriptions

Note:

The following descriptions are divided into five color groups: ✳ White·Green, ★ Yellow·Orange, ● Red·Pink, ■ Blue·Violet, and ▲ Brown. Within each color group, flowers have been arranged in the order of their blooming season, and within each season, according to general visual similarities.

Where several color variants occur within a species, usually the color most frequently encountered is illustrated; the other color variants are noted in the text.

Only the species descriptions illustrated in color bear a number; this is also the number of the color plate.

The simplified keys preceding the text for each color section will aid in the exact identification of a flower of that color. (See *Using the Simplified Keys*, page 13).

The glossary and drawings at the front of the book explain the terms used in this book.

The names of flowers that are relatively rare or endangered by overpicking are marked with a dagger (†) symbol.

White * Green

Key

SPRING (March-early May)	SUMMER (late May-early August)	FALL (late August-October)
Indistinguishable		
Single or two forming "V", palmate	*Basal, entire*	*Alternate, lobed*
26 Jack-in-the-Pulpit	91 Sweet flag	102 Great Ragweed
Basal, entire	*Basal, palmate*	*Opposite, toothed*
3 Field Pussytoes	87 Green Dragon	107 Boneset
28 Wild Calla	*Alternate, entire*	
27 Arrow Arum	56 Curled Dock	
	54 Branching Bur-reed	
	62 Flowering Spurge	
	36 Lizard's-tail	
	Alternate, palmate	
	88 Cow Parsnip	
	Angelica	
	Alternate, pinnate	
	80 Sweet Cicely	
	84 Water Hemlock	
	Alternate, dissected	
	83 Queen Anne's Lace	
	44 Yarrow	
	85 Fool's Parsley	
	Opposite, toothed	
	55 False Nettle	
	82 White Snakeroot	
	Whorled, entire	
	94 Bunchberry	
Regular		
Basal, toothed	*Basal, entire*	
19 Early Saxifrage	32 Flypoison	
Lettuce Saxifrage	52 White Clintonia	
Michaux's Saxifrage	29 Colicroot	
16 Foamflower	50 Water Plantain	
Miterwort	86 Sundew	
Basal, lobed	90 Broad-leaved Arrow-head	
22 Bloodroot	*Basal, toothed*	
Twinleaf	31 Galax	
Alternate, entire	69 Goldthread	
4 Trailing Arbutus	100 Wild Strawberry	
Alternate, toothed	Wood Strawberry	
15 Garlic Mustard	53 Round-leaved Pyrola	
18 Sicklepod	*Basal, palmate*	
Alternate, lobed	101 Common Wood-Sorrel	
12 Fringed Phacelia	*Alternate, entire*	
Oppostie, entire	49 False Hellebore	
7 Star Chickweed	39 Wild Lily-of-the-Valley	
17 Pennywort		

SPRING	SUMMER	FALL
(March-early May)	(late May-early August)	(late August-October)

Regular

Opposite, entire
11 Bladder Campion
   Forking Catchfly
   Evening Lychnis
Opposite, toothed
 9 Golden Seal
   Toothwort
24 Mayapple
Whorled, entire
 2 White Trillium
   Nodding Trillium
   Snow Trillium
 1 Painted Trillium
13 Starry Campion
Whorled, lobed
23 Rue Anemone
Whorled, toothed
14 Cut-leaved Toothwort
Whorled, palmate
   Wood Anemone
10 Dwarf Ginseng
Crowded on stem, entire
 5 Pyxie

Alternate, entire
49 False Hellebore
39 Wild Lily-of-the-Valley
79 Hairy Solomon's Seal
64 False Solomon's Seal
   Starry False Solomon's
    Seal
60 Hedge Bindweed
37 Devil's-bit
47 Featherbells
   Bunchflower
51 Pokeweed
Alternate, toothed
99 Horse-Nettle
43 Meadowsweet
92 White Avens
76 Checkerberry
61 Swamp Rose Mallow
33 Bugbane
   Wild Cucumber
Alternate, palmate
97 Bowman's-root
   American Ipecac
Alternate, pinnate
48 Goatsbeard
73 Virginia Waterleaf
81 White Baneberry
   Red Baneberry
74 Tall Meadow-Rue
Alternate, scale-like
93 Indian Pipe
67 Dodder
Opposite, entire
71 Mountain Sandwort
66 Poke Milkweed
78 Partridgeberry
38 Soapwort
   Intermediate Dogbane
63 Spreading Dogbane
Opposite, pinnate
75 Virgin's-bower
Whorled, entire
77 Indian Cucumber Root
68 Bedstraw

Key

	SPRING (March-early May)	SUMMER (late May-early August)	FALL (late August-October)
Regular			

	98 Maystar	
	Whorled, toothed	
	95 Spotted Wintergreen	
	30 Culver's-Root	
	Whorled, palmate	
	Thimble Weed	
	Single, entire	
	96 Grass-of-Parnassus	
	Floating, entire	
	89 Fragrant Water Lily	
	Leafless, when in bloom	
	65 Wild Leek	

Irregular

SPRING	SUMMER	FALL
Basal, toothed	*Basal, entire*	*Basal, entire*
6 Lance-leaved Violet	46 Bog Twayblade	103 Nodding Ladies Tresses
Basal, dissected	35 Downy Rattlesnake	
Squirrel Corn	Plantain	
25 Dutchman's Breeches	*Alternate, entire*	
Basal, scale-like	41 Helleborine	
20 One-flowered Cancer	42 White Fringed Orchis	
Root	*Alternate, palmate*	
Alternate, entire	45 White Clover	
8 Green Violet	*Alternate, pinnate*	
Alternate, toothed	34 White Sweet Clover	
Pale Violet	*Opposite, toothed*	
Opposite, entire	40 Catnip	
21 Japanese Honeysuckle	57 Bugleweed	
	58 Foxglove Beardtongue	
	59 Turtlehead	

Composite

SPRING	SUMMER	FALL
	Alternate, toothed	*Alternate, toothed*
	72 Daisy Fleabane	104 Silverrod
	70 Ox-eye Daisy	106 Rattlesnake Root
	Alternate, dissected	105 White Wood Aster
	Mayweed	

1 PAINTED TRILLIUM *(Trillium undulatum)*†   Lily family *(Liliaceae)*

Height: 5″-20″ (13-50cm). **Flower:** 2″-2 1/2″ (5-6cm) in diameter; regular, with 3 recurved and wavy-edged petals marked with red at their bases, 3 sepals, 6 stamens, 1 pistil with 3 stigmas; solitary, on upright stalk. **Leaves:** Oval; entire; three, in a whorl. **In bloom:** April-June. **Habitat-Range:** Acid woods and swamps; mainly in northern regions and in mountains in South.

    This trillium is easily recognized by the red color and veining at the base of its white petals.

2 WHITE TRILLIUM *(Trillium grandiflorum)*†   Lily family *(Liliaceae)*

Height: 8″-18″ (20-45cm). **Flower:** 2″-3″ (5-9cm) in diameter; regular, with 3 sepals, 3 petals, 6 stamens, 1 pistil with 3 stigmas; solitary, on slightly arched stalk. **Leaves:** Oval or egg-shaped; entire; three, in a whorl. **In bloom:** April-June. **Habitat-Range:** Rich woods and thickets; throughout, with exception of eastern New England.

    Trillium derives from the Latin *tri*, meaning "three," because trilliums have their parts in threes: three leaves, three sepals, three petals, three-chambered pistil with three stigmas and 6 stamens. The flower often turns pink with age and may then be confused with pink-flowered Catesby's Trillium (*T. catesbaei*) of the piedmont region and lower slopes of the mountains in the Southeast, but this flower has sickle-shaped sepals. A small species (4″-8″, 10-20cm tall) with white flowers that also turn pink with age is Little Trillium (*T. pusillum*). It is found only along the coastal plain from Virginia south and has narrow, oblong leaves. One of the larger and showier of early spring wildflowers, trilliums tend to be overpicked and are now on the conservation list. The plant grows from an underground stem that was chewed by Indians in the belief that it cured snakebite. It was also used as an astringent in diarrhea and as a uterine stimulant in childbirth. A concoction prepared from mashed roots steeped in water served to ease the pain of sore nipples in nursing mothers.

NODDING TRILLIUM *(Trillium cernuum)*†   Lily family *(Liliaceae)*

Height: 10″-18″ (25-45cm). **Flower:** 1 1/2″ (4cm) in diameter; regular, with 3 sepals, 3 petals, 6 stamens, 1 pistil with 3 stigmas; solitary, nodding on slender stalk. **Leaves:** Rhombic, tapering; entire; three, in a whorl. **In bloom:** April-July. **Habitat-Range:** Damp woods and thickets; mostly throughout and in mountains in South.

    Similar to *T. grandiflorum* but the flower is smaller and has purplish anthers and the leaves are rhomboid in shape. In the western part of our range we find Drooping Trillium (*T. flexipes*), which has a small (3/4″, 2cm long) drooping flower with white stamens and large, sessile leaves.

SNOW TRILLIUM *(Trillium nivale)*†   Lily family *(Liliaceae)*

Height: 2″-6″ (5-15cm). **Flower:** 1″ (2.5cm) in diameter; regular, with 3 oval petals, 3 sepals, 6 stamens, 1 pistil with 3 stigmas; solitary, on upright stalk. **Leaves:** Oval, small (1″-2″, 2-5cm long); entire; three, in whorl. **In bloom:** March-May. **Habitat-Range:** Rich woods, clearings; west of Appalachian mountains and south to Kentucky.

    Similar to *T. grandiflorum* but the plant and flower are much smaller.

3 FIELD PUSSYTOES *(Antennaria neglecta)* Composite family *(Compositae)*

Height: 4″-12″ (10-30cm). **Flower:** Tiny; indistinguishable, with many tubular flowers in composite head, dioecious; terminal cluster of several heads. **Leaves:** Spoon-shaped with single vein; entire; basal rosette. **In bloom:** April-July. **Habitat-Range:** Sterile fields, pastures; throughout.

This is the most common of the many species of pussytoes. A similar species, Plantain-leaved Pussytoes (*A. plantaginifolia*) is taller and has larger leaves with 3 to 5 veins. Pussytoes appear wooly and hairy, and the clusters of soft flower heads explains the common name. It spreads by runners and seems to produce a growth inhibitor that prevents other plants from growing near it. Observing this, country people packed dried flower heads with their stored woolens in the hope of keeping clothes moths out. It was also used in a hair shampoo to banish lice.

4 TRAILING ARBUTUS *(Epigaea repens)*† Heath family *(Ericaceae)*

Height: Prostrate, trailing. **Flower:** 5/8″ (1.5cm) long; regular, with tubular corolla spreading into 5 equal lobes, 10 stamens, 1 pistil; several, in axillary or terminal clusters; may sometimes be light pink. **Leaves:** Ovate, leathery, evergreen; entire; alternate. **In bloom:** March-May. **Habitat-Range:** Sandy or rocky woods and banks; throughout; in mountains in South.

Although we may not readily spot this plant in early spring, our attention is often drawn to it by its spicily fragrant flowers. Pushing aside leaf litter exposes a prostrate vine with leaves which may be covered with rust-colored hairs. Because of the shape of its leaves, it is also called Ground Laurel. Many attempts have been made to cultivate it but with little success. It has thus become relatively rare and appears on many conservation lists. The state flower of Massachusetts, it was celebrated by early American poets as the first flower to greet the Pilgrims in their first spring in New England. It was also used as an astringent by Indians and as a diuretic by pioneer doctors. Its species name combines Greek *epi*, "upon" and *gaea*, "earth."

5 PYXIE *(Pyxidanthera barbulata)* Diapensia family *(Diapensiaceae)*

Height: Prostrate, creeping. **Flower:** 1/4″ (6mm) in diameter; regular, with 5 wedge-shaped petals; solitary, but many on plant. **Leaves:** Small (1/4″, 6mm long), narrow, lanceolate; entire; mosslike, crowded on stem. **In bloom:** March-May. **Habitat-Range:** Sandy pine barrens; New Jersey, southeastern Virginia southward.

Because of its small leaves and habit of growing in a mat, the plant, when not in bloom, is often mistaken for moss.

6 LANCE-LEAVED VIOLET *(Viola lanceolata)* Violet family *(Violaceae)*

Height: 2″-6″ (5-15cm). **Flower:** 1/2″ (1cm) in diameter; irregular, with 5 petals, the lowest one extended back as a spur, the 3 lower ones with purple veins, not bearded, 5 stamens, 1 pistil; solitary, on leafless stalk. **Leaves:** Lance-shaped; rounded teeth; basal, upright. **In bloom:** March-July. **Habitat-Range:** Wet meadows, marshy places and bogs; throughout.

Violets are our most common and best known wildflowers. They all have 5 sepals, 5 petals, the lower one being extended back as a hollow spur, 2 side petals and a lower one sometimes with a beard, 5 stamens forming a cone-shaped cluster around the base of the solitary pistil. Besides showy flowers, many violets have flowers that never open but are self-pollinating and produce large quantities of seeds. Identifying a species is difficult because there are so many of them. Some, like *V. lanceolata*, have separate basal leaves and flower stalks; others have the flowers and leaves on the same stalk. The leaves of violets have been used to make expectorants and to relieve hoarseness and inflammation of the throat.

PALE VIOLET *(Viola striata)*   Violet family *(Violaceae)*

Height: 6″-12″ (15-30cm). **Flower:** 3/4″ (2cm) in diameter; irregular, with 5 creamy white petals, the lower one purple-stained and spurred, side ones strongly bearded and striped with purple, 5 stamens, 1 pistil; on slender stalks from leaf axils. **Leaves:** Heart-shaped; toothed; alternate, with fringed stipules. **In bloom:** April-June. **Habitat-Range:** Moist woods and meadows, along streams; throughout.

Similar to *V. lanceolata* but the flower and leaves are on the same stalk. The purple stripes on the lower and side petals and the fringed appendages where the leaves are attached to the stem make this species easy to identify.

7 STAR CHICKWEED *(Stellaria pubera)*   Pink family *(Caryophyllaceae)*

Height: 6″-16″ (15-40cm). **Flower:** 1/2″ (1cm) diameter; regular, with 5 deeply cleft petals, 10 stamens and 3 styles; several, in cyme. **Leaves:** Elliptically oblong, sessile; entire; opposite. **In bloom:** March-May. **Habitat-Range:** Rocky, wooded slopes; south of a line from New Jersey to Illinois.

Of the many species of this common weed, the one with the largest flowers is shown here. It is also called Great Chickweed. The generic name derives from Latin *stella,* "star," in reference to the shape and arrangement of the 5 petals, which are so deeply cleft the flower appears to have 10 pointed petals. The Common Chickweed, *S. media,* an unwelcome occupant of most lawns, has much smaller flowers, 1/4″ (6mm) in diameter, and the sepals are longer than the petals. It blooms throughout most of the year and produces large amounts of seed, which is eaten by many small birds in the wild. The whole plant is relished by canaries and other cage birds; hence the common name.

8 GREEN VIOLET *(Hybanthus concolor)*   Violet family *(Violaceae)*

Height: 1′-3′ (.3-1m). **Flower:** 1/4″ (6mm) diameter; irregular, with sepals and petals about equal in length and shape but lowest petal is sac-like; single or small clusters, drooping from leaf axils. **Leaves:** Elliptical with pointed tips; entire; alternate. **In bloom:** April-June. **Habitat-Range:** Rich woods, ravines; throughout, except upper New England.

The small green flowers only remotely resemble violets but the pistil is clublike and the stamens encircle the ovary in the characteristic violet manner.

9 GOLDEN SEAL *(Hydrastis canadensis)*†   Buttercup family *(Ranunculaceae)*

Height: 8″-12″ (20-30cm). **Flower:** 1/2″ (1cm) diameter; regular, with no petals or sepals, many pistils and stamens; terminal, solitary. **Leaves:** Rounded with 5-7 lobes;

sharply toothed; one opposite pair at summit, single basal leaf. **In bloom:** April-May. **Habitat-Range:** Rich woods; south of a line from Vermont to Minnesota.

The stem is hairy. In summer the pair of stem leaves is overshadowed by a long, stalked basal leaf that is 5″-8″ (13-20cm) broad, and the fruit, a cluster of crimson berries, is conspicuous. The plant arises from a bright yellow underground stem, which accounts for its other common name, Orangeroot. Many Indian tribes extracted the yellow juice and used it as a dye, and some pounded the rootstock along with bear grease and smeared it on their bodies as an insect repellant. The rootstock was also boiled in water by Indians and early settlers and the water served as a wash for skin diseases. The plant was used to treat inflammation of the throat and eyes, stomach ailments, and as a laxative. Because of its popularity as a medicinal plant, it has disappeared from some areas and is on conservation lists.

10 DWARF GINSENG *(Panax trifolius)*   Ginseng family *(Araliaceae)*

Height: 4″-8″ (10-20cm). **Flower:** 1/4″ (6mm) in diameter; regular, with 5 petals, staminate and pistillate flowers on different plants; many, in umbel. **Leaves:** Palmate, 3-5 leaflets; toothed; three, in whorl at summit. **In bloom:** April-June. **Habitat-Range:** Rich woods and damp clearings; throughout northern part of range and in mountains in South.

The generic name combines two Greek words, *pan*, "all," and *akos*, "cure," proclaiming that this plant is a cure-all. It has been used as a medicinal plant for centuries. Its tuber is edible and it was used as a source of starch. A larger, but less common species, *P. quinquefolius*, has 5 leaflets and a large root that is spindle-shaped and is often forked. The root is still used by the Chinese in their medicines.

11 BLADDER CAMPION *(Silene cucubalus)*   Pink family *(Caryophyllaceae)*

Height: 8″-20″ (20-50cm). **Flower:** 3/4″ (2cm) in diameter; regular, with globular calyx, 5 petals with deep clefts, 10 stamens, 3 styles; several, in cyme. **Leaves:** Lanceolate or ovate; entire; opposite. **In bloom:** April-August. **Habitat-Range:** Roadsides, borders of fields; throughout.

The sepals form a sac which is narrower at the open end than in the middle; hence the reference to a bladder in the common name. Early writers say that a thick, downy-leaved plant of this family was dried and used by soldiers in the field as wicks for their lamps. Snowy Campion (*S. nivea*) is a similar species that grows chiefly in the western part of our range but its calyx is bell-shaped and the petals are merely notched.

EVENING LYCHNIS *(Lychnis alba)*   Pink family *(Caryophyllaceae)*

Height: 1′-2′ (.3-.6m). **Flower:** 1″ (2.5cm) in diameter; regular, with globular calyx, 5 petals with deep clefts, 10 stamens, 5 styles; several, in corymb. **Leaves:** Lanceolate; entire; opposite. **In bloom:** May-September. **Habitat-Range:** Roadsides, borders of fields, waste places; mostly throughout.

Similar to *S. cucubalus* but the plant is sticky, flowers have 5 styles instead of 3, and the plant is dioecious with the staminate and the pistillate flowers on different plants. This plant opens at dusk and is very fragrant. It may often be confused with Night-flowering Catchfly (*Silene noctiflora*), but the flowers of the latter have 3 styles.

FORKING CATCHFLY *(Silene dichotoma)*   Pink family *(Caryophyllaceae)*

Height: 2′-3′ (.6-1m). **Flower:** 3/4″ (2cm) in diameter; regular, with tubular calyx, 5 petals with deep clefts, 10 stamens, 3 styles; several, in raceme. **Leaves:** Lanceolate or oblong; entire; opposite. **In bloom:** June-September. **Habitat-Range:** Fields and waste places; throughout.

Similar to *S. cucubalus* but calyx is not inflated and flowers are sessile. The upper stem forks, bearing flowers on only one side of each branch. The plant is very hairy and sticky and this ensnares flying and crawling insects; hence its common name. The generic name is from the Greek *sailon*, meaning "saliva," another allusion to the viscid exudation of the plant.

12 FRINGED PHACELIA *(Phacelia fimbriata)*   Waterleaf family *(Hydrophyllaceae)*

Height: 6″ (15cm). **Flower:** 1/2″ (1cm) diameter; regular, with 5 fringed petals forming a bell-shaped corolla, 5 stamens, 1 pistil; several, in loose cyme. **Leaves:** Oblong, stem leaves sessile, basal leaves with petiole; 5-9 blunt lobes; alternate. **In bloom:** May-June. **Habitat-Range:** Rich woods and along streams; uplands and mountains in West Virginia, western North Carolina and eastern Tennessee.

Its fringes may be pink or lavender. They occur in such masses in some areas that they resemble patches of snow. A more common, taller (12″-18″, 30-45cm) species that grows as far north as Wisconsin is the Pursh Phacelia (*P. purshii*), whose flowers are lavender-blue with a white center.

13 STARRY CAMPION *(Silene stellata)*   Pink family *(Caryophyllaceae)*

Height: 2′-3′ (.6-1m). **Flower:** 3/4″ (2cm) in diameter; regular, with bell-shaped calyx, 5 petals with fringed margins, 10 stamens, 3 styles; several, in upper leaf axils. **Leaves:** Lanceolate; entire; mostly in whorls of four. **In bloom:** June-September. **Habitat-Range:** Woods and clearings; south of a line from Massachusetts to Wisconsin.

Similar to *S. cucubalus* but its petals are fringed and its leaves are mostly in whorls of four.

14 CUT-LEAVED TOOTHWORT *(Dentaria laciniata)*   Mustard family *(Cruciferae)*

Height: 8″-15″ (20-37cm). **Flower:** 1/2″ (1cm) in diameter; regular, with 4 petals in form of cross, 6 stamens, 2 shorter than other 4, 1 pistil; several, in terminal raceme. **Leaves:** Palmate, 3 narrow lobes; sharply toothed; stem leaves in a whorl of three, basal leaves upright. **In bloom:** April-June. **Habitat-Range:** Rich woods, wooded bottoms; mostly throughout.

Similar to *D. diphylla* but leaves are thin-lobed and are arranged in a whorl of three. The rootstock is jointed and not toothed and it tastes peppery, like horseradish. When the flowers fade they may turn pink.

TOOTHWORT *(Dentaria diphylla)*   Mustard family *(Cruciferae)*

Height: 8″-15″ (20-37cm). **Flower:** 1/2″ (1cm) in diameter; regular, with 4 petals in form of cross, 6 stamens, 2 shorter than other 4, 1 pistil; several, in terminal cluster; turns pink when fading. **Leaves:** Palmate, 3 oval leaflets; bluntly toothed; 2 opposite each other on stem and one basal and upright. **In bloom:** April-June. **Habitat-Range:** Rich woods; throughout.

The plant grows from an underground stem that is wrinkled and has small, toothlike projections; hence its common and generic name (from Latin *dentis*, meaning "tooth"). It is also called Crinkleroot. The crisp rhizome can be chopped and added to salads and was boiled and eaten as a root crop by Indians.

15 GARLIC MUSTARD *(Alliaria officinalis)*   Mustard family *(Cruciferae)*

Height: 1'-3' (.3-1m). **Flower:** 1/2" (1cm) in diameter; regular, with 4 petals in form of cross, 6 stamens, 1 pistil; several, in loose raceme. **Leaves:** Triangular or broadly heart-shaped; sharply toothed; alternate. **In bloom:** April-June. **Habitat-Range:** Roadsides, open woods, waste places; mostly throughout.

As a member of the mustard family, the plant produces erect seed pods. But unlike other mustards, it emits the odor of garlic when crushed, which explains its common and generic names (*allium*, the Latin for "garlic"). It was long used as a condiment or salad green by country people.

16 FOAMFLOWER *(Tiarella cordifolia)*   Saxifrage family *(Saxifragaceae)*

Height: 5"-12" (13-30cm). **Flower:** 1/4" (6mm) in diameter; regular, with 5 tapering petals, 10 stamens longer than petals, 2 styles; many, in raceme on leafless stalk. **Leaves:** Heart-shaped, with 3 to 7 shallow lobes; sharply toothed; basal, upright. **In bloom:** April-July. **Habitat-Range:** Rich woodlands; throughout, but mainly in the mountains.

This hairy plant spreads by runners and forms small colonies. The generic name is the diminutive of the Greek *tiara*, a kind of turban worn by ancient Persians, which the pistil was thought to resemble.

MITERWORT *(Mitella diphylla)*   Saxifrage family *(Saxifragaceae)*

Height: 10"-18" (25-45cm). **Flower:** 1/4" (6mm) in diameter; regular, having 5 fringed petals, 10 stamens, 2 styles; several, in slender raceme. **Leaves:** Heart-shaped, with 3 to 5 shallow lobes; sharply toothed; basal leaves upright, 2 stem leaves sessile and opposite. **In bloom:** April-June. **Habitat-Range:** Rocky woods; mostly throughout.

Similar to *T. cordifolia* (often called False Miterwort) but the flower petals are fringed and the flower stalk has a pair of sessile leaves. The much smaller (3"-7", 8-18cm) Naked Miterwort (*Mitella nuda*) which grows in northern regions has greenish yellow flowers, kidney-shaped basal leaves, and a leafless flower stalk. The common and generic names allude to the small seed pod, which has the shape of a bishop's miter, a tall ornamented cap with peaks in front and back.

17 PENNYWORT *(Obolaria virginica)*   Gentian family *(Gentianaceae)*

Height: 3"-6" (8-15cm). **Flower:** 1/2" (1cm) long; regular, with 4 petals and two sepals that resemble leaves; usually group of 3 in leaf axils and single terminal one. **Leaves:** Small (1/2", 1cm long), round; entire; opposite. **In bloom:** March-May, **Habitat-Range:** Moist woods and thickets; south of a line from New Jersey to Illinois.

The plant has a smooth, fleshy, purplish green stem. Although the lower leaves are scale-like, the upper ones are thick and round. Their shape reminded early botanists of a small Greek coin, an *obolos*, similar to a penny; hence the generic and common names.

18 SICKLEPOD *(Arabis canadensis)*   Mustard family *(Cruciferae)*

Height: 1'-3' (.3-1m). **Flower:** 1/4″ (6mm) in diameter; regular, with four petals in form of cross, 6 stamens, 1 pistil; several, in loose raceme. **Leaves:** Basal rosette leaves lanceolate and toothed; stem leaves lanceolate, toothed, alternate. **In bloom:** June-September. **Habitat-Range:** Rich woods, thickets and rocky banks; mostly throughout.

The outstanding feature of this plant is the long (4″, 10cm) seed pods that develop and droop downward. They resemble the blade of a sickle; hence the common name. Smooth Rock Cress (*A. laevigata*) is a similar species but it has a powdery, grayish green bloom and its leaves have clasping bases.

19 EARLY SAXIFRAGE *(Saxifraga virginiensis)*†   Saxifrage family *(Saxifragaceae)*

Height: 4″-12″ (10-30cm). **Flower:** 1/4″ (6mm) diameter; regular, with 5 petals, 10 stamens, 2 pistils; many, in loose panicle, on leafless stalk. **Leaves:** Wedge-shaped or oval; coarsely toothed; basal rosette. **In bloom:** March-May. **Habitat-Range:** Dry or wet rocks, rocky slopes and ledges; throughout.

This is one of the most widespread saxifrages and one of the earliest to bloom. Its leaves are often purplish underneath. Because saxifrages are rooted in cracks in rocks and ledges, early botanists combined two Latin words to name them—*saxum*, "stone," and *fragere*, "to break." This also was taken as a "signature" by herb doctors, who used them to treat kidney stones and gallstones. The flower stalks are usually covered with sticky, glandular hairs which entrap crawling insects and prevent them from taking nectar.

LETTUCE SAXIFRAGE   Saxifrage family (*Saxifragaceae*)
(Saxifraga micranthidifolia)

Height: 1'-3' (.3-1m). **Flower:** 1/4″-1/2″ (.6-1cm) diameter; regular, with 5 petals spotted with yellow, 10 stamens, 2 pistils; many, on widely branched panicle. **Leaves:** Long (6″-12″, 15-30cm), oblong; sharply toothed; basal rosette. **In bloom:** May-June. **Habitat-Range:** Wet rocks, along banks of mountain streams; Pennsylvania, West Virginia and southward to Tennessee and Georgia.

Similar to *S. virginiensis* but it is taller, the petals are spotted with yellow, and the leaves are long and narrow. It is also known as Mountain Lettuce because the leaves are eaten as greens by mountain people.

MICHAUX'S SAXIFRAGE *(Saxifraga michauii)*   Saxifrage family *(Saxifragaceae)*

Height: 6″-20″ (15-50cm). **Flower:** 1/4″-1/2″ (.6-1cm) diameter; regular, with 5 petals spotted with yellow, 3 of them larger than the other two, 10 stamens, 2 pistils; many, on widely branched panicle. **Leaves:** Short (2″-4″, 5-10cm), oblong; coarsely toothed; basal rosette. **In bloom:** June-October. **Habitat-Range:** Rocky cliffs, crevices in rocks; western Virginia, West Virginia southward to Georgia and Tennessee.

Similar to *S. micranthidifolia* but the flower is not symmetrical because its petals are of different sizes and its leaves are much shorter. Its species name honors its discoverer, an 18th-century botanist, André Michaux. Another similar southern species found only in the mountains of West Virginia, western North Carolina and eastern Tennessee is Carolina Saxifrage, *S. caroliniana;* it has oval, coarsely toothed leaves and symmetrical flowers.

20 ONE-FLOWERED CANCER ROOT　　　　Broomrape family *(Orobanchaceae)*
(Orobanche uniflora)

Height: 2″-10″ (5-25cm). **Flower:** 3/4″-1″ (1.5-2.5cm) long; irregular, with 5 petals forming a tubular corolla with two lips, bearded folds in the throat; solitary, at summit of stem; may also be pink or lavender. **Leaves:** White, scale-like; basal. **In bloom:** April-June. **Habitat-Range:** Parasitic on various plants in deep woods and thickets; throughout.

As the common and species names suggest, it bears a single flower. Lacking green foliage it cannot manufacture its own food and is parasitic on the roots of other plants. This "signature" suggested to early herb doctors that the plant could be used to treat cancer, which was considered to be a parasitic-like disease.

21 JAPANESE HONEYSUCKLE　　　　Honeysuckle family *(Caprifoliaceae)*
(Lonicera japonica)

Height: Trailing vine. **Flower:** 1 1/4″ (3cm) long; irregular, with two lips forming tubular corolla, upper lip having 3 lobes, lower lip having 2 lobes, 5 stamens, 1 pistil; usually in pairs from leaf axils. **Leaves:** Oval; entire; opposite. **In bloom:** April-July. **Habitat-Range:** Thickets, borders of woods, roadsides; mostly throughout.

Introduced into America from Asia, especially for its extremely fragrant flowers, which are initially white but turn a buffy yellow, this vine escaped from cultivation. It has become a very troublesome weed, especially in the South, strangling the native flora wherever it grows. Its black berries were used as a diuretic. A tea made from the leaves was used to treat sore throats.

22 BLOODROOT *(Sanguinaria canadensis)*†　　　　Poppy family *(Papaveraceae)*

Height: 6″-12″ (15-30cm). **Flower:** 1 1/2″ (4cm) diameter; regular, with 8-12 oblong petals, numerous stamens, 1 pistil; solitary, terminal, on leafless stem. **Leaves:** Palmate, 5-9 lobes; lobes often cleft; basal, upright. **In bloom:** March-May. **Habitat-Range:** Rich woods, low hillsides; mostly throughout.

This delicate flower is short lived and opens only in full sunshine. The leaf is wrapped around the flower bud as it emerges from the ground and does not expand fully until the flower has bloomed. The underground stem contains a reddish juice that accounts for its common and generic names (from Latin *sanguinarius,* meaning "bleeding"). Indians used the juice as an insect repellant, a treatment for rheumatism and ringworm, a dye for clothing and basketwork, and as a warpaint. In pioneer medicine it was used as an expectorant in bronchitis and asthma.

TWINLEAF *(Jeffersonia diphylla)*　　　　Barberry family *(Berberidaceae)*

Height: 6″-8″ (15-20cm). **Flower:** 1″ (2.5cm) diameter; regular, with 8 oblong petals,

8 stamens, 1 pistil; solitary, terminal, on leafless stalk. **Leaves:** Round, deeply cleft into 2 divisions, entire; upright, on long petiole. **In bloom:** April-May. **Habitat-Range:** Rich shady woods; mostly throughout, with the notable exception of New England.

The flower closely resembles *Sanguinaria canadensis* but the leaf is different. The species name, combining Greek *di*, "two", and Latin *phyllon*, "leaf," describes the distinguishing characteristic of this plant, viz., a leaf so deeply divided that it seems to have two blades. At flowering time the leaf may be only partly developed and folded. The generic name honors Thomas Jefferson.

23 RUE ANEMONE (*Anemonella thallictroides*)†   Buttercup family (*Ranunculaceae*)

Height: 4"-8" (10-20cm). **Flower:** 1/2"-1" (1-2.5cm) in diameter; regular, with 5-10 petal-like sepals, numerous stamens and pistils; 2 or 3, solitary, on thin stalks. **Leaves:** Roundish with 3 round lobes; in whorl of three leaves. **In bloom:** April-June. **Habitat-Range:** Open woods; mostly throughout.

Anemones are characterized by colored, petal-like sepals and an absence of petals. The flowers stand on long thin stalks and tremble in the slightest wind; hence their common name, Windflowers. Their generic name honors the Greek wind god, Anemose. In ancient times it was believed that a wind that had passed over a field of anemones was poisoned and could cause sickness, which may explain why the Persians adopted this flower as an emblem of illness. Most species of anemone contain a caustic juice that was once used to burn out corns and to treat gout and rheumatism.

WOOD ANEMONE (*Anemone quinquefolia*)†   Buttercup family (*Ranunculaceae*)

Height: 4"-12" (10-30cm). **Flower:** 1" (2.5cm) in diameter; regular, with 4-9 petal-like sepals, numerous stamens and pistils; solitary, on thin stalk. **Leaves:** Palmate, 3-5 narrow leaflets; sharply toothed; three, in whorls at stem summit. **In bloom:** April-June. **Habitat-Range:** Open woods, thickets and clearings; mostly throughout.

Similar to *A. thallictroides* but flower is solitary and the leaves are toothed. This is one of the earliest blooming anemones and in the western part of our range the plant stem may be hairy.

THIMBLE WEED (*Anemone virginiana*)   Buttercup family (*Ranunculaceae*)

Height: 2'-3' (.6-1m). **Flower:** 1" (2.5cm) in diameter; regular, with 4-9 petal-like sepals, numerous stamens and pistils; solitary, on thin stalks. **Leaves:** Palmate, 3 leaflets; variously cleft and toothed; three, in whorls at stem summit. **In bloom:** June-August. **Habitat-Range:** Dry or rocky open woods and thickets; mostly throughout.

Similar to *A. quinquefolia* but plant is taller and hairy. The common name derives from the seed head, which is thought to resemble a thimble. A similar northern species, Canada Anemone, *A. canadensis*, is shorter, its leaves are sessile, and the seed head is ball-like.

24 MAYAPPLE (*Podophyllum peltatum*)†   Barberry family (*Berberidaceae*)

Height: 1'-1 1/2' (.3-.5m). **Flower:** 2" (5cm) in diameter; regular, with 6-9 waxy petals, 12-18 stamens, 1 pistil; solitary, nodding in fork between leaves. **Leaves:** Palmate, 5-7 lobes; deeply toothed; two, forming terminal fork. **In bloom:** April-June. **Habitat-**

Range: Rich woods, thickets and pastures; throughout.

Often a pair of umbrella-like leaves catches the eye before the flower is seen nodding underneath. The flower develops into a large, lemon-like berry which is edible and has been made into jams and jellies. Although the leaves and roots are poisonous if a large amount is taken internally, the plant has been used medicinally. Indians used it for its cathartic effect and colonists followed suit. It was also used in the treatment of syphillis, and a compound isolated from the root has found use in treating some human tumors. Locally it is often called Mandrake, but this name belongs to an unrelated European plant.

25 DUTCHMAN'S BREECHES *(Dicentra cucullaria)*†   Poppy family *(Papaveraceae)*

Height: 5"-10" (13-25cm). **Flower:** 3/4" (2cm) long; irregular, flattened, with 4 petals, the two small inner ones with spoon-shaped tips, the two larger outer ones with spurs in the form of the letter V; several, nodding in racemes. **Leaves:** Dissected; basal, upright. **In bloom:** April-May. **Habitat-Range:** Rich woods on rocky slopes; mostly throughout, in mountains in South.

The common name derives from the shape of the flowers, which reminded early botanists of white pantaloons on a clothesline with yellow-belted waists down and the ankles up. The plant grows from a bulb, which was dried and used medicinally as a tonic and blood purifier.

SQUIRREL CORN *(Dicentra canadensis)*   Poppy family *(Papaveraceae)*

Height: 6"-8" (15-20cm). **Flower:** 1/2" (1cm) long; irregular, flattened, with 4 petals, the two small inner ones with spoon-shaped tips, the two large outer ones forming short rounded spurs which point upward; several, nodding in raceme. **Leaves:** Dissected; upright, basal. **In bloom:** April-May. **Habitat-Range:** Rich woods; mostly throughout.

Similar to *D. cucullaria* but the flowers lack the large spurs, are more heart-shaped, and have the odor of hyacinth. The common name refers to the small yellow tubers that occur on its rootstock and resemble grains of corn.

26 JACK-IN-THE-PULPIT *(Arisaema triphyllum)*†   Arum family *(Araceae)*

Height: 1'-3' (.3-1m). **Flower:** Tiny; irregular; many, at base of clublike spadix, hidden by hoodlike spathe, which is often marked with purple or white lines. **Leaves:** Palmate, 3 lanceolate, pointed leaflets; entire; single, upright leaf on long petiole, sometimes two forming a "V". **In bloom:** April-June. **Habitat-Range:** Moist woodlands and thickets; throughout.

The most conspicuous part of this plant, the spathe, forms the "pulpit" and curves over to provide a canopy for the spadix, "Jack." The inconspicuous flowers, which may be staminate and/or pistillate, cluster at the base of the spadix. In late summer the flower is replaced by a clump of glossy red berries. These were once gathered, boiled and eaten by the Indians. They also used the ground-up corm as a pepper substitute, a practice adopted by white settlers. The peppery quality is due to crystals of calcium oxalate which cause a burning sensation in the mouth. Thus, the corm was used as a counterirritant for sore throat and bronchitis. The Indians learned to remove the irritant crystals by boiling the corms and then ate them; hence another common name, Indian Turnip.

27 ARROW ARUM *(Peltandra virginica)* Arum family *(Araceae)*

Height: 1'-4' (.3-1m). **Flower:** Tiny; irregular; many, on spadix enclosed in conical spathe. **Leaves:** Arrow-shaped; entire; upright from base. **In bloom:** May-July. **Habitat-Range:** Swamps, stream and pond borders, wet spots; throughout.

The long (4"-8", 10-20cm), conical green spathe almost conceals the spadix with its many minute flowers. The bulbous, basal portion of the spathe houses the pistillate flowers while its tapered upper part contains staminate flowers. Green berries are produced in the fall, and the plant has a unique way of planting its seeds: the berry stalk, covered with the spathe, which is then dry and leathery, curves and grows downward, boring a hole into the soft mud. The starchy corms from which the plant grows were roasted and eaten by Indians in Virginia. In the southern part of our area the White Arrow Arum, *P. sagittaefolia,* resembles *P. virginica* but has a white spathe and produces red berries.

28 WILD CALLA *(Calla palustris)* Arum family *(Araceae)*

Height: 8"-12" (20-30cm). **Flower:** Tiny; indistinguishable, with many greenish flowers packed on a stubby spike (spadix) behind which is a snow-white, ovoid, modified leaf (spathe); solitary, on leafless stalk. **Leaves:** Large, heart-shaped; entire; basal, upright. **In bloom:** April-August. **Habitat-Range:** Bogs, pond margins; north of a line from New Jersey to Indiana.

Although the flowers are actually green, it is the white spathe that normally attracts attention. The rootstock yields an edible starch if it is dried, ground and the powder heated until its acrid properties are dissipated. In early America this powder was made into "herb cookies" and in Lapland it is made into missebroed, a bread held in high esteem.

29 COLICROOT *(Aletris farinosa)* Lily family *(Liliaceae)*

Height: 1'-3' (.3-1m). **Flower:** 1/2" (1cm) long; regular, with 3 petals and 3 sepals of the same size and color forming a narrow, urn-shaped corolla, 6 stamens, 1 pistil; many, on slender raceme. **Leaves:** Thin, linear; entire; basal rosette. **In bloom:** May-August. **Habitat-Range:** Dry or moist peat, sand and gravel; mostly throughout.

The flowers are wrinkled and on close scrutiny appear to be covered with white meal. This explains both the generic and species names (Aletris was a fabled Greek slave girl who ground corn, and *farina* is the Latin for "flour"). As the common name suggests, the roots were used to treat digestive disorders.

30 CULVER'S-ROOT *(Veronicastrum virginicum)* Figwort family *(Scrophulariaceae)*

Height: 2'-6' (.6-2m). **Flower:** 1/4" (6mm) long; regular, with 5 petals forming a tubular corolla, 2 stamens projecting beyond corolla; many, in slender racemes. **Leaves:** Lanceolate; toothed; 3-7, in whorls along stem. **In bloom:** June-September. **Habitat-Range:** Rich woods, thickets, meadows; south of a line from Vermont to Wisconsin.

The early settlers quickly learned the value of this plant from the Indians. A tea prepared from the roots acted as a laxative, but it proved too drastic and irregular and substitutes such as Blue Flag Iris and American Ipecac were used for this purpose.

31 GALAX *(Galax aphylla)*   Diapensia family *(Diapensiaceae)*

Height: 1′-2′ (30-60cm). **Flower:** 1/2″ (1cm) in diameter; regular, with 5 petals united toward their bases, 5 stamens, 1 pistil; many, on spike. **Leaves:** Roundly heart-shaped; sharply toothed; basal, upright. **In bloom:** May-July. **Habitat-Range:** Open woods; south of a line from Virginia to West Virginia.

The patches of very shiny green leaves with a leathery texture draw attention to these plants. Unfortunately, these attractive leaves are gathered in large quantities by florists for floral arrangements and the plant is becoming rare in some areas. They are also used in Christmas decorations because they turn maroon or bronze in the winter. The generic name derives from the Greek *gala*, meaning "milk," apparently a reference to the color of the flowers.

32 FLYPOISON *(Amianthium muscaetoxicum)*   Lily family *(Liliaceae)*

Height: 1′-4′ (.3-1m). **Flower:** 1/4″ (6mm) in diameter; regular, with 3 sepals and 3 petals of the same size and color, 6 stamens, 3 styles; many, in dense, cylindrical raceme. **Leaves:** Thin, grasslike; entire; basal, upright. **In bloom:** May-July. **Habitat-Range:** Dry, sandy soil, bogs, open woods; Long Island, south along Atlantic coastal plain, and in mountains from Pennsylvania south.

The flower does not wither but persists and turns yellowish green. All parts of the plant are very poisonous to cattle and sheep. The common name and species name (from Latin *musca*, meaning "fly," and *toxicum*, "poison") also suggest that it can kill flies.

33 BUGBANE *(Cimicifuga racemosa)*   Buttercup family *(Ranunculaceae)*

Height: 3′-8′ (1-2.5m). **Flower:** Tiny; regular, with a tuft of stamens and one pistil; many, on slender racemes. **Leaves:** Pinnate, 3 leaflets further divided into threes; cleft or sharply toothed; alternate. **In bloom:** June-September. **Habitat-Range:** Rich woods; south of a line from Massachusetts to Michigan.

The plant is made conspicuous not only by its size and flowers but also its disagreeable odor. This apparently keeps most insects away; hence its common and generic names (from the Greek *cimex*, meaning "bug," and *fugure*, "to drive away"). The only insects that visit the plant are carrion flies. The roots are used in the Blue Ridge Mountains as a diuretic and to stimulate menstrual flow. A tea made from the leaves was used by colonists to treat diarrhea and rheumatism.

34 WHITE SWEET CLOVER *(Melilotus alba)*   Pea family *(Leguminosae)*

Height: 3′-8′ (1-2.5m). **Flower:** 1/4″ (6mm) long; irregular, pealike, with 5 petals, two lower ones form a keel, the two side ones form wings, the upper one forms a banner; many, in long, narrow racemes arising from leaf axils. **Leaves:** Pinnate, three leaflets; finely toothed; alternate. **In bloom:** May-October. **Habitat-Range:** Old fields, waste places; throughout.

This plant and the yellow species, Yellow Sweet Clover, were brought from Europe as a forage crop and also cultivated by beekeepers for the nectar they secrete (*meli* is Greek for "honey"). They were also used to flavor cheeses, snuff and smoking tobacco. They are fragrant, smelling like newmown hay; hence their common name. The dried leaves and flowers were used like camphor to protect furs from moths, and the flower heads have also been used in sachets.

35 DOWNY RATTLESNAKE PLANTAIN   Orchid family *(Orchidaceae)*

(Goodyera pubescens)†

Height: 6"-18" (15-45cm). **Flower:** 1/2" (1cm) long; irregular, with upper sepal and two petals forming a hood over the saclike lip formed by the third petal; many, in densely packed, long raceme. **Leaves:** Ovate; entire; sometimes with wavy edges; basal rosette. **In bloom:** July-September. **Habitat-Range:** Dry or moist woods; mostly throughout.

The leaves, rather than the short-lived, small flowers, often call attention to the plant. They are dark green with a network of whitish veins. They were thought to resemble snakeskin and therefore were supposed to be effective against snakebite if chewed or applied to the bite; hence its common name. Because the leaves are decorative and evergreen and the plant is easy to transplant it is often used in terrariums. The generic name honors John Goodyear, an early English botanist. A smaller species, with fewer white veins and flowers on one-sided raceme, is Dwarf Rattlesnake Plantain, *G. repens.*

36 LIZARD'S-TAIL *(Saururus cernuus)*   Lizard's-tail family *(Saururaceae)*

Height: 1 1/2'-3' (.5-1m). **Flower:** Tiny; indistinguishable; many, on one or more long (4"-12", 10-30cm), drooping spikes. **Leaves:** Heart-shaped; entire; alternate. **In bloom:** June-September. **Habitat-Range:** Swamps and shallow water; mostly throughout, except northern New England.

The flowers have no petals or sepals, the white color being due to the stalks of numerous stamens. A zigzag stem holds the thin drooping spikes from which the plant gets its common and generic names (from Greek *sauros*, meaning "lizard," and *oura*, "tail"). The mashed, boiled roots were applied to wounds as a poultice.

37 DEVIL'S-BIT *(Chamaelirium luteum)*   Lily family *(Liliaceae)*

Height: 1'-3' (.3-1m). **Flower:** 1/4" (6mm) diameter; regular, with 3 petals and 3 sepals of the same size and color, dioecious, having either 6 stamens or 1 pistil; many, on slender spike. **Leaves:** Basal rosette of spatulate leaves; stem leaves are small, narrow, entire, alternate. **In bloom:** June-July. **Habitat-Range:** Woods and bogs; south of a line from Massachusetts to Michigan.

Since the plant is dioecious, the flowers on any given plant are staminate or pistillate. The staminate spike most resembles Lizard's-tail *(Saururus cernuus)* because it tapers to a point and droops. The pistillate spike is evenly thick and remains upright. When eaten it causes vomiting and dizziness, but it is used externally to treat dandruff.

38 SOAPWORT *(Saponaria officinalis)*   Pink family *(Caryophyllaceae)*

Height: 1'-2' (.3-.6m). **Flower:** 1" (2.5cm) diameter; regular, with shallowly notched petals, 10 stamens, 1 pistil; many, in dense cymes. **Leaves:** Broadly lanceolate, 3-5 ribs; entire; opposite. **In bloom:** July-September. **Habitat-Range:** Roadsides, railroad beds, waste places; throughout.

A native of Europe, this sometimes pink-tinged flower escaped from Colonial gardens. The common and generic names (from *sapon*, the Latin for "soap") refer to the soap-like lather which forms when crushed leaves (containing saponins, detergent-like substances) are agitated in water. The cleaning action was utilized in treating skin disorders and poison ivy. It was also used, and is still used, to restore color and sheen to old china and precious glass.

39 WILD LILY-OF-THE-VALLEY   Lily family *(Liliaceae)*
(Maianthemum canadense)[†]

Height: 3″-6″ (8-15cm). **Flower:** 1/4″ (6mm) long; regular, with two sepals and two petals of the same size and color, 4 stamens, 1 pistil; several, in a raceme. **Leaves:** Heart-shaped with clasping bases; entire; 2 or 3 alternating on stem. **In bloom:** May-June. **Habitat-Range:** Woods and clearings; mostly throughout, uplands in South.

The plant is first seen in spring as widespread patches of shiny, heart-shaped leaves on zigzag stems. Its generic name combines the Latin *Maius*, "May," and the Greek *anthemon*, "flower," since it grows in profusion in the Canadian woodlands in May; hence its other common name, Canada Mayflower. In summer it develops small clusters of green berries speckled with red. It is also called Two-leaved Solomon's Seal and closely resembles Three-leaved Solomon's Seal (*Smilacina trifolia*), but the latter has three leaves with sheathing bases and bears its flowers on a sparse raceme, each flower having 3 sepals and 3 petals of the same size and color.

40 CATNIP *(Nepeta cataria)*   Mint family *(Labiatae)*

Height: 6″-24″ (15-60cm). **Flower:** 1/2″ (1cm) long; irregular, with two-lipped corolla, upper lip erect, concave, 2 clefts, lower lip 3 clefts; many, in terminal head. **Leaves:** Arrow-shaped; coarsely toothed; opposite. **In bloom:** June-September. **Habitat-Range:** Roadsides, waste places; throughout.

The flowers appear purplish because the white corolla is dotted with purple. The Mohegan Indians made tea from the leaves to treat infantile colic. Early settlers followed their example and this remedy is still used in some regions. A catnip tea was used to induce sweating to cure colds and for relief of insomnia, flatulence and halitosis. The leaves and dried flowerheads were widely used to promote suppressed menstruation. The plant odor is apparently irresistable to cats; hence the common name.

41 HELLEBORINE *(Epipactis helleborine)*   Orchid family *(Orchidaceae)*

Height: 1′-4′ (.3-1m). **Flower:** 1″ (2.5cm) diameter; irregular, having 3 strongly keeled sepals, 2 shorter lateral petals, saclike 3rd petal with a triangular lip that is bent back under the sac; several, in raceme, emerging from axils of narrow bracts. **Leaves:** Lanceolate, strongly veined, mostly sessile, clasping; entire; alternate. **In bloom:** June-September. **Habitat-Range:** Woods, thickets, roadside banks; throughout Northeast and southwestward to Maryland and Illinois.

This relatively unattractive orchid was introduced into America from Europe and has spread across the Northeast.

42 WHITE FRINGED ORCHIS   Orchid family *(Orchidaceae)*

(Habenaria blephariglottis)†

Height: 1'-2' (30-60cm). **Flower:** 1 1/2" (4cm) long; irregular, with upper sepal and 2 petals forming hood, 2 lateral sepals, lower petal forming fringed lip and long spur; many, in plumelike spike. **Leaves:** Lanceolate, sessile, clasping, upper ones smallest; entire; alternate. **In bloom:** June-September. **Habitat-Range:** Bogs, swamps, wet meadows; mostly throughout.

There are a number of white orchids with spurs but this is the largest and showiest. The Leafy White Orchis (*H. dilatata*) has a lip (as long as the spur) that extends outward and is not fringed. The Small Woodland Orchis (*H. clavellata*) has a short, blunt lip and one clasping leaf on the flowering stem. Two flat, roundish leaves at the base of the flowering stalk bearing small white orchids with a thin tapering lip identify the Round-leaved Orchis, *H. orbiculata.*

43 MEADOWSWEET *(Spiraea latifolia)*   Rose family *(Rosaceae)*

Height: 2'-5' (.6-1.5m). **Flower:** 1/4" (6mm) diameter; regular, having 5 petals, numerous stamens, 5-8 pistils; many, on densely packed panicles forming pyramid. **Leaves:** Oval; coarsely toothed; alternate. **In bloom:** June-September. **Habitat:** Damp meadows; throughout northern regions; in mountains in South.

This plant grows from red or purplish brown woody stems and is included here only because it will be seen with many herbaceous plants in summer meadows. An infusion of the dried leaves sweetened with honey was a favorite diet drink of the colonists. It was also used as an astringent and diuretic. An extract of the roots in white wine was considered a specific for fever. Fresh leaves were strewn on the floor of banqueting houses in the summertime because, it was said, "the smell thereof makes the heart merrie and joyful and delighteth the senses."

44 YARROW *(Achillea millefolium)*   Composite family *(Compositae)*

Height: 1'-3' (.3-1m). **Flower:** Tiny; indistinguishable; many, in flat-topped corymb. **Leaves:** Dissected, fernlike; alternate. **In bloom:** June-September. **Habitat-Range:** Fields and roadsides; throughout.

A common roadside plant that may sometimes have pink flowers, its feathery leaves often cause it to be mistaken for a fern. The leaves explain its species name which combines two Latin words meaning "thousand-leaved." It escaped from cultivation after being brought from Europe, where it was considered a valuable medicinal plant. Achilles was said to have discovered its healing properties and used it to treat the wounds of his troops at the siege of Troy; hence the generic name. The leaves were chewed by colonists for stomachache and toothache. A tea made from the leaves was used to treat chills, fever, and gout and for hair and scalp care. The plant was effective in stopping a bleeding wound or a nosebleed and was often called Woundwort or Nosebleed Plant. (Recent chemical analysis of the plant yielded a blood-clotting substance.) Yarrow was also an ingredient in witches' brews designed to conjure up devils or prepare love potions.

45 WHITE CLOVER *(Trifolium repens)*   Pea family *(Leguminosae)*

Height: 4"-10" (10-25cm). **Flower:** 3/8" (1cm) long; irregular, pealike, tubular; many, clustered in a globular head. **Leaves:** Palmate, 3 leaflets; entire; alternate, on creeping stem. **In bloom:** May-October. **Habitat-Range:** Fields, lawns, roadsides; throughout.

The fresh leaves can be added to salads or cole slaw. The pink-tinged blossoms were steeped to make tea. It was an important survival food in times of famine in Ireland and Scotland. A bread was made from flour obtained by grinding the dried flower heads and seed pods. The flowers are an important source of honey for hive bees.

46 BOG TWAYBLADE *(Liparis loeselii)*†   Orchid family *(Orchidaceae)*

Height: 4″-8″ (10-20cm). **Flower:** 3/4″ (2cm) long; irregular, having 3 narrow sepals, 2 threadlike lateral petals rolled lengthwise, one concave, liplike petal; several, in raceme. **Leaves:** Lanceolate, keeled; entire; two basal, upright. **In bloom:** June-July. **Habitat-Range:** Bogs, peaty meadows and damp thickets; mostly throughout; in mountains in South.

Everything about the plant is yellow-green; flowers, stem and leaves. The common name derives from the two large basal leaves.

47 FEATHERBELLS *(Stenanthium gramineum)*   Lily family *(Liliaceae)*

Height: 3′-5′ (1-1.5m). **Flower:** 1/2″ (1cm) long; regular, with 3 sepals and 3 petals of the same color and shape, 6 stamens, 1 pistil; many, in long panicle (1′-2′, .3-.6m); may also be greenish or purplish. **Leaves:** Linear, grasslike, folded lengthwise; entire; alternate, most numerous toward base of stem. **In bloom:** June-September. **Habitat-Range:** Moist meadows and open woods, bogs; south of a line from Pennsylvania to Illinois; in mountains in South.

The flowers appear starlike because the sepals and petals are very narrow; hence the generic name (from Greek *stenos*, meaning "narrow," and *anthos*, "flower"). The drooping side branches of the inflorescence are mostly staminate while those of the main stalk have both stamens and pistils.

BUNCHFLOWER *(Melanthium virginicum)*   Lily family *(Liliaceae)*

Height: 3′-5′ (1-1.5m). **Flower:** 3/4″ (2cm) diameter; regular, with 3 sepals and 3 petals having narrow bases, 6 stamens, 1 pistil; many, in panicle with pyramid shape; creamy white or greenish white initally but later purplish or blackish. **Leaves:** Linear, grasslike; entire; alternate, most numerous at base of stem. **In bloom:** June-July. **Habitat-Range:** Moist meadows, wet woods, bogs; south of a line from southern New York to Illinois.

Similar to *Stenanthium gramineum* but the flowers are less numerous. The stem is rough and hairy. Its later color accounts for its generic name (from the Greek *melas*, "black," and *anthos*, "flower").

48 GOATSBEARD *(Aruncus dioicus)*   Rose family *(Rosaceae)*

Height: 3′-6′ (1-2m). **Flower:** 1/4″ (6mm) diameter; regular, with 5 oval petals, staminate flowers with 15 stamens, pistillate flowers with 3 pistils; dioecious, many in plumelike panicle. **Leaves:** Pinnate, divided two or three times into oval leaflets; coarsely toothed; alternate. **In bloom:** May-July. **Habitat-Range:** Rich woods and ravines; south of a line from Pennsylvania to Illinois.

Although each flower is small, the large, feathery spray of the inflorescence makes a striking display. Pistillate flowers occur on different plants from staminate flowers; hence the species name, combining two Greek words, *di* "two," and *oikos*, "house."

49 FALSE HELLEBORE *(Veratrum viride)*   Lily family *(Liliaceae)*

Height: 2'-8' (.6-2.5m). **Flower:** 3/4" (2cm) diameter; regular, with 3 sepals and 3 petals of the same color and size forming a star-shaped corolla, 6 curved stamens, 1 pistil with 3 styles; many, on 8"-20" (20-50cm) panicle. **Leaves:** Broadly oval, pointed, heavily ribbed, sessile, clasping base; entire; alternate. **In bloom:** May-July. **Habitat-Range:** Swamps and wet woods; throughout, but more common in uplands in southern regions.

The star-shaped flowers, initially a greenish yellow, turn to a dull green and are relatively inconspicuous; thus the many heavily ribbed leaves are what usually catch the eye. Although this plant doesn't bloom until May, it becomes noticeable as green spears projecting aboveground in March. The young plant is attractive to cattle that have been feeding on dry hay throughout the winter, but eating it is fatal to them because the entire plant is highly poisonous. Small amounts of this plant were used by the Indians to lower heart rate and blood pressure in cases of high blood pressure. They also used it in an "ordeal by trial" to choose a chief; the one whose stomach could withstand the action the longest was obviously entitled to command.

50 WATER PLANTAIN *(Alisma triviale)*   Arrowhead family *(Alismataceae)*

Height: 1'-3' (.3-1m). **Flower:** 1/4" (6mm) diameter; regular, with 3 roundish petals, 6 stamens, many pistils; many, in whorls on loose panicles. **Leaves:** Ovate, with rounded bases; entire; basal, upright. **In bloom:** June-September. **Habitat-Range:** Shallow water, swamps, muddy shores; throughout.

A similar species, *A. subcordatum*, commonly found in more southern regions, has smaller flowers (1/8", 3mm). The bulbous base of water plantain was dried and cooked as a starchy vegetable. A drug from this base was used to treat kidney stones, dysentery and epilepsy. It also enjoyed some repute as a cure for hydrophobia; hence another of its common names, Mad-dog Weed.

51 POKEWEED *(Phytolacca americana)*   Pokeweed family *(Phytolaccaceae)*

Height: 4'-10' (1-3m). **Flower:** 1/4" (6mm) diameter; regular, with 5 petal-like sepals, 10 stamens, 1 pistil; many, on terminal, nodding racemes. **Leaves:** Lanceolate; entire; alternate. **In bloom:** July-October. **Habitat-Range:** Open woods, thickets, old fields; mostly throughout.

The stem takes on a reddish tinge as the plant matures and the berries are a purplish black. The berries, when crushed, yield a bright purple juice which was used as a dye and ink; hence another common name, Inkberry. The juice was also added to cheap whisky by frugal colonial Pennsylvanians who then served it to guests as expensive "port wine." The followers of President Polk wore sprigs of this plant in their lapels as campaign buttons. Poke root tea has laxative and narcotic properties and was considered useful in treating rheumatism. The young shoots (about 6", 15cm high) were boiled and eaten like asparagus, but the mature stem is poisonous.

52 WHITE CLINTONIA *(Clintonia umbellulata)* Lily family *(Liliaceae)*

Height: 8″-20″ (20-50cm). **Flower:** 1/2″ (1cm) long; regular, with 3 sepals and 3 petals of the same size and color, forming a bell-shaped corolla, 6 stamens, 1 pistil; many, in compact umbel on leafless stalk. **Leaves:** Oval; entire, but hairy; 2-5, in basal whorl. **In bloom:** May-July. **Habitat-Range:** Rich woods; in the mountains south of a line from western New York to eastern Ohio.

The flowers are speckled with green and purple, which accounts for its other common name, Speckled Wood Lily. The pollinated flowers eventually develop a cluster of round, shiny dark blue or black berries that are often more conspicuous than the small flowers. The young leaves were used in salads or as a pot herb.

53 ROUND-LEAVED PYROLA Wintergreen family *(Pyrolaceae)*
(Pyrola rotundifolia)

Height: 6″-15″ (15-37cm). **Flower:** 3/4″ (2cm) diameter; regular, with 5 petals, 10 stamens, 1 pistil with curved style; several, nodding in raceme. **Leaves:** Oval or roundish; slightly toothed; basal, upright. **In bloom:** June-August. **Habitat-Range:** Woods and clearings; throughout northern regions; in mountains in South.

The several species of Pyrola derive their generic name from a fancied resemblance of their leaves to those of the pear tree, *Pyrus*. The One-sided Pyrola (*P. secunda*) has nodding flowers arranged on only one side of the stalk. The Shinleaf (*P. elliptica*) has elliptical leaves which are thin and not shiny, in contrast to the leathery, shiny leaves of *P. rotundifolia*. The leaves were applied directly to bruises and sores to relieve pain. They contain a drug closely related to the pain reliever, aspirin. The English peasants called any plaster a "shin-plaster" regardless of where it was applied; hence the common name Shinleaf.

54 BRANCHING BUR-REED Bur-reed family *(Sparganiaceae)*
(Sparganium americanum)

Height: 1′-3′ (.3-1m). **Flower:** Tiny; indistinguishable; many, in dense, round heads. **Leaves:** Linear; entire; alternate, usually erect, sometimes floating. **In bloom:** May-September. **Habitat-Range:** Muddy or peaty shores, shallow water; throughout.

Of the several species in our area, this is the most widely distributed. The flowers, which have neither sepals nor petals, are crowded into ball-like heads along a zigzag stem. The heads on the upper part of the stem are staminate and soon wither and disappear after shedding their pollen. The heads near the base contain pistillate flowers which form a bur-like cluster of seedlike fruits with sharp beaks; hence the common name.

55 FALSE NETTLE *(Boehmeria cylindrica)* Nettle family *(Urticaceae)*

Height: 1′-3′ (.3-1m). **Flower:** Tiny; indistinguishable; compact clusters along slender inflorescences from leaf axils. **Leaves:** Ovate; coarsely toothed; opposite. **In bloom:** July-October. **Habitat-Range:** Moist or shady ground; throughout.

The nettles and their close relatives have almost feather-like inflorescences emerging from leaf axils. The tiny greenish white flowers are unisexual, being either pistillate or staminate. Some species have both kinds of flowers on the plant and are thus monoecious. Other species are dioecious, having only one kind of flower on a plant. The family name derives from the Latin *uro*, "to burn," referring to the fact that many nettles are covered with fine hairs containing crystals of oxalic acid that cause skin irritation and a burning sensation. False Nettle lacks stinging hairs whereas Stinging Nettle, *Urtica dioica*, which closely resembles it, is covered with them. These hairs were regarded as a "signature" so that a tea made from the leaves was used to stimulate hair growth. Early Scottish settlers brought this plant from Europe where they had cultivated it and served its tender tops like spinach. They also used the juice of the plant to curdle milk and thus thicken soups.

CLEARWEED *(Pilea pumila)*   Nettle family *(Urticaceae)*

Height: 4″-20″ (10-50cm). **Flower:** Tiny, monoecious or dioecious; indistinguishable; many, in short clusters drooping from leaf axils. **Leaves:** Ovate, relatively few rounded teeth; opposite. **In bloom:** July-September. **Habitat-Range:** Swampy, shady places; throughout.

It resembles *Urtica dioica* but lacks stinging hairs and its leaves are lustrous and translucent; hence its common name.

56 CURLED DOCK *(Rumex crispus)*   Buckwheat family *(Polygonaceae)*

Height: 1′-4′ (.3-1m). **Flower:** Tiny; indistinguishable; many, in wandlike raceme. **Leaves:** Lanceolate; wavy and curled borders; alternate. **In bloom:** June-August. **Habitat-Range:** Waste places and fields; throughout.

Twenty species of dock grow in our area. Their dark green color accounts for their common name, a corruption of Old English *docce*, "a dark-colored plant." Curled Dock has leaves with curled borders; hence the common name. A common species with long leathery leaves that grows in wet meadows and swamps is Water Dock, *R. orbiculatus*. Seabeach Dock, *R. pallidus*, is found in coastal marshes and its narrow leaves are covered with a white bloom. The leaves of Broad Dock, *R. obtusifolius*, usually have red veins. All are characterized by wandlike clusters of tiny green flowers. These flowers give rise to seed stalks which develop a rich brown color after drying and are much used in dried floral arrangements. The seeds are almost unique because they usually have heart-shaped wings. Often it is the seed stalks and not the tiny flowers that catch the eye. The young leaves of Curled Dock were prized as a green vegetable in Europe, particularly when boiled with meat such as bacon. The young stems were also used by George Washington Carver as a rhubarb substitute in pies. According to the "doctrine of signatures," the "signature" was the yellow roots; hence, an infusion of the roots was prepared to treat jaundice. A tea made from the leaves was taken as a spring tonic and mild laxative.

57 BUGLEWEED *(Lycopus virginicus)*   Mint family *(Labiatae)*

Height: 6″-24″ (15-60cm). **Flower:** Tiny; irregular, with two-lipped, bell-shaped corolla; many, in whorls at leaf axils. **Leaves:** Ovate; sharply toothed; opposite, held horizontal. **In bloom:** July-October. **Habitat-Range:** Rich, moist soil; mostly throughout.

Although a member of the mint family, it lacks the minty odor. There are 8 species in our area but this is the only one with dark green, purple-tinged leaves. The common name derives from a fancied resemblance of the plant to a "bugle," a sort of pin worn as decoration in the hair of medieval ladies. The rootstock of this plant was cooked and eaten by Indians.

58 FOXGLOVE BEARDTONGUE   Figwort family *(Scrophulariaceae)*
(Penstemon digitalis)

Height: 2'-4' (.6-1m). **Flower:** 1" (2.5cm) long; irregular, with 5 petals forming a tubular corolla with the opening having a 2-lobed upper lip and a 3-lobed lower lip, 4 anther-bearing stamens and 1 sterile, hairy filament; many, in open panicle. **Leaves:** Lanceolate, sessile; toothed; opposite. **In bloom:** May-July. **Habitat-Range:** Open woods, meadows; mostly throughout.

There are several species of Beardtongue but the most widespread is illustrated here. They have 4 stamens with anthers and a fifth filament without an anther but usually covered with hairs—the "beardtongue." Tea made from its leaves was used as a laxative by Indians. They also boiled the flower tops, adding sugar until they obtained a syrup, which was given to babies for whooping cough. Some Indians considered a wet dressing of pounded leaves an "absolute antidote" to rattlesnake bite.

59 TURTLEHEAD *(Chelone glabra)*†   Figwort family *(Scrophulariaceae)*

Height: 2'-5' (.6-1.5m). **Flower:** 1" (2.5cm) long; irregular, with 5 petals forming a broadly tubular 2-lipped corolla, upper lip arched, swollen and slightly notched lower lip 3-lobed, 5 stamens, 1 pistil; several, in dense spike. **Leaves:** Lanceolate, sessile or nearly so; sharply toothed; opposite. **In bloom:** August-October. **Habitat-Range:** Low places, margins of streams, wet thickets; throughout.

The common and generic names (from the Greek *chelone*, meaning "tortoise") derive from the fancied resemblance of the corolla to a turtle's head. Sometimes, as a bee struggles between the two lips to get at the nectar, it looks like a turtle eating a bee. The flower occasionally may be pink, but the pink-flowered species, *C. obliqua*, has stalked leaves. A southern species, *C. lyoni*, with a crimson corolla, has stalked leaves with a round base to the blades. Turtleheads have been used in preparing a tonic to treat indigestion and gall bladder complaints, and to expel worms.

60 HEDGE BINDWEED   Morning-glory family *(Convolvulaceae)*
(Convolvulus sepium)

Height: Twining vine. **Flower:** 2"-3" (5-7.5cm) diameter; regular, with 5 petals united to form a funnel-shaped corolla, 5 stamens, 1 pistil; solitary, from leaf axils. **Leaves:** Sagittate with blunt basal lobes; entire; alternate. **In bloom:** May-August. **Habitat-Range:** Thickets, waste places; mostly throughout.

It is also called the Wild Morning Glory, which it resembles. The flower, which may also be pink, has a pair of heart-shaped bracts at its base, which is not found in the Morning Glory. All bindweeds are twining vines, a fact reflected in their generic name (from the Latin *convolvere*, "to entwine"). Field Bindweed (*C. arvensis*) has smaller leaves and flowers and the bracts are halfway up the flower stem. It is used to flavor "noyeau," a liquor imported from Martinique.

61 SWAMP ROSE MALLOW *(Hibiscus moscheutos)*†   Mallow family *(Malvaceae)*

Height: 5′-7′ (1.5-2m). **Flower:** 6″-8″ (15-20cm) diameter; regular, having 5 petals forming a bell-shaped corolla, numerous stamens forming a collar around the style with anthers on the outside, 1 pistil with 5-knobbed stigma; few, on terminal stem. **Leaves:** Narrowly ovate with 3 lobes; irregularly toothed; alternate. **In bloom:** July-September. **Habitat-Range:** Marshes; south of a line from Maryland to Indiana.

This large, spectacular white flower has a red or purple center.

62 FLOWERING SPURGE *(Euphorbia corollata)*   Spurge family *(Euphorbiaceae)*

Height: 1′-3′ (.3-1m). **Flower:** Tiny; indistinguishable, in center of 5 white, rounded petal-like leaves; many, in branching flower clusters at summit. **Leaves:** Oblong, sessile; entire; alternate on stem, whorled at base of inflorescence. **In bloom:** June-October. **Habitat-Range:** Dry open woods, clearings, roadsides; mostly throughout but rare in New England.

What appears to be a cup-shaped flower is 5 petal-like leaves in the center of which is a cluster of minute flowers. The plant has a milky juice which is acrid enough to burn skin and raise blisters. For this reason it was used by Indians, but sparingly, in a laxative preparation. The common name comes from the Latin *expurgare,* "to purge."

63 SPREADING DOGBANE   Dogbane family *(Apocynaceae)*
(Apocynum androsaemifolium)

Height: 1′-4′ (.3-1m). **Flower:** 1/4″ (6mm) long; regular, having 5 petals with recurved ends, 5 stamens with arrow-shaped anthers; several in cyme, at summit and in leaf axils. **Leaves:** Ovate; entire; opposite. **In bloom:** June-August. **Habitat-Range:** Dry thickets, woodland borders; throughout.

The numerous bell-shaped flowers with recurved petal tips are marked with deep rose stripes. The stem is reddish and contains a milky juice that was coagulated and used as chewing gum by Indians. They also used the bark for weaving baskets and mats. Early settlers used the plant to treat dropsy and as a heart stimulant. The root is still used to treat heart irregularities because it contains an ingredient similar to digitalis, a cardiac stimulant. The attractive Dogbane Beetles that often feed on the leaves are an iridescent blue-green with a coppery tinge.

INTERMEDIATE DOGBANE   Dogbane family *(Apocynaceae)*
(Apocynum medium)

Height: 1′-4′ (.3-1m). **Flower:** 1/2″ (1cm) long; regular, having 5 petals forming a bell-shaped corolla, 5 stamens with arrow-shaped anthers; many, in terminal cymes; may range from white to pale pink. **Leaves:** Elliptical; entire; opposite. **In bloom:** June-August. **Habitat-Range:** Dry or moist ground, throughout northern regions.

Similar to *A. androsaemifolium* but flower petals are not recurved, flower stalks do not emerge from leaf axils, and the leaves are elliptical. The white form may be mistaken for *A. cannabinum,* commonly called Indian Hemp, but the latter species has small greenish white flowers and much narrower leaves.

64 FALSE SOLOMON'S SEAL *(Smilacina racemosa)*   Lily family *(Liliaceae)*

Height: 2′-3′ (.6-1m). **Flower:** 1/8″ (3mm) long; regular, with 3 petals and 3 sepals of the same size and color, 6 stamens, 1 pistil; many, in a branched raceme. **Leaves:** Lanceolate with conspicuous ribs; entire; alternate. **In bloom:** May-July. **Habitat-Range:** Woods, clearings and rocky slopes; mostly throughout, uplands in South.

The inflorescence is found at the end of an arching, zigzag stem. In the fall it bears a cluster of ruby-red berries. The young shoots can be chopped and added to a salad or eaten boiled. This plant has been used medicinally in the same manner as true Solomon's Seal.

65 WILD LEEK *(Allium tricoccum)*   Lily family *(Liliaceae)*

Height: 6″-18″ (15-45cm). **Flower:** 1/4″ (6mm) diameter; regular, with 3 petals and 3 sepals the same size and color, forming a cuplike corolla, 6 stamens, 1 pistil; several, in umbel. **Leaves:** Elliptical, large (6″-10″, 15-25cm long); entire; basal, upright, not present when plant is in bloom. **In bloom:** June-July. **Habitat-Range:** Rich woods and bottoms; throughout northern regions; in uplands in South.

The large leaves emerge early in the spring and have a distinct onion-like odor. The flowers emerge only after the leaves have withered in early summer. The young leaves may be chopped and added to salads and the underground bulbs are good in salads, soups and stews. Like other members of this genus, it is also thought to be good for the treatment of respiratory ailments. A Midwest Indian tribe named a place that was crowded with this plant, *shika'ko*, or skunk place. The area was eventually settled and the Indian term Anglicized to Chicago.

66 POKE MILKWEED *(Asclepias exaltata)*   Milkweed family *(Asclepiadaceae)*

Height: 3′-6′ (1-2m). **Flower:** 3/8″ (1cm) diameter; regular, with 5 recurved petals that form a cup supporting 5 little horns curving onto a central structure of 5 united stamens and a column of 5 pistils; many, in drooping clusters from leaf axils; may be tinged with green or lavender. **Leaves:** Broadly lanceolate, tapering to points at both ends; entire; opposite. **In bloom:** June-August. **Habitat-Range:** Rich, open woods and thickets; mostly throughout.

An earlier blooming species, the White Milkweed (*A. variegata*), has an upright umbel of white flowers with purple centers and broadly oval leaves.

67 DODDER *(Cuscuta* spp.*)*   Morning-glory family *(Convolvulaceae)*

Height: Climbing vine. **Flower:** 1/8″ (3mm) diameter; regular, with 4 or 5 petals forming globular corolla; many, in dense cymes. **Leaves:** Few scales; alternate. **In bloom:** July-October. **Habitat-Range:** Low ground, thickets; mostly throughout.

The small flower would go unnoticed were it not for the bright orange or yellow, slender, vinelike stems on which they grow. These climbing stems form threadlike masses on other plants, sometimes covering them. The dozen species in our area can only be distinguished by botanists. Lacking chlorophyll, they are parasitic and send rootlike structures into the stems of their host plant.

68 BEDSTRAW *(Galium* spp.*)*   Madder family *(Rubiaceae)*

Height: Reclining or leaning on other plants. **Flower:** Tiny; regular, with 4 petals, 4 stamens, 2 styles; many, in terminal or axillary clusters. **Leaves:** Small, narrow; entire; in whorls of 4, 6 or 8 along stem. **In bloom:** May-September. **Habitat-Range:** Woods, thickets, fields, roadsides; mostly throughout.

About 60 species of bedstraw are found in America and only their general characteristics are described here. The flowers of bedstraw are small and may be white, yellow or purple, but the plant is conspicuous because of its mass of attractive foliage. This was gathered and dried by Colonists and used as bedding for themselves and their cattle. The leaves have an astringent property causing blood to coagulate. They were also used in Europe to curdle milk in cheesemaking.

69 GOLDTHREAD *(Coptis groenlandica)*   Buttercup family *(Ranunculaceae)*

Height: 3″-6″ (8-15cm). **Flower:** 1/2″ (1cm) in diameter; regular, with 5-7 white sepals, no petals, numerous stamens, several pistils; solitary, on leafless stalks. **Leaves:** Palmate, 3 rounded leaflets; sharply toothed; basal, upright. **In bloom:** May-July. **Habitat-Range:** Damp woods, swamps, bogs, throughout northern regions and in mountains in South.

Although its flowers are small, patches of glistening, evergreen leaves catch the eye. The common name alludes to the bright yellow, threadlike rhizomes (underground stems). Many tribes of Indians used the root as a remedy for sore or ulcerated mouths; hence its other common name, Canker-root. The root has been found to contain the alkaloid berberine, which has a mild sedative action. The colonists, imitating the Indians, used the root in remedies for inflammation of the mouth or eyes. Autumn was supposedly the ideal time for collecting roots and as late as 1908 they brought a relatively high price.

70 OX-EYE DAISY   Composite family *(Compositae)*
(Chrysanthemum leucanthemum)

Height: 1′-3′ (.3-1m). **Flower:** 2″ (5cm) diameter; composite, with flattened or depressed yellow disc surrounded by 20-30 white rays; solitary, terminal. **Leaves:** Narrow, sessile; toothed or lobed; alternate. **In bloom:** June-August. **Habitat-Range:** Roadsides, fields; throughout.

A native of Europe, it escaped cultivation and invaded fields and meadows where it is difficult to eradicate. Since it contains an acrid juice, it is avoided by cattle and thus ruins good pastureland. However, the crushed leaves were used for bruises; hence another common name, Bruisewort. The juice was also thought to be good for gout. An early superstition held, "The same given to little dogs with milk, keepeth them from growing great."

MAYWEED *(Anthemis cotula)*   Composite family *(Compositae)*

Height: 8″-20″ (20-50cm). **Flower:** 1/2″-1″ (1-2.5cm) diameter; regular, composite, with dome-shaped yellow disc surrounded by white rays; solitary, terminal. **Leaves:** Dissected, fernlike; alternate. **In bloom:** May-August. **Habitat-Range:** Roadsides and waste places; throughout.

Similar to *Chrysanthemum leucanthemum* but flower is smaller, the central disc is dome-shaped and the leaves are fernlike. It has a fetid odor and, if picked, its acrid juice can cause blisters. A tea from the leaves was used to treat chronic rheumatism and hysteria.

71 MOUNTAIN SANDWORT   Pink family *(Caryophyllaceae)*
(Arenaria groenlandica)

Height: 2″-6″ (5-15cm). **Flower:** 1/2″ (1cm) in diameter; regular, with 5 slightly notched petals, 10 stamens, 1 pistil; solitary, but many in matted plants. **Leaves:** Needle-like; crowded basal cluster, opposite along stem. **In bloom:** June-August. **Habitat-Range:** Granite ledges and gravel; mountains of New York and New England, coast of Maine.

Sandworts tend to grow in tufts or mats. The common name and generic name (from Latin *arena*, meaning "sandy place") allude to the type of soil in which many of the species grow. The Indians used hot tea made from the whole plant to induce a high fever as a treatment for venereal disease. The dried leaves were also substituted for, or blended with, tobacco. The Rock Sandwort (*A. stricta*) commonly found throughout our range has oblong petals without notches, and the Pine Barren Sandwort (*A. caroliniana*) found locally on eastern coastal plains has spatulate petals.

72 DAISY FLEABANE *(Erigeron annuus)*   Composite family *(Compositae)*

Height: 1′-5′ (.3-1.5m). **Flower:** 1/2″ (1cm) diameter; regular, with disc flowers encircled by 80-125 ray flowers; several, in single cluster or branching corymb; daisy-like and may be white or lavender. **Leaves:** Ovate; toothed; alternate. **In bloom:** May-November. **Habitat-Range:** Fields, waste places; throughout.

There are many species of fleabane, so named from the belief that when dried and burned they were an insect repellant. They were hung in country cottages for this purpose. The generic name combines the Greek *eri*, "early," and *geron*, "old man," an allusion to the white hair covering this early-blooming plant. A similar but taller species, *E. strigosus*, has fewer leaves, most of which are not toothed or only slightly toothed.

73 VIRGINIA WATERLEAF   Waterleaf family *(Hydrophyllaceae)*
(Hydrophyllum virginianum)

Height: 1′-2 1/2′ (.3-.8m). **Flower:** 1/4″ (6mm) long; regular, with 5 petals united to form a bell-shaped corolla, 5 stamens extending beyond petals, 1 pistil; several, in cyme above leaves; may also be violet or purple. **Leaves:** Pinnate, 5 to 7 lanceolate-ovate leaflets; sharply toothed; alternate. **In bloom:** May-August. **Habitat-Range:** Rich woods and damp clearings; throughout.

The common and generic names (from the Greek *hydro*, "water" and *phyllon*, "leaf") apparently were applied to a species that had juicy leaves. However, some writers claim the name derives from the "watermarks" (gray-green patches) on the leaves of some species. A number of species differ mainly in the shape of their leaves: *H. macrophyllum* is rough and hairy and its leaves are larger and have 7 to 13 oval leaflets; *H. appendiculatum* has palmate leaves with 5 lobes, and *H. canadense* has broadly palmate leaves that tower above the inflorescence.

74 TALL MEADOW-RUE   Buttercup family *(Ranunculaceae)*
(Thalictrum polygamum)

Height: 3′-8′ (1-2.5m). **Flower:** 3/4″ (2cm) long; regular, with 5 sepals, no petals, numerous threadlike stamens in staminate flowers, other flowers with 1 pistil and a few stamens; many, in panicle. **Leaves:** Pinnate, with 3 or more leaflets; rounded lobes; alternate. **In bloom:** June-August. **Habitat-Range:** Meadows, low thickets, swamps; throughout.

The generic name indicates that this is a "polygamous" plant with both staminate and pistillate flowers. Hippocrates listed Rue as a "soothing herb" and the Indians used it as an antispasmodic. The lore of many Indian tribes says that the smoke of tobacco made from Rue leaves would cure deafness when blown into the ear.

75 VIRGIN'S-BOWER *(Clematis virginiana)*†   Buttercup family *(Ranunculaceae)*

Height: Climbing vine. **Flower:** 1/2″-3/4″ (1-2cm) diameter; regular, having 4 petal-like sepals, many stamens and pistils; many, in corymbs arising from leaf axils. **Leaves:** Pinnate, 3 egg-shaped leaflets; sparsely toothed; opposite. **In bloom:** July-September. **Habitat-Range:** Edges of woods, thickets, streambanks; throughout.

This vine commonly climbs over other plants and forms a shaded retreat; hence its common name. The clusters of creamy white flowers have no petals but have petal-like sepals. The seeds have gray, plumelike tails that account for the common name, Old Man's Beard.

WILD CUCUMBER *(Echinocystis lobata)*   Gourd family *(Cucurbitaceae)*

Height: Climbing vine. **Flower:** 1/4″ (6mm) diameter; regular, with 6 petals, staminate flowers in long racemes, pistillate flowers solitary or in small clusters. **Leaves:** Sharply and deeply 5-lobed; toothed; alternate. **In bloom:** June-October. **Habitat-Range:** Streambanks, thickets; throughout.

Similar to *Clematis virginiana* but its clustered flowers are unisexual and have six petals, its leaves are 5-lobed, and it produces a single, prickly fruit. The oval prickly fruit accounts for its generic name, a combination of the Greek *echinos*, meaning "hedgehog," and *cystis*, "a bladder." The juice from the bruised fruit was used to treat sunburn and remove freckles. The Bur-Cucumber, *Sicyos angulatus*, is a similar plant but has clusters of 5-petaled flowers which produce clusters of small, bristly fruit.

76 CHECKERBERRY *(Gaultheria procumbens)*†   Heath family *(Ericaceae)*

Height: 2″-6″ (5-15cm). **Flower:** 3/8″ (1cm) long; regular, with 5 petals forming an urn-shaped corolla, 10 stamens, 1 pistil; usually solitary, nodding from leaf axils. **Leaves:** Elliptical or oval; bristly teeth; alternate. **In bloom:** July-August. **Habitat-Range:** Sterile woods and clearings; throughout.

The new leaves are bright yellowish green but the older ones are dark green and often tinged with red. The evergreen leaves form large patches on the ground, even in winter. The plant has an oil of wintergreen odor and taste; hence another common name, Wintergreen. The leaves are refreshing when chewed raw, and in tea form are effective in treating fever and minor aches. A substance similar to aspirin has been extracted from them. The Indians used the leaves to treat rheumatism. The red berries that form in the fall can be eaten and are a principle food of partridges and grouse.

*

BEARBERRY (*Arctostaphylos uva-ursi*)   Heath family (*Ericaceae*)

Height: Trailing shrub. **Flower:** 1/4″ (6mm) long; regular, with 5 united petals in shape of urn, 10 stamens, 1 pistil; several, in terminal raceme. **Leaves:** Small, spatulate, evergreen; entire; opposite. **In bloom:** May-July. **Habitat-Range:** Exposed rocks or sands; locally, in northern regions.

Similar to *Gaultheria procumbens* but it is a trailing shrub with paddle shaped leaves and is found only in the northern regions. It forms spreading mats of evergreen leaves in colder, drier areas. The flowers are followed by clusters of red berries supposedly relished by bears. This belief is expressed in both the generic name (from Greek *arcto*, "bear" and *staphylo*, "cluster of grapes") and the species name (from Latin *ursus*, "bear" and *uva*, "grapes"). The berries are also eaten by game birds. The leaves were steeped in water and used as a diuretic by Indians and later by white settlers. It was officially used for this purpose in American medicine until 1936.

77 INDIAN CUCUMBER ROOT (*Medeola virginiana*)   Lily family (*Liliaceae*)

Height: 1′-3′ (.3-1m). **Flower:** 3/4″ (2cm) diameter; regular, with 3 sepals and 3 petals of the same size and color curved backward, 6 reddish stamens, 1 pistil with 3 long, recurved, reddish-brown stigmas; several, nodding in umbel, from axils of upper leaves. **Leaves:** Oval or lanceolate; entire; whorl of 5-9 near middle of stem, whorl of 3-5 at summit. **In bloom:** May-June. **Habitat-Range:** Moist woods; throughout.

The two whorls of leaves on a slender stem often draw attention to this plant since the few nodding, yellow-green flowers are almost inconspicuous. These small flowers eventually develop dark crimson, upright berries which attract attention in the fall. The common name is derived from the tuberous rootstock which resembles a cucumber in shape and taste. The raw root makes a delightful addition to a tossed salad and was used in soups and stews by the Indians.

78 PARTRIDGEBERRY (*Mitchella repens*)†   Madder family (*Rubiaceae*)

Height: Short (6″-12″, 15-30cm), trailing stem. **Flower:** 1/2″ (1cm) long; regular, with four fringed petals forming a funnel-shaped corolla, 4 stamens, 4 stigmas; in pairs, terminal; may also be pink. **Leaves:** Roundish; entire; opposite. **In bloom:** June-July. **Habitat-Range:** Dry or moist woods; mostly throughout.

The flowers always occur in pairs and when the fruit develops it fuses to form a single red berry with two scars; hence another common name, Two-eyed Berry. The berries persist and the leaves are evergreen, so the plant is often gathered during the winter holidays and used in small terrariums called Partridgeberry bowls. As a result, the plant is now on conservation lists. Frequent doses of a tea prepared from the leaves were taken by pregnant Indian women to speed childbirth; hence another common name, Squawberry. Until as recently as 1947 this use of the plant was officially recognized by the medical profession.

79 HAIRY SOLOMON'S SEAL (*Polygonatum pubescens*)   Lily family (*Liliaceae*)

Height: 1′-3′ (.3-1m). **Flower:** 1/2″ (1cm) long; regular, with 3 sepals and 3 petals of the same color and size forming a bell-shaped corolla, 6 stamens, 1 pistil; usually in pairs, dangling. **Leaves:** Elliptical-oval, sessile or short petiole; entire; alternate. **In bloom:** April-June. **Habitat-Range:** Woodlands; throughout, but in the South more common in mountains.

There are several species of Solomon's Seal; this one has minute hairs along the veins on the underside of its leaves whereas the almost identical Smooth Solomon's Seal, *P. biflorum*, is hairless. The Great Solomon's Seal, *P. canaliculatum*, is the tallest (usually over 4', 1m) species and has wavy, corrugated leaves. All of these plants are characterized by an arched stem with small tubular flowers dangling along the axis. The stem grows from a creeping underground stem (rhizome) which is jointed and scarred. The shape of the rhizome explains the plant's generic name, which combines the Greek *polys*, "many" and *gonu*, "knee," an allusion to the many joints of the rhizome. The common name is explained by the scars on the rhizome left by earlier flower stalks; these were thought to resemble King Solomon's official seal. The juice from crushed rhizomes was used to treat earache and sunburn. A tea made from the leaves served as a contraceptive. In addition, the starchy rhizomes were eaten by Indians and the early settlers. Even today some woodsmen eat the tender new shoots, which are said to taste like asparagus.

STARRY FALSE SOLOMON'S SEAL *(Smilacina stellata)*   Lily family *(Liliaceae)*

Height: 8"-20" (20-50cm). **Flower:** 1/4" (6mm) long; regular, with 3 petals and 3 sepals of the same size and color, 6 stamens, 1 pistil; several, in uncrowded raceme. **Leaves:** Lanceolate, conspicuous ribs, sessile; entire; alternate. **In bloom:** May-August. **Habitat-Range:** Open meadows, thickets, rocky slopes; mostly throughout northern regions, and uplands to West Virginia.

Similar to *S. racemosa* but has larger flowers in a loose, unbranched raceme; its leaves are sessile and its berries are black when ripe.

80 **SWEET CICELY** *(Osmorhiza claytonia)*   Parsley family *(Umbelliferae)*

Height: 1 1/2'-3' (.3-1m). **Flower:** Tiny; indistinguishable; many in clusters, clusters sparse in umbel. **Leaves:** Pinnate; deeply toothed; alternate. **In bloom:** June-August. **Habitat-Range:** Woods and wooded slopes; mostly throughout.

The stem of this species is hairy. A more southern species, *O. longstylis*, is nearly smooth. The carrot-like roots of both species have a pleasant licorice or anise-like odor. Hence, the generic name, which combines the Greek *osme*, "scent," and *rhiza*, "a root." Crushing a leaf yields a similarly pleasant odor. The common name is a corruption of *seseli*, an old Greek name for a sweet-smelling plant.

81 **WHITE BANEBERRY** *(Actaea pachypoda)*   Buttercup family *(Ranunculaceae)*

Height: 1'-2' (.3-.6m). **Flower:** 1/4" (6mm) diameter; regular, with 4-10 small, spoon-shaped petals, numerous stamens, 1 pistil; many, in dense, oblong raceme. **Leaves:** Pinnate, divided two or three times into lanceolate leaflets; sharply toothed; alternate. **In bloom:** May-June. **Habitat-Range:** Rich woods and thickets; mostly throughout.

The petals of the small flowers do not last long. The stalk of each flower in the raceme is relatively thick, the species name (from Greek *pachys*, "thick," and *podos*, "foot") reflecting this. This stalk gets red as the fruit ripens. The fruit consists of white, egg-shaped berries with a dark spot at their ends that resemble the china eyes once used in dolls; hence another common name, Doll's Eyes. As the common name suggests, these berries are very poisonous and the Indians warned colonists against them. However, an infusion of the leaves was drunk by nursing squaws to stimulate the flow of milk.

RED BANEBERRY *(Actaea rubra)*   Buttercup family *(Ranunculaceae)*

Height: 1'-2' (.3-.6m). **Flower:** 1/4" (6mm) diameter; regular, with 4-10 small spoon-shaped petals, numerous stamens, 1 pistil; many, in dense, oval raceme. **Leaves:** Pinnate, divided two or three times into lanceolate leaflets; sharply toothed; alternate. **In bloom:** May-July. **Habitat-Range:** Woods and thickets; mostly throughout, commoner northward.

Similar to *A. pachypoda* but has oval-shaped raceme, the fruit stalk is thin, and the berries are usually red.

82 WHITE SNAKEROOT *(Eupatorium rugosum)*†   Composite family *(Compositae)*

Height: 1'-5' (.3-1.5m). **Flower:** Tiny; indistinguishable; many, in corymb. **Leaves:** Heart-shaped; coarsely toothed; opposite. **In bloom:** July-October. **Habitat-Range:** Rich woods, thickets; throughout.

The clusters of bright white flowers add sparkle to the shaded places in which the plant is found. As the common name signifies, it was used to cure snakebite, but the plant is poisonous. The poison can even be transferred through cows who graze the plant; anyone who drinks their milk gets "milk sickness."

83 QUEEN ANNE'S LACE *(Daucus carota)*   Parsley family *(Umbelliferae)*

Height: 1'-5' (.3-1.5m). **Flower:** Tiny; indistinguishable; many, in flat-topped umbel 3"-4" (8-10cm) wide. **Leaves:** Dissected, fernlike; alternate. **In bloom:** May-October. **Habitat-Range:** Dry fields and waste places; throughout.

This very bristly and hairy weed plant has historic interest since early man developed the common garden carrot from an Asiatic form of it. When crushed, the leaf gives off a carrot odor. The roots of this so-called Wild Carrot can be cooked and eaten but excessive amounts will turn the skin yellow and jaundiced. Perhaps because they saw this as a "signature," Indians used the plant to treat liver diseases. The seeds served as seasoning for soups and stews, and medicinally they were used to treat colic, chronic coughs and dysentery. The common name originated from the notion that the inflorescence resembled Queen Anne's lace headdress. Before the umbel is in full bloom, and again as seed forms, it is hollow and has the shape of a bird's nest, which is another of its common names.

84 WATER HEMLOCK *(Cicuta maculata)*   Parsley family *(Umbelliferae)*

Height: 3'-6' (1-2m). **Flower:** Tiny; indistinguishable; many in loose, flat-topped umbel. **Leaves:** Twice or thrice pinnate; coarsely toothed; alternate. **In bloom:** June-September. **Habitat-Range:** Wet meadows, swamps; mostly throughout; in mountains in South.

Although it resembles other flat-topped plants, the distinguishing characteristic is its purple-streaked stem as suggested by its species name *maculata*, the Latin for "blotched or spotted." This identifies it as the most poisonous plant in the United States.

Its roots look and smell like parsnips but one mouthful can kill a man. A similar appearing plant, Poison Hemlock (*Conium maculatum*), also has stems which are spotted with purple but its leaves are finely dissected like those of Queen Anne's Lace. The leaves and seeds are extremely toxic when eaten, causing paralysis and death. The ancient Greeks used a decoction of these parts to execute criminals and this was the hemlock that Socrates drank.

85 FOOL'S PARSLEY (*Aethusa cynapium*)　　　Parsley family (*Umbelliferae*)

Height: 6"-30" (15-75cm). **Flower:** Tiny; indistinguishable; many, in flat-topped umbel 1"-2" (2.5-5cm) wide. **Leaves:** Dissected, fernlike; alternate. **In bloom:** June-August. **Habitat-Range:** Fields and waste places; mostly throughout.

Similar to *D. carota* but has a smaller umbel with forked bracts hanging down underneath and shiny leaves. Although its shiny leaves somewhat resemble those of parsley, they are poisonous; hence its common name.

86 SUNDEW (*Drosera* spp.)†　　　Sundew family (*Droseraceae*)

Height: 3"-9" (7-21cm). **Flower:** 1/4" (6mm) diameter; regular, with 5 petals, 5 stamens, 1 pistil; several, on slender, usually curved spike. **Leaves:** Shape is species variable; entire; basal. **In bloom:** June-August. **Habitat-Range:** Acid or peaty bogs; mostly throughout.

There are several species of sundew distinguished mainly by the shape of their leaves, such as Thread-leaved Sundew (*D. filiformis*), shown here. But sundews are all similar in having leaves covered with gland-tipped red hairs that exude droplets of sticky fluid. In the sunlight these droplets sparkle like dewdrops. Hence the common and generic names (from Greek *droseros*, meaning "dewy"). The sticky droplets trap small insects which are then gradually digested. Since the plant lives in nitrogen-poor soil, this is its main source of nitrogen. The plant juice is acrid and was used to remove warts and corns. In Italy a liquor called *rossali* is distilled from its juices. The dried plant was used medicinally as an antispasmodic.

87 GREEN DRAGON (*Arisaema dracontium*)　　　Arum family (*Araceae*)

Height: 1'-4' (.3-1m). **Flower:** Tiny; irregular; many, at base of spadix, hidden by spathe. **Leaves:** Palmate, with lateral segments 2-cleft, 5-15 oblong-lanceolate pointed segments; entire; single, upright. **In bloom:** May-July. **Habitat-Range:** Moist woodlands and banks of shady streams; throughout.

The unique characteristic of this plant is the slender, pointed, greenish white spadix that projects 4" (10cm) or more beyond the green spathe. The tiny pistillate and staminate flowers are found at the base of this elongated spadix. They eventually develop into large, ovoid heads of conspicuous reddish orange berries in the fall. The roots of this plant were chewed by the colonists as a cure for asthma.

88 COW PARSNIP (*Heracleum maximum*)　　　Parsley family (*Umbelliferae*)

Height: 4'-8' (1-2.5m). **Flower:** Tiny; indistinguishable; many, in flat-topped umbel 6"-8" (15-20cm) in diameter. **Leaves:** Palmate, 3 broadly oval leaflets, inflated sheath at base of petiole; lobed and irregularly toothed; alternate. **In bloom:** June-August. **Habitat-Range:** Moist ground; mostly throughout, in mountains in South.

Notable is the very stout, ridged, hairy stem with large leaves. The leaves have an inflated sheath at their base that clasps the stem. The cooked roots taste like rutabaga. The young stems can be eaten raw or cooked. Young leaves may be used in salads. Mature leaves may be dried and burned to serve as a substitute for salt. Although many parts of this plant may be eaten, care must be taken not to mistake it for Water Hemlock (*Cicuta maculata*).

ANGELICA *(Angelica atropurpurea)*   Parsley family *(Umbelliferae)*

Height: 3'-10' (1-3m). **Flower:** Tiny; indistinguishable; many, in flat-topped umbel 4"-8" (10-20cm) in diameter. **Leaves:** Palmate, 3 leaflets which may be further divided, inflated sheath at base of petiole; lobed and irregularly toothed; alternate. **In bloom:** July-October. **Habitat-Range:** Rich thickets, bottomlands, swamps; north of a line from Delaware to Illinois.

Similar to *Heracleum maximum* but has a smooth, purple stem and the compound leaves have more leaflets. The young stems may be used as an asparagus substitute. It has aromatic properties which made it useful as a sweat inducer and expectorant for colds.

89 FRAGRANT WATER LILY   Water-lily family *(Nymphaeaceae)*
(Nymphaea odorata)†

Height: Floating on water. **Flower:** 3"-6" (7-15cm) diameter; regular, with numerous petals diminishing in size toward the center, numerous stamens, 1 large pistil; solitary, floating on water. **Leaves:** Roundish, large (4"-10", 10-25cm diameter) with V-shaped notch at base; entire; floating. **In bloom:** June-September. **Habitat-Range:** Ponds, quiet waters, bog pools; throughout.

The flowers, which remain open for several days, are very fragrant. The large leaves are shiny green above and purple below. The young, unopened leaves and flowers may be boiled in salted water and served with butter. The seeds can be popped like popcorn. Indians cooked the seeds and ground them into a meal resembling cornmeal. They also ate the starchy rootstock. An odorless species found mainly in northern regions, the Tuberous White Water Lily (*N. tuberosa*), has larger flowers (4"-8", 10-20cm diameter) and larger leaves that are green on both sides.

90 BROAD-LEAVED ARROWHEAD   Water-plantain family *(Alismataceae)*
(Sagittaria latifolia)†

Height: 1'-2' (.3-.6m). **Flower:** 1"-1 1/2" (2.5-4cm) diameter; regular, with 3 petals, variable number of stamens and pistils; in whorls of 3 along flower stems. **Leaves:** Arrow-shaped; entire; basal, upright. **In bloom:** July-September. **Habitat-Range:** In water or wet places; throughout.

The leaf shape explains both the common and generic names (from Latin *sagitta*, meaning "arrow"). But the leaf shape varies from species to species, and even the leaf of this species is broad when growing in a relatively dry place and narrower in a very damp situation. The flowers, which occur in whorls of three, also vary, those in the uppermost whorls having only stamens, whereas those in the lower whorls have pistils or sometimes both pistils and stamens. The plant grows from underground stems, the ends of which develop into starchy tubers. These were a favorite food among Indians, who called them *wapato*. The Indians would enter the water, root out the tubers with their toes and let them float to the surface. The Indians also raided muskrat lairs because these animals stored the tubers. The white settlers learned to gather the tubers and called them Duck Potatoes. The Lewis and Clark expedition used the tubers as their chief source of starch.

91 SWEETFLAG *(Acorus calamus)*   Arum family *(Araceae)*

Height: 1'-5' (.3-1.5m). **Flower:** Tiny; indistinguishable; many, crowded on long, narrow spadix. **Leaves:** Long, swordlike; entire; basal, upright. **In bloom:** May-August. **Habitat-Range:** Swamps and along streams; throughout.

This plant, and especially the rhizome, has a sweetish, aromatic odor. The Indians chewed the root for toothache and other ills and the early settlers chewed it for stomach-ache. One of the most common colonial confections was candied Sweetflag root.

92 WHITE AVENS *(Geum canadense)*   Rose family *(Rosaceae)*

Height: 18"-30" (.4-.7m). **Flower:** 1/2" (1cm) diameter; regular, with 5 petals and 5 sepals of equal lenght, numerous stamens, numerous pistils with hooked styles; solitary, terminal, from leaf axils. **Leaves:** Stem leaves ovate and toothed or 3-lobed and toothed, alternate; basal leaves divided into 3-5 toothed leaflets. **In bloom:** June-August. **Habitat-Range:** Open woods and thickets; throughout.

A similar species, the Rough Avens (*G. virginianum*), has more hair and its petals are pale yellow or creamy white and are shorter than the sepals. The seed pods are hooked and travel far by attaching themselves to animal fur or human clothing. The roots were used in olden times to impart an agreeable taste to beer and ale. Indians boiled the roots and made a tasty beverage to treat disorders of the stomach and bowels.

93 INDIAN PIPE *(Monotropa uniflora)*†   Wintergreen family *(Pyrolaceae)*

Height: 4"-10" (10-25cm). **Flower:** 3/4" (2cm) long; regular, having 4 or 5 petals, 10 stamens, 1 pistil; solitary, terminal, nodding. **Leaves:** Scale-like; few, alternate. **In bloom:** June-September. **Habitat-Range:** Shady, moist woods; throughout.

Lacking chlorophyll, this waxy white or sometimes pinkish plant obtains its food from mycorhiza, tiny fungi that are associated with the roots of many photosynthetic plants. The single nodding flower turns upright as seeds are forming. The plant is cool and clammy to the touch, readily turns black and decays when touched, and its pallor probably earned it its other name, Corpse Plant. Indians and early settlers used a clear juice extracted from crushed stems for eye problems.

94 BUNCHBERRY *(Cornus canadensis)*   Dogwood family *(Cornaceae)*

Height: 3"-9" (7-21cm). **Flower:** Tiny; indistinguishable; many, in dense, terminal cluster surrounded by 4 white, petal-like bracts. **Leaves:** Oval; entire; usually 6 in a whorl. **In bloom:** May-July. **Habitat-Range:** Woods, thickets and damp openings; throughout northern parts, and in mountains to West Virginia.

Most members of this family are trees or shrubs. This small plant grows in woods and bogs in colder climates. The tiny flowers grow in a greenish yellow cluster surrounded by 4 conspicuous, white bracts. A cluster of red fruit develops; hence the common name. These berries are edible and because they seem to stimulate the appetite Scottish immigrants called Bunchberry "plant of gluttony."

95 SPOTTED WINTERGREEN   Wintergreen family *(Pyrolaceae)*
(Chimaphila maculata)†

Height: 4″-12″ (10-30cm). **Flower:** 1/2″-1″ (1-2.5cm) diameter; regular, with 5 petals, 10 stamens. 1 thick, knobbed pistil; few, nodding in umbel. **Leaves:** Lanceolate; teeth widely spaced; whorled in tiers. **In bloom:** June-August. **Habitat-Range:** Dry woods; mostly throughout.

While most plants are blooming in sun-drenched meadows, this plant blooms in the summer woods. The nodding flowers are often overlooked but the dark, shiny leaves with their white markings catch the eye. The leaves, which are refreshing when chewed, are evergreen and even in winter draw our attention. Hence the common and the generic name (from *cheima,* Greek for "winter," and *philein,* "to love"). The plant was once used to treat kidney stones.

96 GRASS-OF-PARNASSUS *(Parnassia glauca)*†   Saxifrage family *(Saxifragaceae)*

Height: 8″-16″ (20-40cm). **Flower:** 1″ (2.5cm) diameter; regular, with 5 petals, 5 true stamens alternate with clusters of gland-tipped, sterile filaments, 1 pistil; solitary, terminal. **Leaves:** Roundish with heart-shaped bases; entire; mostly basal and upright, one sessile leaf halfway up flower stalk. **In bloom:** July-October. **Habitat-Range:** Wet, limy soil; north of a line from New Jersey to Illinois.

The flower petals are usually green-veined and the 5 true stamens alternate with clusters of 3-pronged, glandular filaments. Nothing about the plant is grasslike but the common name originated with the ancient Greek naturalist Dioscorides who saw a similar plant growing in masses in meadows around Mount Parnassus, sacred to Apollo and the Muses.

97 BOWMAN'S-ROOT *(Gillenia trifoliata)*   Rose family *(Rosaceae)*

Height: 2′-3′ (.6-1m). **Flower:** 1″ (2.5cm) diameter; regular, with 5 thin, twisted petals, numerous stamens, 5 pistils; several, in panicle. **Leaves:** Palmate, 3 stalkless leaflets; sharply toothed; alternate. **In bloom:** May-July. **Habitat-Range:** Rich woods; mostly throughout.

The twisted petals and stems give this plant an untidy appearance. In many instances the calyx is reddish. The root contains a very bitter substance and was used by Indians and colonists as a mild emetic.

AMERICAN IPECAC *(Gillenia stipulata)*   Rose family *(Rosaceae)*

Height: 2′-3′ (.6-1m). **Flower:** 1″ (2.5cm) diameter; regular, with 5 thin, twisted petals, numerous stamens, 5 pistils; several, in panicle. **Leaves:** Palmate, 3 stalkless leaflets and 2 leaflike structures at base; sharply toothed; alternate. **In bloom:** May-July.

Habitat-Range: Woods, thickets and rocky slopes; south of a line from southern New York to Illinois.

Similar to *G. trifoliata* but has two large stipules (leaflet-like structures at base of leaf) which make it appear to have 5 leaflets. another common name is Indian Physic, suggesting that it was used medicinally by Indians.

98 MAYSTAR *(Trientalis borealis)*   Primrose family *(Primulaceae)*

Height: 3″-9″ (8-23cm). **Flower:** 1/2″ (1cm) diameter, regular, usually with 7 finely pointed petals, 4 or 5 stamens, 1 pistil; 1 or 2, on thin stalks. **Leaves:** Lanceolate; entire; in whorls at summit. **In bloom:** May-June. **Habitat-Range:** Damp woods, slopes; northern regions, in mountains in South.

Although the names of many flowers suggest that they appear starlike, the arrangement of the finely pointed petals of this flower is truly star-shaped. The whorl of 7 to 9 shiny, tapering leaves adds to this illusion.

99 HORSE-NETTLE *(Solanum carolinense)*   Nightshade family *(Solanaceae)*

Height: 1′-2′ (.3-.6m). **Flower:** 3/4″(2cm) diameter; regular, with 5 wide, pointed petals forming a starlike corolla, 5 stamens whose anthers form a "beak," 1 pistil; several, in raceme. **Leaves:** Elliptical or oval; widely toothed; alternate. **In bloom:** May-October. **Habitat-Range:** Fields and waste places; mostly throughout, commoner southward.

The flower and/or buds may also be blue or lavender. The slender, yellowish prickles on the stem and midrib of its leaves make it difficult to clear this weed from a pasture. A member of the nightshade family, its plant parts contain solanine, a violently toxic chemical. Nevertheless, its orange berries, which contain relatively small amounts of the chemical, were dried and used as a sedative and anti-spasmodic by herb doctors.

BLACK NIGHTSHADE   Nightshade family *(Solanaceae)*
(Solanum americanum)

Height: 1′-3′ (.3-1m). **Flower:** 1/2″ (1cm) diameter; regular, with 5 turned-back petals, 5 stamens forming a "beak," 1 pistil; 2-4 flowers in nodding umbels. **Leaves:** Ovate, translucent; entire; opposite. **In bloom:** May-November. **Habitat-Range:** Rocky or dry open woods, thickets, waste places; mostly throughout.

Similar to *S. carolinense* but the flowers are smaller and the stem and leaves lack prickles. The common name refers to the lustrous black berries used to make nightshade jam and pies. Although these berries contain the poisonous alkaloid solanine, the Indians and early settlers learned to eliminate this by cooking, and some Indian tribes prepared a remedy for insomnia by steeping a few leaves in a large quantity of water. Another similar species with dull black berries and triangular, toothed leaves is Common Nightshade, *Solanum nigrum.*

100 WILD STRAWBERRY *(Fragaria virginiana)*   Rose family *(Rosaceae)*

Height: 2″-6″ (5-15cm). **Flower:** 3/4″ (2cm) diameter; regular, with 5 rounded petals, numerous stamens and pistils on cone-shaped structure in center; several, in flat cyme. **Leaves:** Palmate, 3 oval leaflets; sharply toothed; basal, upright. **In bloom:** May-July.

Habitat-Range: Fields, open slopes, borders of woods; mostly throughout.

Like the cultivated strawberry, it grows from a prostrate stem that runs along the ground. The fruit is an oval red berry with seedlike objects embedded in pits on its surface. It has a flavor some consider superior to that of the cultivated strawberry. Indians used strawberry juice and water to treat inflamed eyes. Root infusions were used to treat gonorrhea and mouth sores. A tea made from the leaves was reputed to remove cataracts and kidney stones. Linnaeus, the renowned Swedish plant taxonomist, was said to have successfully treated his gout with this plant.

WOOD STRAWBERRY *(Fragaria vesca)*   Rose family *(Rosaceae)*

Height: 2″-6″ (5-15cm). **Flower:** 3/4″ (2cm) diameter; regular, with 5 rounded petals, numerous stamens and pistils on a cone-shaped structure in center; several, in flat cyme. **Leaves:** Palmate, 3 narrow, oval leaflets; sharply toothed; basal, upright. **In bloom:** May-August. **Habitat-Range:** Rocky woods and openings; north of a line from Virginia to Illinois.

Similar to *F. virginiana* but is pale green and its leaflets are more narrow. Its fruit, which is rather dry and tasteless, is cone-shaped, with seedlike objects on the surface but not in pits.

101 COMMON WOOD SORREL   Wood-sorrel family *(Oxalidaceae)*
(Oxalis montana)†

Height: 2″-6″ (5-15cm). **Flower:** 3/4″ (2cm) diameter; regular, with 5 notched petals having deep pink veins, 10 stamens, 1 pistil; solitary, on leafless stalk. **Leaves:** Palmate, 3 heart-shaped leaflets; entire; basal, upright. **In bloom:** May-August. **Habitat-Range:** Damp woods; northernmost regions and in mountains in South.

Large colonies grow in the cool dampness of mountain woodlands. Because of the shape of the leaves it is also called Wood Shamrock. In Europe it is called Hallelujah Flower because it usually blooms between Easter and Pentacost Sunday. The slightly sour-tasting leaves make an interesting addition to a green salad. Indians made a tea from the leaves and drank it as a treatment for worms.

102 GREAT RAGWEED *(Ambrosia trifida)*   Composite family *(Compositae)*

Height: 1′-15′ (.3-4.5m). **Flower:** Tiny; indistinguishable; many, nodding in racemes. **Leaves:** Trilobed; upper leaves alternate, lower leaves opposite. **In bloom:** July-October. **Habitat-Range:** Dry soil, cultivated and waste lands; throughout.

Like many noxious weeds. this plant seems to grow anywhere. It can easily take over pasture land since it is not touched by grazing cattle because of its bitter taste. Although its flowers are small and inconspicuous, its trilobed leaves usually identify it. The leaves of Common Ragweed (*A. artemisiifolia*) a much smaller species, are finely dissected. These leaves provided a tea that was thought by early settlers to be helpful for upset stomach. The generic name, a term from classical mythology signifying the food of the gods, has become rather inappropriate since the plant is avoided by man because the pollen from its flowers is a chief cause of hay fever in late summer. The plant's seeds make an excellent bird food.

103 NODDING LADIES' TRESSES
(*Spiranthes cernua*)†

Orchid family *(Orchidaceae)*

Height: 6″-18″ (15-45cm). **Flower:** 1/4″ (6mm) long; irregular, with 1 sepal and 2 petals forming a hood, the third petal forms a lip with wavy edges; many, nodding in 3 or 4 spiral rows on long spike. **Leaves:** Grasslike; entire; basal, upright. **In bloom:** August-October. **Habitat-Range:** Moist or dry fields, bogs, moist thickets; mostly throughout.

The dozen or so species of Ladies' Tresses in our area are all similar to the one illustrated here. They are characterized by flowers in a more or less spirally twisted spike; hence the generic name, combining the Greek *speira*, "spiral," and *anthos*, "flower." The twisted spikes were also said to resemble the silken laces women used to gird themselves. These were called "ladies' traces," and the common name is a corruption of this. The Slender Ladies' Tresses (*S. gracilis*) has only a single spiral of flowers, and each flower has a green blotch on the lip. The flowers of the Hooded Ladies' Tresses (*S. romanzofiana*) do not nod and the lip is narrow toward the middle. The flowers of a coastal species, Spring Ladies' Tresses (*S. vernalis*), are covered with fine red hair and start blooming in the spring.

104 SILVERROD (*Solidago bicolor*)

Composite family *(Compositae)*

Height: 1′-3′ (.3-1m). **Flower:** Tiny; regular, composite with only 7-9 rays; many, on interrupted spike. **Leaves:** Spatulate, basal leaves stalked, stem leaves small and sessile; toothed; alternate. **In bloom:** July-October. **Habitat-Range:** Dry, open, sterile soil; throughout.

This is the only goldenrod whose flower is cream-colored or white; hence its common name. The stem is grayish and covered with fine hair.

105 WHITE WOOD ASTER (*Aster divaricatus*)

Composite family *(Compositae)*

Height: 1 1/2′-2 1/2′ (.5-.8m). **Flower:** 1″ (2.5cm) diameter; composite, with a circular cluster of disc flowers surrounded by relatively few ray flowers; many, in cymes. **Leaves:** Heart-shaped; toothed; alternate. **In bloom:** July-October. **Habitat-Range:** Dry, open woods, clearings; throughout.

There are may species of white aster but this is one of the earliest blooming. It grows on a zigzag stem and the flower disc, initially yellow, turns purple or brown as it ages. Indians used the young leaves of asters as a pot herb and made a tonic from the dried leaf stems.

106 RATTLESNAKE ROOT (*Prenanthes alba*)

Composite family *(Compositae)*

Height: 2′-5′ (.6-1.5m). **Flower:** 1/4″ (6mm) long; regular, composite, with rays forming bell-shaped head; many, in panicle in drooping clusters. **Leaves:** Variable (oval, triangular or heart-shaped); coarsely toothed, lobed or deeply cleft; alternate. **In bloom:** August-September. **Habitat-Range:** Rich woods and thickets; mostly throughout.

The drooping flowers (from the Greek *prenes*, "drooping," and *anthos*, "flower") are characteristic and are responsible for the generic name. Ten species are found in our area. The species illustrated has a purplish stem that exudes a milky juice when broken. A very bitter tonic made from the roots was used to treat snakebite; hence its common name.

107 BONESET *(Eupatorium perfoliatum)*   Composite family *(Compositae)*

Height: 2′-5′ (.6-1.5m). **Flower:** Tiny indistinguishable, tubular; many, in flat-topped, terminal cymes. **Leaves:** Lanceolate; finely toothed; opposite, clasping or often united at their bases. **In bloom:** August-October. **Habitat-Range:** Moist thickets, open woods, meadows; throughout.

An unusual feature is the way the hairy stem seems to grow through leaves that are united at their base. Hence the species name, combining the Latin words *per,* meaning "through," and *folium,* "leaf." Herb doctors took this as a "signature," and leaves of the plant were wrapped into the splint or bandage for a broken bone in the belief that they aided, as the common name suggests, in setting it. Dried leaves and flower tops were used as a tea in treating colds and breakbone fever (similar to grippe).

Yellow ★ Orange

Key

SPRING (March-early May)	**SUMMER** (late May-early August)	**FALL** (late Auguste-October)

Indistinguishable

Basal, entire
110 Golden Club
Alternate, pinnate
124 Golden Alexanders

Regular

Basal, tubular	*Basal, entire*
108 Trumpets	153 Bullhead-lily
Basal, entire	131 Corn Lily
113 Trout Lily	155 Yellow Iris
Basal, toothed	126 Blackberry Lily
121 Coltsfoot	125 Common Day-lily
Alternate, entire	142 Yellow Stargrass
119 Frostweed	*Alternate, entire*
116 Sessile Bellwort	160 Common Mullein
114 Hairy Puccoon	Tiger Lily
Alternate, toothed	137 Nodding Mandarin
123 Winter Cress	*Alternate, toothed*
120 Marsh Marigold	168 Moth Mullein
Alternate, palmate	165 Velvet Leaf
115 Common Cinquefoil	*Alternate, wavy-toothed*
Alternate, pinnate	169 Evening Primrose
117 Celandine	*Alternate, palmate*
Opposite, entire	143 Common Buttercup
111 Trumpet Honeysuckle	144 Yellow Wood-Sorrel
Opposite, pinnate	167 Flower-of-an-Hour
118 Celandine Poppy	*Alternate, pinnate*
	145 Yellow Avens
	161 Agrimony
	141 Wild Radish
	157 Partridge-Pea
	159 Wild Senna
	Opposite, entire
	164 Common St. Johnswort
	130 St. Andrew's Cross
	Opposite, lobed or toothed
	171 Yellow False Foxglove
	Opposite, pinnate
	138 Trumpet-creeper
	Whorled, entire
	162 Whorled Loosestrife
	128 Wood Lily
	129 Canada Lily
	127 Turk's-cap Lily

SPRING	SUMMER	FALL
(March-early May)	(late May-early August)	(late August-October)

Irregular

Basal, wavy-toothed	*Alternate, entire*	
112 Round-leaved Yellow Violet	156 Yellow Lady Slipper	
	166 Butter-and-Eggs	
Alternate, toothed	134 Yellow Fringed Orchis	
Downy Yellow Violet	132 Butterfly-Weed	
Whorled, entire	*Alternate, toothed*	
109 Whorled Pogonia	136 Spotted Touch-me-not	
	Alternate, palmate	
	139 Wild Indigo	
	Hop Clover	
	Alternate, pinnate	
	140 Birdsfoot Trefoil	
	163 Yellow Sweet Clover	
	Alternate, finely dissected	
	154 Bladderwort	
	Opposite, toothed	
	135 Horsemint	

Composite

Basal, pinnately lobed and toothed	*Basal, entire*	*Alternate, entire*
122 Common Dandelion	175 King Devil	180 Hard-leaved Goldenrod
	133 Orange Hawkweed	181 Showy Goldenrod
	Alternate, entire	*Alternate, toothed*
	148 Gray-headed Coneflower	178 Orange Coneflower
	173 Yellow Goatsbeard	176 Canada Goldenrod
	147 Black-eyed Susan	179 Blue-stemmed Goldenrod
	170 Wild Lettuce	177 Elm-leaved Goldenrod
	Alternate, toothed	
	149 Purple-headed Sneeze-weed	
	150 Woolly Ragwort	
	151 Elecampane	
	174 Field Sow-Thistle	
	172 Gumweed	
	146 Common Sunflower	
	Alternate, finely dissected	
	158 Common Tansy	
	Opposite, entire	
	152 Tickseed Coreopsis	

108 TRUMPETS *(Sarracenia flava)*† Pitcher-plant family *(Sarraceniaceae)*

Height: 1′-3′ (.3-1m). **Flower:** 3″-4 1/2″ (7-11cm) diameter; regular, with 5 oblong, incurving petals, numerous stamens, 1 pistil with umbrella-like stigma; solitary, terminal, nodding. **Leaves:** Long (1 1/2′-4′, 4.5-1m), hollow, trumpet-shaped with narrow wing along one side, hood at opening; basal, upright. **In bloom:** April-May. **Habitat-Range:** Wet pinelands, bogs; from southeastern Virginia south.

The trumpet-shaped leaves account for the common name. The hood is often yellowish and is veined with purple or red. This plant is insectivorous and the mechanism by which it captures and digests insects is similar to that of the Pitcher Plant, *S. purpurea.*

109 WHORLED POGONIA *(Isotria verticillata)*† Orchid family *(Orchidaceae)*

Height: 6″-12″ (15-30cm). **Flower:** 1 1/2″ (4cm) long; irregular, with 2 lateral petals and ridged lower lip with purple streaks, 3 long, narrow, purplish brown sepals; solitary, terminal. **Leaves:** Elliptical or oblong; entire; 5 in a whorl just below flower. **In bloom:** May-June. **Habitat-Range:** Moist woodlands and thickets; mostly throughout.

The outstanding feature of the flower is the three long, wide-spreading sepals. This is reflected in the generic name which combines the Greek *isos,* "equal," and *treis,* "three." A smaller, less flamboyant species commonly called Small Whorled Pogonia, *I. medeoloides,* has arching sepals that are not much longer than the petals. It is a rare plant because the bulb remains dormant for 10 to 20 years underground before producing a flower.

110 GOLDEN CLUB *(Orontium aquaticum)* Arum family *(Araceae)*

Height: 1′-2′ (.3-.6m). **Flower:** Tiny; indistinguishable; many, crowded on clublike spadix. **Leaves:** Oblong-elliptic; entire; basal, floating or erect. **In bloom:** April-June. **Habitat-Range:** Shallow ponds, shores, swamps; south of a line from Massachusetts to Kentucky, mainly in coastal states.

The club is a spadix whose tip is crowded with tiny yellow flowers. The plant is also called Never-wet because the leaves, which show a silvery iridescence while underwater, come up perfectly dry. After repeated boilings and washings, the rootstocks were eaten by the Indians of New York and Virginia.

111 TRUMPET HONEYSUCKLE Honeysuckle family *(Caprifoliaceae)*
(Lonicera sempervirens)

Height: Climbing vine. **Flower:** 1 1/2″-2″ (4-5cm) long; regular, with 5 petals forming a trumpet-shaped corolla, 5 stamens, 1 pistil; several, in cluster in upper leaf axils. **Leaves:** Elliptical or ovate; entire; opposite. **In bloom:** March-July. **Habitat-Range:** Borders of woods, thickets and fencerows; throughout, but more common southward.

This garden escape is sometimes called Coral Honeysuckle because the flowers, which are scarlet on the outside and yellow within, are said to resemble the red corals. The upper one or two pairs of leaves are fused at their bases and appear to be perforated by the stem. The fruit, an orange or red berry, forms late in the summer and early fall. The rather tasteless berries were eaten by Indians who also made a decoction from the leaves for treating sore throats and coughs. The leaves were also dried and used as an ingredient in herbal tobacco smoked in the treatment of asthma.

112 ROUND-LEAVED YELLOW VIOLET
(*Viola rotundifolia*)
Violet family (*Violaceae*)

Height: 2″-5″ (5-12cm). **Flower:** 1/2″ (1cm) diameter; irregular, with 5 yellow petals, the 3 lower ones veined with brown, side petals bearded, 5 stamens, 1 pistil; solitary, terminal on leafless stalk. **Leaves:** Roundish; wavy-toothed; basal. **In bloom:** April-May. **Habitat-Range:** Rich woods; throughout.

At flowering time the leaves are partly curled but later they spread out flat on the ground. Of the many species of yellow violets this is the only one that does not have stem leaves. The leaves of all yellow violets can be eaten in salads or used to thicken soups and stews.

DOWNY YELLOW VIOLET (*Viola pubescens*)†
Violet family (*Violaceae*)

Height: 6″-16″ (15-40cm). **Flower:** 1/2″ (1cm) diameter; irregular, with 5 yellow petals, the 3 lower ones veined with purple, side petals bearded, 5 stamens, 1 pistil; few, from leaf axils. **Leaves:** Heart-shaped; irregularly toothed; alternate. **In bloom:** May-June. **Habitat-Range:** Dry woodlands; mostly throughout.

This yellow violet is characterized by hairy stems and heart-shaped stem leaves, whereas the similar appearing Smooth Yellow Violet, *V. pensylvanica*, has smooth stems and stem leaves and several basal leaves. The stem leaves of the Three-parted Yellow Violet, *V. tripartita*, which grows in the southern part of our area, are cleft into three lobes. The small bulbs from which violets grow were boiled and dried by Indians and stored for winter use.

113 TROUT LILY (*Erythronium americanum*)†
Lily family (*Liliaceae*)

Height: 4″-10″ (10-25cm). **Flower:** 1 1/2″ (4cm) diameter; regular, with 3 petals and 3 sepals of same size and color which are curved backwards, 6 stamens, 1 pistil; solitary, nodding. **Leaves:** Elliptical, clasping petiole; entire; upright basal pair. **In bloom:** March-May. **Habitat-Range:** Moist woods, thickets; throughout.

The plant usually grows in patches that catch one's eye because the leaves are mottled with purplish brown. Its leaves are responsible for several of its common names. The mottling was said to resemble the marking of a brook trout; hence Trout Lily. The two upright leaves suggest alert fawn's ears; hence the name Fawn Lily. Adder's Tongue, another name, refers to the sharp, purplish points of the leaves as they emerge from the ground in early spring. Young leaves were cooked as greens or added to soups and stews by the Indians. They were also made into a poultice for swellings and ulcers. A leaf tea was used to treat dropsy, hiccoughs and vomiting. The plant's small underground bulb was eaten by the Indians. The shape of the bulb, which resembles a canine tooth, accounts for the common name Dog's-tooth Violet.

114 HAIRY PUCCOON
(*Lithospermum croceum*)
Forget-me-not family (*Boraginaceae*)

Height: 1′-3′ (.3-1m). **Flower:** 1″ (2.5cm) diameter; regular, with 5 petals forming a funnel-shaped corolla with flared opening; many, on crowded raceme. **Leaves:** Lanceolate; entire; alternate. **In bloom:** May-July. **Habitat-Range:** Sands, gravel, dry woods; north of a line from western New York to Illinois.

As the common name suggests, the leaves and stem are very hairy. The roots yield a purple stain which explains the name Puccoon, an Indian word given to many plants that yielded a coloring material. An infusion made of the root, taken daily as a drink for 6 months, was believed by Indians to result in sterility. A shorter, less leafy species with smaller flowers, Hoary Puccoon (*L. canascens*), yields a yellow dye that was used as war paint and is commonly called Indian Paint. Narrow-leaved Puccoon, *L. incisum*, has very narrow leaves and its flowers have toothed petals. The generic name (from the Greek *lithos*, "stone," and *sperma*, "seed") derives from the small, hard nut they produce.

115 COMMON CINQUEFOIL *(Potentilla simplex)*   Rose family *(Rosaceae)*

Height: Crawling runners 6″-20″ (15-50cm). **Flower:** 1/2″ (1cm) diameter; regular, with 5 round petals, numerous stamens and pistils; single, or few in cyme. **Leaves:** Palmate, with elliptical leaflets; toothed; alternate. **In bloom:** April-June. **Habitat-Range:** Dry or moist fields, thickets, open woods; throughout.

The common name is derived from the shape of the leaf (from French *cinque*, "five," and *feuille*, "leaves"). Indians made a tea from boiled leaves and mixed it with wine or brandy and used it to treat diarrhea and stomachache. When boiled or roasted the roots taste like parsnips and have been used as famine food. Silvery Cinquefoil (*P. argentea*) has leaves with lobed margins and with silvery-silky undersides. Rough-fruited Cinquefoil (*P. recta*) is an upright species with 5-7 narrow leaflets and a flat terminal cluster of pale yellow flowers. Another upright species, Tall Cinquefoil (*P. arguta*), has white or creamy flowers and a stem covered with brownish hair.

116 SESSILE BELLWORT *(Uvularia sessilifolia)*   Lily family *(Liliaceae)*

Height: 4″-12″ (10-30cm). **Flower:** 1″ (2.5cm) long; regular, with 3 sepals and 3 petals of the same size and color and forming a bell-shaped corolla, 6 stamens, 1 pistil; several, drooping from leaf axils. **Leaves:** Oval, tapering at tip, sessile; entire; alternate. **In bloom:** May-June. **Habitat-Range:** Woods and thickets; throughout.

The drooping flowers reminded Linnaeus of the uvula, the flap of tissue hanging from the roof of the oral cavity; hence the generic name. The common and species names indicate that the leaf lacks a stalk. A species whose leaf bases surround the stem and it appears to grow through them is Perfoliate Bellwort (*U. perfoliata*). Another perfoliate species which is much taller (1′-2′, .3-.6m) and has larger flowers (1 1/2″, 4cm long) is the Large-flowered Bellwort (*U. grandiflora*). The young shoots of all bellworts were once used as a substitute for asparagus.

117 CELANDINE *(Chelidonium majus)*   Poppy family *(Papaveraceae)*

Height: 1′-2′ (.3-.6m). **Flower:** 3/4″ (2cm) diameter; regular, having 4 petals, numerous stamens, 1 pistil; several, in loose umbel. **Leaves:** Pinnately divided; lobed; alternate. **In bloom:** March-August. **Habitat-Range:** Moist soil, waste places; mostly throughout.

The leaves, stems and flower buds are whitish and hairy. The broken stem exudes an acrid, saffron-colored juice that was once used as a dye and to remove warts, corns and freckles. Herb doctors interpreted the color as a "signature" and used the plant to treat jaundice and liver problems. The generic name is derived from the Greek *chelidon*, "swallow," because according to Aristotle and others, swallows bathed the eyes of their young in the juice to strengthen eyesight. Herb doctors also used it as a cure for sore eyes.

118 CELANDINE POPPY *(Stylophorum diphyllum)*   Poppy family *(Papaveraceae)*

Height: 12″-18″ (30-45cm). **Flower:** 1 1/2″ (4cm) diameter; regular, with 4 petals, numerous stamens, 1 pistil; 1-4 at the summit. **Leaves:** Pinnately divided; lobed; one opposite pair just below flower, others basal. **In bloom:** March-May. **Habitat-Range:** Rich woods and bluffs; south of a line from western Pennsylvania to Wisconsin.

Just below the deep yellow flower is a pair of stem leaves with white bloom on their undersides.

119 FROSTWEED *(Helianthemum canadense)*   Rockrose family *(Cistaceae)*

Height: 8″-16″ (20-40cm). **Flower:** 1″ (2.5cm) diameter; regular, with 5 petals, numerous stamens, 1 pistil; solitary, from leaf axils. **Leaves:** Lanceolate, sessile or almost so; entire; alternate. **In bloom:** May-July. **Habitat-Range:** Dry, sandy soil; throughout.

If the sun is shining the plant produces a single showy flower which only lasts one day. Later in the summer it produces inconspicuous, budlike flowers that yield most of the seed. The common name derives from the fact that late in autumn the stem cracks near its base and the leaking sap freezes and forms feathery ice crystals. The dried herb was used as a tonic and astringent. The Carolina Rockrose, *H. carolinianum*, which has a hairy stem and mainly basal leaves, is found in the drier coastal plains in the southernmost part of our range.

120 MARSH MARIGOLD *(Caltha palustris)*†   Buttercup family *(Ranunculaceae)*

Height: 8″-24″ (20-60cm). **Flower:** 1″-1 1/2″ (2.5-4cm) diameter; regular, with 5-9 petal-like sepals, numerous stamens, many pistils; few, terminal or in leaf axils. **Leaves:** Heart-shaped or kidney-shaped, upper ones sessile; toothed; alternate. **In bloom:** April-June. **Habitat-Range:** Swamps, wet woods, wet meadows; mostly throughout.

As the common and species names suggest (*palustris* is Latin for "of the swamps") the plant is found in wet situations. The name Marigold is said to be due to the use of the flower in Medieval church festivals dedicated to the Virgin Mary. The leaves, which are poisonous if eaten uncooked, were used as a cooked green. They are very rich in iron and were used to treat anemia. The flower buds can also be boiled and eaten; they are pickled in the southern states.

121 COLTSFOOT *(Tussilago farfara)*   Composite family *(Compositae)*

Height: 6″-18″ (15-45cm). **Flower:** 1″ (2.5cm) diameter; composite, with many thin, bright yellow rays around a dull yellow disc; solitary, terminal. **Leaves:** Roundly heart-shaped; sparsely toothed; basal, upright. **In bloom:** March-May. **Habitat-Range:** Roadsides, waste places, eroded banks; north of a line from New Jersey to Illinois.

It is often mistaken for a dandelion but study reveals that the flower stem is covered with reddish scales and the flowers appear long before the leaves. The leaves, which are white and hairy underneath, were thought to resemble a colt's foot; hence the common name. The plant was brought from Europe as a cure for coughs (*tussis* is Latin for "cough") and its leaves served as an ingredient in herbal tobacco, which was smoked as a treatment for asthma. Coltsfoot tea sweetened with honey was used for colds and asthma. The flower stalks were made into a preparation, "Syrup of Coltsfoot," recommended for chronic bronchitis.

122 COMMON DANDELION   Composite family *(Compositae)*
(Taraxacum officinale)

Height: 2″-18″ (5-45cm). **Flower:** 1 1/2″ (4cm) diameter; composite, with 150-200 ray flowers; solitary, terminal. **Leaves:** Oblong; pinnately lobed and toothed; basal rosette. **In bloom:** March-October. **Habitat-Range:** Lawns, roadsides, fields; throughout.

Because of the sharp projections from the borders of the leaves early botanists described it as *dent de lion* — French for "teeth of a lion" — which was eventually corrupted into the common name. The hollow flower stalk contains a milky juice which was used to remove warts. In time the flowers produce balls of feathery, tufted seeds which are dispersed by the wind. Because the leaves lie flat the plant is usually unharmed by the passage of a lawnmower, and most attempts to pull it up merely remove some of the leaves because they grow from a long, tough root. The roots were gathered by Europeans and early Americans, dried and ground, and steeped in hot water to make a substitute for coffee. The young leaves can be gathered in the spring and served as salad greens or cooked and eaten like spinach. The flower stalk of the Fall Dandelion (*Leontodon autumnalis*) does not have the milky juice and the underside of the outer ray flowers are usually reddish. The Red-seeded Dandelion (*Taraxacum erythrospermum*) has a smaller flower head, very deeply cut leaves and, as the common name suggests, red seeds.

123 WINTER CRESS *(Barbarea vulgaris)*   Mustard family *(Cruciferae)*

Height: 1′-2′ (.3-.6m). **Flower:** 3/8″ (8mm) diameter; regular, with 4 petals which spread out to form a cross, 6 stamens, 1 pistil; many, in raceme. **Leaves:** Upper ones ovate, sessile, clasping, deeply toothed, alternate; lower ones lyre-shaped, deeply lobed with terminal lobe larger than the 1 or 2 pairs of lateral lobes, alternate. **In bloom:** April-August. **Habitat-Range:** Meadow, brooksides, damp woods; north of a line from Virginia to Illinois.

This is one of the earliest blooming members of the large mustard family. The long, thin seed pods either stand upright and hug the stem or spread horizontally. The leaves, which are gathered until the flowers show their full yellow, were used in salads or as a cooked green. Early Winter Cress, *B. verna*, closely resembles *B. vulgaris*, but its lower leaves have 4-8 pairs of lateral lobes and its seed pods are sharply four-sided.

124 GOLDEN ALEXANDERS *(Zizia aurea)*   Parsley family *(Umbelliferae)*

Height: 1′-3′ (.3-1m). **Flower:** Tiny; indistinguishable; many, in umbels. **Leaves:** Pinnate, lanceolate leaflets; finely toothed; alternate. **In bloom:** April-June. **Habitat-Range:** Damp thickets, wet woods, meadows, swamps; throughout.

The generic name honors Johann Ziz, a German botanist. The central flower in each umbel lacks a stalk. A similar species but with heart-shaped basal leaves is Heartleaf Parsnip, *Z. aptera*. The Yellow Pimpernel, *Taenidia interrima*, also has umbels of yellow flowers but its pinnate leaves are not toothed and its thin stem often has a whitish bloom.

125 COMMON DAY-LILY *(Hermerocallis fulva)*   Lily family *(Liliaceae)*

Height: 3′-6′ (1-2m). **Flower:** 5″ (13cm) diameter; regular, with 3 petals and 3 sepals the same color and size forming a bell-shaped corolla, 6 stamens, 1 pistil; single, with several additional buds on forked stalk. **Leaves:** Long, swordlike; entire; upright, basal. **In bloom:** June-August. **Habitat-Range:** Border of fields and woods, roadsides; locally throughout northern part of range, south to Virginia.

The flower of this garden escape is only open for one day. Hence its common and generic names, *Hemerocallis* being a combination of two Greek words, *hemera*, "a day," and *callos*, "beauty." The upward-facing flower has petals with wavy margins. A smaller yellow species, *H. flava*, is less common and is found in scattered locations. Many parts of the plant are edible. Unopened flower buds may be fried in egg batter. The young, crisp tubers add a nutty flavor to salads. The young stems also make a tender vegetable when boiled and seasoned with butter and salt.

126 BLACKBERRY LILY *(Belamcanda chinensis)*   Iris family *(Iridaceae)*

Height: 1 1/2′-4′ (.4-1m). **Flower:** 1 1/2″-2″ (4-5cm) diameter; regular, with 3 petals and 3 sepals the same size and color, 3 stamens, 1 pistil; several, on branched stem. **Leaves:** Flat, swordlike; entire; upright, rising from basal cluster. **In bloom:** June-July. **Habitat-Range:** Thickets, open woods, waste places; south of a line from Connecticut to Indiana and South to Georgia.

Introduced from Asia where it was used by the Chinese as a medicinal plant for complaints of the chest and liver, it now adds color to our open woods and roadsides. The flowers, which last only one day, are marked with crimson-purple spots. The common name is derived from its mature seed pod which splits open to reveal a mass of black, shining seeds resembling a blackberry.

127 TURK'S-CAP LILY *(Lilium superbum)*†   Lily family *(Liliaceae)*

Height: 3′-8′ (1-2.5m). **Flower:** 5″ (13cm) diameter; regular, with 3 petals and 3 sepals the same size and color and markedly curled back, 6 stamens, 1 pistil; several, nodding. **Leaves:** Lanceolate; entire; usually in whorls along stem. **In bloom:** June-August. **Habitat-Range:** Moist meadows and swampy woods; mostly throughout.

An endangered species, the spotted petals and sepals of the nodding flowers are curled back markedly, giving the flower a shape like the cap worn by ancient Turks. The inner bases of the petals and sepals are green, forming a green star in the center of the flower. Thoreau once said that the bulbs of this plant were gathered in the fall by Maine Indians and were used in soups. A shorter species (2′-3′, .6-1m) that closely resembles the Turk's-Cap Lily is the Carolina Lily (*L. michauxii*) found in Virginia, West Virginia and southward. It differs in having bluntly pointed leaves tapering to narrow bases that may be scattered or arranged in whorls along the stem.

TIGER LILY *(Lilium tigrinum)* Lily family *(Liliaceae)*

Height: 2′-5′ (.6-1.5m). **Flower:** 5″ (13cm) diameter; regular, with 3 petals and 3 sepals the same size and color and markedly curled back, 6 stamens, 1 pistil; several, nodding. **Leaves:** Lanceolate; entire; alternate. **In bloom:** July-August. **Habitat-Range:** Roadside and thickets; locally throughout most of our range.

Although similar to *L. superbum*, the flower lacks the green central star and the leaves, which are alternate, have small black bulbets in their axils. Purple spots mottle the flower like the markings of a tiger; hence its common name. A native of Eastern Asia, this plant was used by Chinese physicians to prevent the nausea and vomiting of pregnancy. The bulbs were also cultivated as a vegetable in Japan but when the plant was brought to this country for its beauty, it escaped from gardens and is now found in meadows and along roadsides.

128 WOOD LILY *(Lilium philadelphicum)*† Lily family *(Liliaceae)*

Height: 2′-4′ (.6-1m). **Flower:** 4″ (10cm) diameter; regular, with 3 petals and 3 sepals the same size and color and tapering at their bases and forming a bell-shaped corolla, 6 stamens, 1 pistil; solitary, terminal, upright. **Leaves:** Lanceolate; entire; in whorls along stem. **In bloom:** June-August. **Habitat-Range:** Dry, open woods, clearings; throughout northern part of range, in uplands in South.

The beauty of this rather rare orange-red lily is accentuated by its bleak habitat in small, woodland clearings. The petals and sepals are mottled with purple-brown spots and are tapered to slender stalks. Because the flower head holds no water it remains erect, even in rain. The plant grows from a bulb which was dug by Indians and eaten like a potato.

129 CANADA LILY *(Lilium canadense)*† Lily family *(Liliaceae)*

Height: 2′-5′ (.6-1.5m). **Flower:** 2″-3″ (5-8cm) long; regular, with 3 petals and 3 sepals the same size and color with tips curved outwards forming a bell-shaped corolla, 6 stamens, 1 pistil; one or several, nodding. **Leaves:** Broadly lanceolate; entire; in whorls along stem. **In bloom:** June-August. **Habitat-Range:** Meadows, low thickets and wet woods; throughout northern part of range, in Southern uplands.

The nodding bells of the Canada Lily grace wet meadows and clearings. Although orange is the more common form, there are also red and yellow forms. The petals and sepals display brownish-purple spots. The flower buds were picked by the Indians and prepared like green beans. Indians also ate the rootstock and by soaking the roots in vinegar, herb doctors prepared a medicine for removing corns. A smaller, nodding lily (2′-3′ .6-1m) found in Virginia and North Carolina is Gray's Lily (*L. grayi*). It resembles the Canada Lily but its petals and sepals are not curved as much, the color is a deeper orange, and it is more heavily spotted.

130 ST. ANDREW'S CROSS St. Johnwort family *(Hypericaceae)*
(Ascyrum hypericoides)

Height: 6″-18″ (15-45cm). **Flower:** 3/4″ (2cm) diameter; regular, having 4 unequal sepals, 4 oblong petals, numerous stamens, 1 pistil; few, terminal and from upper leaf axils, **Leaves:** Oblong, narrowed at the base; entire; opposite. **In bloom:** July-September. **Habitat-Range:** Dry, sandy soil; south of a line from Massachusetts to Illinois.

The similar, but taller, St. Peterswort (*A. stans*) has larger flowers with 2 pairs of unequal sepals, one pair broad and one narrow.

131 CORN LILY (*Clintonia borealis*)   Lily family *(Liliaceae)*

Height: 6″-18″ (15-45cm). **Flower:** 3/4″ (2cm) long; regular with 3 sepals and 3 petals of the same size and color forming a bell-shaped corolla, 6 stamens, 1 pistil; few, nodding in umbel. **Leaves:** Oval; entire; with hairy fringe; three, basal, upright. **In bloom:** May-July. **Habitat-Range:** Cool, moist woods and thickets; throughout northern areas, in mountains in the South.

Oval-shaped blue berries develop from the greenish yellow flowers. The dark shiny leaves were added to salads or boiled and served as greens. This plant and a similar white-flowered species, White Clintonia (*C. umbellulata*), are dedicated to De Witt Clinton, early 19th-century governor of New York.

132 BUTTERFLY-WEED   Milkweed family *(Asclepidaceae)*
(*Asclepias tuberosa*)

Height: 2′-3′ (.6-1m). **Flower:** 3/8″ (1cm) diameter; regular, with 5 curved-back petals that form a cup that supports 5 small horns curving onto a central structure of 5 united stamens and a column of 5 pistils; many, in terminal, flat cluster. **Leaves:** Oblong-ovate, almost sessile; entire; mostly alternate. **In bloom:** June-September. **Habitat-Range:** Dry, open soil; mostly throughout.

This is an unusual member of the milkweed family because its sap is not milky but is a watery juice. The brilliant coloring of its flowers at the tip of a rough, hairy stem is what attracts many butterflies; hence its common name. Indians chewed the tough, underground stem as a cure for pleurisy and other pulmonary complaints; hence another common name, Pleurisy Root. The young tender shoots were used by Indians as a green vegetable and some Indians ate the young, spindle-shaped seed pods with buffalo meat.

133 ORANGE HAWKWEED   Composite family *(Compositae)*
(*Hieracium aurantiacum*)

Height: 1′-2′ (.3-.6m) **Flower:** 3/4″ (1.5cm) diameter; composite, with rays overlapping in several concentric circles; several, in terminal cluster. **Leaves:** Elliptical-oval, hairy; entire; basal rosette. **In bloom:** June-September. **Habitat-Range:** Roadsides, fields; throughout northern part of range, south to Virginia.

A European emigrant, it invaded fields and meadows so profusely it ruined good pastureland and was cursed by farmers as the Devil's Paintbrush. It apparently was not eaten by cattle because of its hairy stems and leaves. It is futile to gather the bright orange flowers for a bouquet since they close tightly soon after being picked. The common name refers to an ancient superstition (reflected in the generic name, derived from the Greek *hierax* meaning "hawk") that hawks ate the plant to strengthen their eyesight. This is also why hawkweeds were used by herb doctors in eye lotions.

134 **YELLOW FRINGED ORCHIS**   Orchid family *(Orchidaceae)*
(Habenaria ciliaris)†

Height: 1'-2' (.3-.6m). **Flower:** 1 1/2″ (4cm) long; irregular, having 3 petals and 3 sepals the same color, upper sepal and 2 lateral petals erect, lower petal a fringed lip and projecting backward with downward-pointing spur; many, in dense spike. **Leaves:** Lanceolate, sessile, clasping; entire; alternate. **In bloom:** July-August. **Habitat-Range:** Moist meadows, sandy bogs; mostly throughout, with exception of upper New England.

   The color ranges from yellow to deep orange in these long-spurred flowers. The spur is shorter than the fringed lip in the Crested Yellow Orchis, *H. cristata.*

135 **HORSEMINT** *(Monarda punctata)*   Mint family *(Labiatae)*

Height: 1'-3' (.3-1m). **Flower:** 1″ (2.5cm) long; irregular, having 2-lipped yellow corolla dotted with purple, upper lip arched, lower lip pointing downward; several, in axils of white or purplish bracts. **Leaves:** Lanceolate; toothed; opposite. **In bloom:** July-October. **Habitat-Range:** Sandy soil along or near coastal plain; Long Island south.

   The cluster of white or purplish bracts usually catch the eye. The purple spots on the pale yellow flower account for the species name, Latin *punctatum* meaning "a point."

136 **SPOTTED TOUCH-ME-NOT**   Jewelweed family *(Balsaminaceae)*
(Impatiens capensis)

Height: 2'-6' (.6-2m). **Flower:** 1″ (2.5cm) long; irregular, with 3 petals emerging from a colored, bell-shaped sepal extended backward as a spur, 2 smaller, green sepals, 5 stamens, 1 pistil; on slender stalks from leaf axils. **Leaves:** Oval; rounded teeth; alternate. **In bloom:** June-September. **Habitat-Range:** Wet, shady places; mostly throughout.

   This plant grows in fairly large patches in moist, shaded ground and in open areas along streams. When touched, even very lightly, its mature seed pods burst open and scatter their seeds; hence, the common and generic names (*impatiens,* a Latin word meaning "impatient"). The dangling flowers with red spots consist of a sac with a spur that is bent back parallel with the sac. The hollow, succulent stem contains a watery juice which can be used as an emergency prophylactic against the itch of poison ivy. The Indians also used the juice to treat athlete's foot and other fungal skin ailments. Recent scientific analysis confirms that it has fungicidal agents. A less common pale yellow species, *I. pallida,* may also be found. Its flowers have a red-spotted sac but the spur is pointed downward.

137 **NODDING MANDARIN** *(Disporum maculatum)*   Lily family *(Liliaceae)*

Height: 8″-24″ (20-60cm). **Flower:** 1″ (2.5cm) long; regular, with 3 petals and 3 sepals of the same size and color forming a bell-shaped corolla, 6 stamens projecting beyond corolla; solitary, or few nodding in umbel. **Leaves:** Ovate, sessile; entire; alternate. **In bloom:** April-May. **Habitat-Range:** Rich woods; west of a line from Ohio to Tennessee.

   The stem and lower leaf surfaces are covered with small stiff hairs and the yellow flowers are spotted with purple; hence another common name, Spotted Disporum. A more eastern species, Yellow Mandarin (*D. lanuginosum*), has smaller flowers that are not spotted and its stamens are shorter than the corolla.

138 TRUMPET-CREEPER *(Campsis radicans)* Bignonia family *(Bignoniaceae)*

Height: Climbing vine. **Flower:** 3″ (8cm) long; regular, with 5 petals united to form a tubular corolla, 5 stamens, 1 pistil; several, in terminal clusters. **Leaves:** Compound, 7-11 ovate, pointed leaflets; toothed; opposite. **In bloom:** July-September. **Habitat-Range:** Low woods and thickets; throughout the area south of a line from New Jersey to Illinois, locally northward.

This creeping vine escaped from cultivation and has become a troublesome weed, especially in the South. Farmers, whose cattle-grazed meadows were surrounded by this vine, claimed it gave the cattle an itch; hence, its other common name, Cow-Itch Vine. A more southern species that resembles Trumpet Creeper is Cross Vine (*B. capreolata*). Its leaves consist of two oblong leaflets with heart-shaped bases. Its flowers are red on the outside and orange within and emerge from leaf axils; when cut, the center of the stem is marked with a Maltese cross; hence its common name.

139 WILD INDIGO *(Baptisia tinctoria)* Pea family *(Leguminosae)*

Height: 1′-3′ (.3-1m). **Flower:** 1/2″ (1cm) long; irregular, pealike; several, in loose racemes. **Leaves:** Palmate, 3 ovate leaflets; entire; alternate. **In bloom:** June-September. **Habitat-Range:** Dry, sandy soil; throughout.

The many-branched stem and its leaves are bluish green. The leaves turn black when dried. The dried bushy stem is used as a fly brush by southern mountain people, and farmers tied it to the harness to brush flies from their plow-horses. When steeped in water and allowed to ferment, the leaves yield a blue dye; hence the common and generic names (from Greek *baptizein*, "to dye").

140 BIRDSFOOT TREFOIL *(Lotus corniculatus)* Pea family *(Leguminosae)*

Height: 6″-24″ (15-60cm). **Flower:** 1/2″ (1cm) diameter; irregular, pealike, yellow sometimes tinged with red; solitary, or several in umbel. **Leaves:** Pinnate, 5 leaflets, basal pair looking like stipules; entire; alternate. **In bloom:** June-September. **Habitat-Range:** Fields, roadsides, waste places; north of a line from Virginia to Ohio.

The common name derives from the palmate arrangement of the seed pods, which resembles a bird's foot, and the three end segments of the pinnate leaves. The cooked seed pods were eaten by Indians.

141 WILD RADISH *(Raphanus raphanistrum)* Mustard family *(Cruciferae)*

Height: 1′-2 1/2′ (.3-.8m). **Flower:** 1/2″ (1cm) diameter; regular, having 4 petals forming crosslike corolla, 6 stamens, 1 pistil; several, in raceme. **Leaves:** Pinnately lobed with roundish terminal lobe; lobes toothed; alternate. **In bloom:** April-November. **Habitat-Range:** Weed of grainfields, waste places; throughout, except southernmost areas.

As the pale yellow flowers of this hairy plant age, they turn whitish with violet veins. The upright, beaked seed pods have beadlike constrictions. The generic name derives from the Greek *raphanos*, meaning "quickly appearing," alluding to the rapid germination of the seeds.

142 **YELLOW STARGRASS** *(Hypoxis hirsuta)*   Amaryllis family *(Amaryllidaceae)*

Height: 2″-6″ (5-15cm). **Flower:** 1/2″ (1cm) diameter; regular, with 3 petals and 3 sepals of the same color and size forming a star-shaped corolla, 6 stamens, 1 pistil; one or a few, at summit of stem. **Leaves:** Narrow, grasslike; entire; basal, upright. **In bloom:** April-September. **Habitat-Range:** Open woods and meadows; mostly throughout.

Although the open flower is bright yellow, the underside of the petals and sepals is greenish and hairy and the stem is hairy; hence the species name, *hirsutus* being the Latin for "hairy."

143 **COMMON BUTTERCUP** *(Ranunculus acris)*   Buttercup family *(Ranunculaceae)*

Height: 2′-3′ (.6-1m). **Flower:** 1″ (2.5cm) diameter; regular, with 5 bright yellow petals, numerous stamens; several, in loose corymb. **Leaves:** Palmate, 5-7 narrow leaflets; toothed; stem leaves sessile and alternate, basal leaves upright with long petioles. **In bloom:** May-August. **Habitat-Range:** Fields, meadows, roadsides; mostly throughout.

This naturalized, hairy native of Europe is one of the commonest species of buttercup. As the generic name (from Latin *ranunculus*, "little frog") suggests, many species of buttercup are found in moist situations. The Swamp Buttercup, *R. septentrionalis*, has a smooth, hollow stem and palmate leaves with 3 leaflets. A common species that grows in large patches because it spreads by runners is Creeping Buttercup, *R. repens*. It is easily identified because its leaves are often mottled with pale blotches. Buttercups can easily take over a meadow because they contain an acrid juice that makes them distasteful to grazing animals. This juice was often used by beggars to produce ulcerations of the skin and thus attract sympathy. Indians boiled and ate the roots and some Indian tribes crushed the leaves and inhaled the vapor as a cure for headache.

144 **YELLOW WOOD-SORREL** *(Oxalis stricta)*   Wood-sorrel family *(Oxalidaceae)*

Height: 6″-15″ (15-37cm). **Flower:** 1/2″ (1cm) diameter; regular, with 5 petals sometimes red at the base, 10 stamens, 1 pistil; few, on long stalks in sparse umbel. **Leaves:** Palmate, 3 heart-shaped leaflets; entire; alternate. **In bloom:** May-October. **Habitat-Range:** Dry, open woods and fields; throughout.

The pencil-shaped seed pods are bent upright on the stalk. A taller species (1′-3′, .3-1m) with larger flowers and unbent seed pods is the Large Yellow Wood-Sorrel, *O. grandis*. Creeping Wood-Sorrel, *O. corniculata*, grows from a creeping stem. The leaves of wood-sorrel add a pleasantly sour taste to a green salad but they should be used sparingly because they contain oxalic acid (from Greek *oxys*, "sour").

145 **YELLOW AVENS** *(Geum aleppicum)*   Rose family *(Rosaceae)*

Height: 1′-5′ (.6-1.5m). **Flower:** 1″ (2.5cm) diameter; regular, with 5 petals, numerous stamens, numerous pistils with hooked styles; solitary, terminal. **Leaves:** Pinnate, 5-9 wedge-shaped leaflets, sometimes interspersed with small ones; toothed; alternate. **In bloom:** June-August. **Habitat-Range:** Thickets, moist meadows; north of a line from New Jersey to Illinois.

The stem of this species and that of Large-leaved Avens (*G. macrophyllum*), which has basal leaves that end in very large round segments, are hairy. The roots, which have a delicate aromatic flavor, were chewed for halitosis and were added to freshly brewed ale to enrich the flavor and improve the keeping qualities. A cordial against the plague was made by boiling the roots in wine.

146 COMMON SUNFLOWER *(Helianthus annuus)*   Composite family *(Compositae)*

Height: 3′-12′ (1-3.5m). **Flower:** 4″-6″ (10-15cm) diameter; composite, with many rays surrounding a brownish disk; solitary, terminal. **Leaves:** Broadly ovate; toothed; alternate. **In bloom:** July-October. **Habitat-Range:** Waste places, roadsides; mostly throughout.

There are over 20 species of sunflower in our area, this being a native western species that became established in the East. Some species have yellow disks but this one has a brownish disk. The generic name combines the Greek *helios*, "sun," and *anthos*, "flower." They were worshipped by the early Incas as a symbol of the sun. American Indians ate the seeds or boiled them to obtain oil to dress their hair. They also used the stalks for textile fibers and the dried leaves as a substitute for tobacco.

147 BLACK-EYED SUSAN *(Rudbeckia serotina)*   Composite family *(Compositae)*

Height: 1′-2′ (.3-.6m). **Flower:** 2″-4″ (5-10cm) diameter; composite, having 10-20 dark yellow rays around a dark brown disk; single, terminal. **Leaves:** Linear-lanceolate; entire, rarely toothed; alternate. **In bloom:** June-October. **Habitat-Range:** Waste places, roadsides, dry fields; throughout.

Originally a native of the western United States, it was introduced into our range in samples of clover seed. It closely resembles a rough, hairy species with ovate leaves, *R. hirta*. Herbalists used the plant to treat skin infections, and recent research has shown that extracts from the plant have antibiotic properties.

148 GRAY-HEADED CONEFLOWER   Composite family *(Compositae)*
(Ratibida pinnata)

Height: 3′-5′ (1-1.5). **Flower:** 3″-4″ (8-10cm) long; composite, oblong disk surrounded by 4-7 drooping rays; solitary, terminal. **Leaves:** Pinnate, 3-7 lanceolate leaflets; entire; alternate. **In bloom:** June-September. **Habitat-Range:** Dry, open woods, prairies; west of a line from western New York to Georgia.

The oblong disk, which is gray but may become brownish, and the drooping rays give the flower a cone shape; hence the common name. When crushed, the disk emits the odor of anise.

149 PURPLE-HEADED SNEEZEWEED   Composite family *(Compositae)*
(Helenium nudiflorum)

Height: 1′-3′ (.3-1m). **Flower:** 1″-2″ (1-2.5cm) diameter; composite, with 10-15 3-lobed rays drooping around a purplish-brown, ball-shaped disk; several, in corymb. **Leaves:** Narrowly lanceolate; sparsely toothed; alternate. **In bloom:** June-October. **Habitat-Range:** Moist meadows, fields, roadsides; mostly throughout, except for upper New England.

The plant was used in folk medicine to rid the body of evil spirits that were believed to cause disease. The treatment consisted of driving the spirit out by violent means such as sneezing. The dried and powdered leaves were used in making snuff; hence its common name. Indians used the greens to give a "biting taste" to salads. The Common Sneezeweed, *H. autumnale*, is taller than *H. nudiflorum* and has a greenish yellow disk. The short (1'-2', .3-.6m) Fine-leaved Sneezeweed, *H. tenuifolium*, found mainly in the southeast has grasslike, branched leaves and flowers with a greenish yellow disk.

150 WOOLLY RAGWORT   Composite family *(Compositae)*
(Senecio tomentosus)

Height: 6"-30" (15-75cm). **Flower:** 1" (2.5cm) diameter; composite, having densely packed disc flowers and sparse ray flowers; several, in corymb. **Leaves:** Stem leaves lanceolate, toothed, alternate; basal leaves oval, hairy, toothed. **In bloom:** May-July. **Habitat-Range:** Sandy open woods, clearings, fields; coastal plain from New Jersey southward.

The stem and basal leaves are very woolly. The irregularly spaced ray flowers give the plant a ragged appearance; hence the common name. The seed head, which is a ball of silky down, explains the generic name (from *senex*, a Greek word for "old man"). It is also called Squawweed because it was used by several Indian tribes to treat ailments of the female reproductive organs. A smooth species with tapering oval, basal leaves is the Round-leaf Ragwort, *S. obovatus*. Finely cut stem leaves characterize the Tansy Ragwort or Stinking Willie, *S. jacobaea*.

151 ELECAMPANE *(Inula helenium)*   Composite family *(Compositae)*

Height: 2'-6' (.6-2m). **Flower:** 2"-4" (5-10cm) diameter; composite, having many thin, fringed, dishevelled rays surrounding a brownish disk; solitary, terminal. **Leaves:** Ovate, upper leaves sessile and clasping, lower ones with petioles; toothed; alternate. **In bloom:** July-September. **Habitat-Range:** Pastures, roadsides, clearings; throughout.

The upper leaf surface is rough and the lower surface is woolly. The common name is a corruption of *ala Campania* referring to an ancient province in southern Italy where the plant grew in profusion, It was also called Horseheal in England where the root was used as a horse medicine. It was used by early Americans as an expectorant and for lung disorders. Recent clinical work indicates an extract of the plant is useful as an antiseptic. It is also a source of inulin, a sugar used in kidney-function tests.

152 TICKSEED COREOPSIS   Composite family *(Compositae)*
(Coreopsis lanceolata)

Height: 1'-2' (.3-.6m). **Flower:** 1 1/2"-2 1/2" (4-6cm) diameter; composite, 6-8 deeply lobed rays, flat yellowish disc; solitary, terminal. **Leaves:** Lanceolate, sometimes with two basal lobes; entire; opposite. **In bloom:** May-August. **Habitat-Range:** Dry sandy or rocky woods, thickets, clearings; mostly throughout.

Because of their large, showy flowers, many species of Coreopsis have been cultivated. The disc soon turns brown and produces seeds that resemble small ticks; hence the common and generic names (from Greek *coris*, "a bug," and *opis*, "appearance"). The Tall Tickseed, *C. tripteris*, grows up to 3 feet (1m) tall and has palmate leaves with

3 leaflets. Narrowleaf Tickseed, *C. angustifolia,* has very narrow leaves and grows in wet coastal pine barrens. The Whorled Tickseed, *C. verticillata,* which grows in the southern part of our range, has whorled leaves dissected into thin segments.

153 BULLHEAD-LILY *(Nuphar variegatum)*   Water-lily family *(Nymphaeaceae)*

Height: Floating on water. **Flower:** 2″-3″ (5-8cm) diameter; regular, with 6 concave yellow sepals forming globular corolla open at the top, numerous small scale-like petals, many stamens, 1 pistil with many radiating stigmas; solitary, terminal. **Leaves:** Broadly ovate, with deep V-cleft at base; entire; basal, upright, blade floating. **In bloom:** May-September. **Habitat-Range:** Pond margins, slow streams, pools; north of a line from Delaware to northern Illinois.

The sepals may be red on their inner surfaces and the petioles are flat. A very similar species, *N. advena,* commonly called Spatter-dock, has erect leaves. The Small Pond-lily, *N. microphyllum,* has a small (1″, 2.5cm diameter) flower and narrow, ribbon-like leaves. The Arrow-leaf Pond-lily, *N. sagittifolium,* has arrow-shaped leaves and is found in our southern coastal regions. The seeds of these lilies were roasted and eaten or ground into flour. The rootstocks were often roasted with meat or used in a poultice to treat boils and skin inflammation.

154 BLADDERWORT *(Utricularia* spp.*)*   Bladderwort family *(Lentibulariaceae)*

Height: 3″-12″ (8-30cm). **Flower:** 1/2″ (1cm) diameter; irregular, with two-lipped corolla, upper lip erect, lower lip slightly 3-lobed and spurred at the base, 2 stamens, 1 pistil; several, in a raceme on leafless stalk. **Leaves:** Very finely dissected, threadlike segments bearing little bladders; alternate. **In bloom:** June-August. **Habitat-Range:** Muddy soil or floating in ponds or sluggish streams; throughout.

There are about a dozen species in our area that can be distinguished only by their technical characteristics. They have small inflated bladders on their leaves, which accounts for the common and generic names (from Latin *utriculus,* "little bladder"). The bladders have bristled trap doors that capture insects or small aquatic organisms, which are then digested and nourish the plant. The bladders are filled with water and anchor the plant as it grows, but as flowering season approaches they fill with air and float the plant to the surface.

155 YELLOW IRIS *(Iris pseudacorus)*   Iris family *(Iridaceae)*

Height: 1′-3′ (.3-1m). **Flower:** 3″ (8cm) diameter; regular, having 3 yellow petal-like sepals that curve downward and outward, 3 smaller yellow upright petals, 3 petal-like yellow styles that arch over the sepals, 3 stamens hidden under the styles; solitary, terminal. **Leaves:** Flat, swordlike; entire; upright, rising from basal cluster. **In bloom:** June-August. **Habitat-Range:** Marshes, streamsides; locally throughout.

This is the only yellow iris found growing wild.

156 YELLOW LADY SLIPPER   Orchid family *(Orchidaceae)*
(Cypripedium calceolus)†

Height: 8″-24″ (20-60cm). **Flower:** 2″ (5cm) long; irregular, with long, thin, brown-streaked sepals, two twisted, brown-streaked, lateral petals, 1 pouchlike lip; 1-3, terminal. **Leaves:** Oval, parallel veins, sessile, clasping base; entire; alternate. **In bloom:** May-July. **Habitat-Range:** Wet woods, shady swamps, bogs; throughout.

There are several varieties of this orchid. The large-flowered one is hairy and may cause dermatitis when handled by a sensitive person. The dried and powdered underground stem was used by Indians as a remedy for insomnia.

157 PARTRIDGE-PEA *(Cassia fasciculata)*   Pea family *(Leguminosae)*

Height: 1'-2' (.3-.6m). **Flower:** 1 1/2" (4cm) diameter; regular, having 5 rounded, somewhat unequal petals often spotted with red or purple at the base, 10 stamens, 4 of them yellow, the others purple, 1 pistil; several, on slender stalks from leaf axils. **Leaves:** Pinnate, 10-15 pairs of linear-oblong leaflets; entire; alternate. **In bloom:** July-September. **Habitat-Range:** Sandy, open soil; throughout, except upper New England.

Seeds in the flat seed pods provide food for some game birds; hence the common name. The seeds were roasted and used as a coffee substitute by early Americans. The pairs of leaflets, which close at night, are somewhat sensitive and will also close when touched. A species with very sensitive leaves is Wild Sensitive Plant, *C. nictitans*, which has much smaller flowers with only 5 stamens and much smaller leaflets.

158 COMMON TANSY *(Tanacetum vulgare)*   Composite family *(Compositae)*

Height: 1'-3' (.3-1m). **Flower:** 1/2" (1cm) diameter; composite, having dense cluster of disc flowers; many discs in flat-topped corymb. **Leaves:** Pinnate and dissected, fernlike; alternate. **In bloom:** July-September. **Habitat-Range:** Roadsides, borders of fields; throughout.

Tansies look like daisies without petals and the leaves have a strong smell and bitter taste. A tea from its leaves has been used medicinally since the Middle Ages for boils, pimples, sunburn and intestinal worms. The tea was also thought to promote menstruation and, in a pregnant woman, an abortion. As a herb in cooking it was used as a substitute for sage.

159 WILD SENNA *(Cassia hebecarpa)*   Pea family *(Leguminosae)*

Height: 3'-6' (1-2m). **Flower:** 3/4" (2cm) diameter; regular, having 5 unevenly spread petals (3 upper and 2 lower), 10 unequal stamens; 1 pistil; several, in clusters in upper leaf axils. **Leaves:** Pinnate, 6-10 pairs of lanceolate leaflets; entire; alternate. **In bloom:** July-August. **Habitat-Range:** Dry thickets, roadsides; mostly throughout.

It has a cone-shaped gland near the base of the petiole. The seed pod is flat and slightly curved. A tea made from the leaves was widely used by American Indians as a laxative.

160 COMMON MULLEIN *(Verbascum thapsus)*   Figwort family *(Scrophulariaceae)*

Height: 2'-6' (.6-2m). **Flower:** 3/4" (2cm) diameter; regular, having 5 petals, 5 stamens, 1 pistil; only a few blooming on tightly packed terminal spike. **Leaves:** Elliptical, pointed at both ends, very woolly; entire; alternate. **In bloom:** June-September. **Habitat-Range:** Fields, waste places, roadsides; throughout.

This biennial grows a basal rosette of large woolly leaves the first year; the second year it grows a woolly stalk with woolly leaves topped by a densely packed spike on which only a few of the flowers are open at one time. The ancient Romans dipped the dried stalks in suet and used them as torches in funeral processions. Ancient Greeks used the leaves as lamp wicks. American Indians used the leaves as innersoles in moccasins and early settlers lined their stocking with leaves to keep their feet warm. Herb doctors prepared a tea from the leaves for chest complaints or mixed them with tobacco to be smoked for asthma. Quaker maidens who were forbidden to use any kind of make-up brought a pleasant glow to their cheeks by rubbing them with the slightly abrasive leaves.

161 AGRIMONY *(Agrimonia pubescens)*   Rose family *(Rosaceae)*

Height: 3'-4' (1m). **Flower:** 1/2" (1cm) diameter; regular, having 5 petals, 5-15 stamens, 1 pistil; several, on long, thin raceme. **Leaves:** Pinnate, 5-9 lanceolate leaflets separated by pairs of tiny leaflets; toothed; alternate. **In bloom:** July-September. **Habitat-Range:** Rich woods, thickets; mostly throughout.

There are several species of agrimony in our area and they all produce top-shaped seed pods ringed with hooked bristles that attach to clothing or fur, thus assuring distribution. Europeans used the leaves to make a tea with an apricot-like aroma. Agrimony is the chief ingredient in Eau d'Arquelius, a lotion sold in France for cuts, scratches, sprains and strains. In Colonial times the leaves and stems were used to make a yellow dye.

162 WHORLED LOOSESTRIFE   Primrose family *(Primulaceae)*
(Lysimachia quadrifolia)

Height: 1'-3' (.3-1m). **Flower:** 1/2" (1cm) diameter; regular, having 5 yellow petals forming a star-like corolla with reddish center, 5 stamens, 1 pistil; several, on thin stalks from leaf axils. **Leaves:** Lanceolate; entire; usually whorls of 4 along stem. **In bloom:** June-August. **Habitat-Range:** Open woods, thickets, shores; mostly throughout.

The generic name honors Lysimachus, a king of ancient Sicily, who, according to tradition, was being chased by a maddened bull and in desperation seized the plant and waved it before the bull, pacifying him, i.e., released the bull from its strife. Thus the plant was fed to yokes of oxen by Colonial farmers in the belief that it pacified the animals and enabled them to work harmoniously together. The common name derives from the whorls of flowers emerging from the axils of the whorled leaves. The flowers of the Fringed Loosestrife, *L. ciliata*, emerge from the axils of opposite leaves that have fringed petioles. The flowers of the Yellow Loosestrife, *L. terrestris*, which grows in swampy places, are crowded onto a slender terminal spike.

163 YELLOW SWEET CLOVER   Pea family *(Leguminosae)*
(Melilotus officinalis)

Height: 2'-5' (.6-1.5m). **Flower:** 1/4" (6mm) long; irregular, pealike; many, in long, narrow racemes arising from leaf axils. **Leaves:** Pinnate, 3 leaflets; finely toothed; alternate. **In bloom:** May-October. **Habitat-Range:** Fields, waste places, roadsides; throughout.

★ _____

This is very similar to White Sweet Clover. The young leaves can be added to salads or used as cooked greens. Young shoots were eaten like asparagus and the pealike seeds were added to soups and stews. If the plant is gathered and allowed to rot, dicoumarin, an anticoagulant, is produced.

164 COMMON ST. JOHNSWORT   St. Johnswort family *(Hypericaceae)*
(Hypericum perforatum)

Height: 1'-2 1/2' (.3-8m). **Flower:** 3/4" (2cm) diameter; regular, having 5 yellow petals usually spotted with black, numerous stamens, 1 pistil with 3 styles; several, in cyme. **Leaves:** Oblong, spotted with translucent dots; entire; opposite. **In bloom:** June-September. **Habitat-Range:** Open woods, thickets, roadsides; throughout.

Emigrants from Europe gathered these plants on St. John's Eve, June 24, and hung them in the doors of homes to ward off evil spirits and protect from lightning. Dew gathered from the plants on St. John's Day was believed valuable as an eye lotion. Gerade, a famous herbalist wrote "...flowers and seed boyled and drunken, provoketh urine, and is right good against stone in the bladder." Several species of St. Johnswort are found in our area and all have tiny translucent or black dots on their leaves. They contain oil which was extracted and used for healing wounds and skin irritations.

165 VELVET LEAF *(Abutilon theophrasti)*   Mallow family *(Malvaceae)*

Height: 3'-5' (1-1.5m). **Flower:** 1" (2.5cm) diameter; regular, having 5 petals; few, growing on short, stout stalks from leaf axils. **Leaves:** Heart-shaped, large (4"-10", 10-25cm), velvety; toothed; alternate. **In bloom:** July-October. **Habitat-Range:** Waste places, vacant lots; mostly throughout.

The common name derives from the soft, velvety leaf. It is also called Pie-marker, an allusion to the large seed pod whose edges resemble the crimped edges of a pie crust. The plant was originally imported from India for its stem fibers, which were used to make cloth and rope.

166 BUTTER-AND-EGGS *(Linaria vulgaris)*   Figwort family *(Scrophulariaceae)*

Height: 1'-2' (.3-.6m). **Flower:** 1" (2.5cm) long; irregular, 2-lipped corolla spurred at base, 2-lobed erect upper lip, 3-lobed spreading lower lip with orange colored base closing the throat; many, in dense raceme. **Leaves:** Linear, grasslike; entire; upper leaves alternate, lower leaves opposite or whorled. **In bloom:** May-October. **Habitat-Range:** Waste places, fields, roadsides; throughout.

This plant was introduced from Europe because it contained an ingredient used in colonial skin lotions. The "butter" yellow flower has an orange blotch ("eggs") on its lower lip. The juice of the plant was mixed with milk and served as a fly poison around barns. A tea from the leaves was used to treat constipation.

167 FLOWER-OF-AN-HOUR *(Hibiscus trionum)*   Mallow family *(Malvaceae)*

Height: 1'-2' (.3-.6m). **Flower:** 2"-3" (5-7.5cm) diameter; regular, having 5 yellow petals with a dark purple eye, bladder-like calyx; several, on long stalks from upper leaf axils. **Leaves:** Palmate, 3 lanceolate segments, the middle segment the longest; bluntly toothed or lobed; alternate. **In bloom:** July-September. **Habitat-Range:** Waste places, fields, roadsides; throughout.

The flower is open only a few hours; hence the common name.

168 MOTH MULLEIN *(Verbascum blattaria)*   Figwort family *(Scrophulariaceae)*

Height: 2'-4' (.6-1m). **Flower:** 1" (2.5cm) diameter; regular, having 5 rounded petals, 5 stamens on filaments bearded with violet wool, 1 pistil; several, in terminal raceme. **Leaves:** Lanceolate, upper ones sessile and clasping, lower ones with petioles; toothed; alternate. **In bloom:** June-September. **Habitat-Range:** Fields, waste places, roadsides; throughout.

A white flower is more common in some places, the yellow in other places. The common name derives from a fancied resemblance of the woolly anther filaments to the antennae and tongue of a moth.

169 COMMON EVENING PRIMROSE   Evening-primrose family *(Onagraceae)*
(Oenothera biennis)

Height: 1'-5' (.3-1.5m). **Flower:** 1"-2" (2.5-5cm) diameter; regular, having 4 reflexed sepals, 4 broad petals, 8 stamens, 1 pistil with cross-shaped stigma; several, from axils of upper leaflike bracts. **Leaves:** Lanceolate; wavy-toothed; alternate. **In bloom:** June-October. **Habitat-Range:** Roadsides, waste places; throughout.

The angled stems are often tinged with reddish purple. In most species the flowers open in the evening and close the following morning; hence the common name. A day-blooming species, *O. fruticosa* (commonly called Sundrops), is hairy and has linear leaves. The young stems and leaves of all species have been eaten as cooked greens. The roots, when boiled, taste like parsnip. The seed pods were eaten by Indians.

170 WILD LETTUCE *(Lactuca canadensis)*   Composite family *(Compositae)*

Height: 3'-10' (1-3m). **Flower:** 1/4" (6mm) diameter; composite, with many square-tipped rays; many, in elongated panicle. **Leaves:** Upper ones lanceolate and toothless, lower ones wavy lobed or pinnate; alternate. **In bloom:** July-September. **Habitat-Range:** Roadsides, open ground, thickets; throughout.

Although the flowers are small and almost inconspicuous, the great height of the plant and feathery seed heads catch the eye. The generic name derives from the milky juice (from Latin *lac*, meaning "milk") that oozes from the plant when a leaf is removed or the stem is bruised. Indians rubbed this juice on the skin to cure poison ivy. The plant was also called Wild Opium because the appearance and scent of the latex resembled that of the opium plant. It has therefore been used since antiquity by various cultures as a sedative, but modern science has found that it has no such power.

171 YELLOW FALSE FOXGLOVE   Figwort family *(Scrophulariaceae)*
(Aureolaria flava)†

Height: 3'-6' (1-2m). **Flower:** 2" (5cm) long; regular, having trumpet-shaped corolla with 5 roundish lobes, 4 stamens, 1 pistil; several, on short stalks from upper leaf axils. **Leaves:** Elliptical; lower leaves deeply pinnately cleft, upper leaves lobed or toothed; opposite. **In bloom:** July-September. **Habitat-Range:** Deciduous woods; mostly throughout.

The stem is often purplish. The several species of yellow-flowered false foxglove are thought to be parasitic on the roots of oak trees. The Downy False Foxglove, *A. virginica*, has deeply lobed hairy leaves and a hairy stem. Smooth False Foxglove, *A. laevigata*, grows chiefly in mountains, is smooth and its leaves are unlobed and nearly sessile.

172 GUMWEED *(Grindelia squarrosa)*   Composite family *(Compositae)*

Height: 1'-4' (.3-1m). **Flower:** 1 1/2″ (4cm) diameter; composite, having many rays encircling a dark yellow or brownish disk; several, terminal on branched stem. **Leaves:** Linear-oblong, sessile; toothed; alternate. **In bloom:** July-September. **Habitat-Range:** Prairies, waste places; New York, Pennsylvania and westward.

Of the several species of this plant most are found in the West. The generic name honors David Grindel, a 19th-century Russian botanist. The common name refers to the gummy resin that exudes from the cluster of recurved bracts below the flower head. The gum has the odor of balsam and a bitter taste and was used by Indians to treat asthma, bronchitis and whooping cough.

173 YELLOW GOATSBEARD *(Tragopogon pratensis)*   Composite family *(Compositae)*

Height: 1'-3' (.3-1m). **Flower:** 1″ (2.5cm) diameter; composite, overlapping square-tipped rays, slender green bracts extending beyond rays; solitary, terminal. **Leaves:** Grasslike, sessile, clasping base; entire; alternate. **In bloom:** May-October. **Habitat-Range:** Fields, rocky banks, roadsides; mostly throughout.

The dandelion-like flowers close by midday. If you overlook the flower, the large fluffy seed head will catch your attention. This seed head accounts for its common and generic names (from Greek *tragos*, "goat" and *pogon* "beard"). Milky juice from the stem and roots was used to treat gallstones, and the Indians coagulated it into a chewing gum used for indigestion. Boiled roots were used as cooked vegetables and young lower leaves served in salads or as cooked greens. A purple-flowered species, *T. porrifolius*, was commonly called Oyster Plant because the raw roots had an oyster-like flavor.

174 FIELD SOW-THISTLE *(Sonchus arvensis)*   Composite family *(Compositae)*

Height: 1'-4' (.3-1m). **Flower:** 1″ (2.5cm) diameter; composite, with many overlapping rays; several heads, in umbels. **Leaves:** Oblong, pinnately lobed; prickly toothed; alternate. **In bloom:** July-October. **Habitat-Range:** Fields, roadsides, waste places; north of a line from Maryland to Illinois.

This species has a hairy stem. The Common Sow-Thistle, *S. oleraceus*, is smooth and the pointed bases of its prickly leaves extend on either side of the stem. The Spiny-leaved Sow-Thistle, *S. asper*, is also smooth and the rounded lobes at the base of its prickly, curled leaves embrace the stem.

175 KING DEVIL *(Hieracium pratense)*   Composite family *(Compositae)*

Height: 1'-3' (.3-1m). **Flower:** 3/4″ (2cm) diameter; composite, with rays overlapping in several concentric circles; several, in compact cyme. **Leaves:** Elliptical-oval, hairy; entire; basal rosette. **In bloom:** May-August. **Habitat-Range:** Fields, clearings, road-sides; mostly throughout.

The stem and basal leaves of this common hawkweed are covered with bristly black hairs. It resembles Orange Hawkweed except for flower color. A short species, Mouse-ear Hawkweed (*H. pilosella*), has white hair on the underside of its leaves and forms clusters of creeping runners. It was once given to horses in the belief that the horse "shall not be hurt by the smith that shoeth him." The basal leaves of Rattlesnake-weed, *H. venosum*, which were used to treat snakebite, are purple underneath and have purple veining. Some species of Hawkweed like the Common Canada Hawkweed (*H. canadense*) do not have basal leaves but have alternate, toothed, sessile, lanceolate, stem leaves.

176 CANADA GOLDENROD *(Solidago canadensis)*   Composite family *(Compositae)*

Height: 1'-5' (.3-1.5m). **Flower:** Tiny; composite, with 9-15 rays; many, in plumelike, terminal cluster. **Leaves:** Lanceolate, parallel veins; toothed; crowded, alternate. **In bloom:** July-September. **Habitat-Range:** Roadsides, clearings, thickets; throughout.

Many species of Goldenrod were used in herbal medicine; this accounts for their generic name, which is derived from the Latin *solidus*, meaning "whole" in the sense of "to make whole." Most botany manuals list over 60 species of Goldenrod in our area. Although Goldenrods are easy to recognize it is difficult even for botanists to identify some of the species; thus, only a few of the more distinctive species will be described here. The above species and the four other Goldenrods illustrated in this book were chosen because their inflorescences have a relatively distinctive shape that can aid in their identification. Canada Goldenrod is one of the commonest tall Goldenrods and has a plumelike cluster of flowers, i.e., they are crowded on terminal branches resembling an arching plume. The similar Tall Goldenrod, *S. altissima*, has a downy stem with parallel-veined lanceolate leaves that have a rough texture and few teeth. Late Goldenrod, *S. gigantea*, has either a smooth green or purplish stem (usually with a whitish bloom) topped with a plumelike inflorescence. Early Goldenrod, *S. juncea*, (whose inflorescence may also be elmlike) has small winglike leaflets in the axils of the upper, feather-veined stem leaves. Rough-stemmed Goldenrod, *S. rugosa* (another whose inflorescence may be elmlike) has a hairy stem, and wrinkled, hairy, deeply toothed, elliptical, feather-veined leaves. Gray Goldenrod, *S. nemoralis*, one of the first Goldenrods to bloom, is a short species usually with a narrow plumelike inflor-escence, its stem and leaves densely covered with hair, and tiny leaflets in the axils of its upper, narrow, feather-veined leaves.

177 ELM-LEAVED GOLDENROD   Composite family *(Compositae)*
(Solidago ulmifolia)

Height: 2'-5' (.6-1.5m). **Flower:** Tiny; composite, with 3-5 rays; many, in elmlike cluster of arching branches. **Leaves:** Elliptical, feather-veined; coarsely toothed; alter-nate. **In bloom:** August-October. **Habitat-Range:** Dry woods, thickets; mostly through-out, except upper New England.

The flowers occur on several upright but arching, slender branches near the end of the stem, the whole resembling the shape of an elm tree. A similar species is Rough-leaved Goldenrod, *S. patula*; it has sharply 4-angled stems, elliptical leaves that are very rough on their upper surface and smooth underneath, and large lower leaves with a broadly margined petiole.

178 ORANGE CONEFLOWER *(Rudbeckia fulgida)*   Composite family *(Compositae)*

Height: 1′-3′ (.3-1m). **Flower:** 1 1/2″ (4cm) diameter; composite, having 8-15 yellow rays with orange bases encircling a dark brown disk; single, terminal. **Leaves:** Linear-elliptical; slightly toothed; alternate. **In bloom:** August-October. **Habitat-Range:** Open woods, dry fields, roadsides; south of a line from New Jersey to Indiana.

This plant is very similar to the Black-eyed Susan (**R.** *serotina*) but its rays have an orange base.

179 BLUE-STEMMED GOLDENROD   Composite family *(Compositae)* (*Solidago caesia*)

Height: 1′-3′ (.3-1m). **Flower:** Tiny; composite, with 3-5 rays; many, in clusters in upper leaf axils. **Leaves:** Lanceolate; toothed; alternate. **In bloom:** August-October. **Habitat-Range:** Woods, thickets; throughout.

The stem of this plant is bluish or purplish and is covered with a whitish bloom. The small tufts of flowers in the upper leaf axils give the flower cluster a slender, wand-like appearance. Hairy Goldenrod, *S. hispida*, appears similar but differs in that it has very hairy stems and leaves and its leaves are elliptical and tapering toward their base. The flower cluster in Wandlike Goldenrod, *S. stricta*, is slender and compact because the flowers emerge from small, bractlike leaves that hug the stem.

180 HARD-LEAVED GOLDENROD   Composite family *(Compositae)* (*Solidago rigida*)

Height: 1′-5′ (.3-1.5m). **Flower:** Tiny; composite, with 6-14 rays; many, in flat-topped cluster. **Leaves:** Oval, sessile, clasping; entire; alternate. **In bloom:** August-October. **Habitat-Range:** Dry, open places; throughout, except upper New England.

The flowers in this species are in a flat-topped cluster. A flat-topped inflorescence is also found in Lance-leaved Goldenrod but its leaves are narrow and linear with 3-7 parallel veins. A similar species is Slender Fragrant Goldenrod, *S. tenuifolia*, which has grasslike leaves with only one vein.

181 SHOWY GOLDENROD *(Solidago speciosa)*   Composite family *(Compositae)*

Height: 2′-6′ (.6-2m). **Flower:** Tiny; composite, with 5-6 rays; many, in a clublike cluster. **Leaves:** Elliptical, tapering to stalklike proportions; obscurely toothed; alternate. **In bloom:** August-October. **Habitat-Range:** Thickets, openings, fields; throughout, except upper New England.

The flowers of this goldenrod, which has a reddish stem, are found near the top of the plant in a broad, clublike cluster. A similar species that often has a reddish stem is Stout Goldenrod, *S. squarrosa*, but its basal leaves are strongly toothed and often form a rosette. In coastal marshes the clublike (or plumelike) inflorescence of the Seaside Goldenrod, *S. sempervirens*, tops a stem with fleshy, oblong, toothless, alternate leaves.

Red•Pink

Key

	SPRING (March-early May)	SUMMER (late May-early August)	FALL (late August-October)

Indistinguishable

Alternate, entire
226 Field Milkwort
    Cross-leaved Milkwort
231 Smartweed
    Arrow-leaved
       Tearthumb
209 Blazing-star
Alternate, pinnately lobed
223 Nodding Thistle
220 Knapweed

Regular

Basal, lobed
183 Round-lobed Hepatica
Basal, entire
200 Swamp Pink
192 Shooting Star
195 Field Garlic
196 Wild Garlic
Basal, tubular
201 Pitcher Plant
Alternate, dissected
191 Wild Columbine
Opposite, entire
187 Fire Pink
182 Spring Beauty
Opposite, palmate
186 Wild Geranium
    Herb Robert
Whorled, entire
189 Red Trillium
    Sessile Trillium
184 Moss Pink

Basal, entire
221 Wild Onion
Basal, toothed
208 Pink Pyrola
Alternate, entire
212 Fireweed
Alternate, toothed
207 Steeplebush
214 Seashore Mallow
    Marsh Mallow
Opposite, entire
188 Garden Phlox
    Wild Sweet William
185 Deptford Pink
217 Ragged-Robin
222 Scarlet Lychnis
215 Rose Pink
Opposite, toothed
228 Pipsissewa
213 Virginia Meadow Beauty

Irregular

Leafless, when in bloom
197 Dragon's-mouth
Single leaf, entire
    Snake-mouth
Basal, entire
206 Pink Lady Slipper
202 Showy Orchis
Basal, dissected
193 Wild Bleeding Heart
Alternate, lobed
205 Wood Betony

Basal, entire
    Grass Pink
Alternate, entire
230 Rosebud Orchid
232 Three-Birds Orchis
Alternate, toothed
210 Cardinal Flower
Alternate, palmate
211 Castor Bean
229 Tick-trefoil
225 Pink Wild Bean

Key

	SPRING (March-early May)	SUMMER (late May-early August)	FALL (late August-October)

Irregular

SPRING	SUMMER	FALL
Alternate, lobed 204 Indian Paintbrush	*Alternate, pinnate* 227 Crown Vetch	
Alternate, entire 198 Fringed Polygala	*Opposite, toothed* 218 Beebalm	
Alternate, palmate 199 Red Clover 203 Rabbit-Foot Clover	216 Hairy Beardtongue 224 Teasel 219 Wild Bergamot	
Alternate, dissected 194 Pale Corydalis		

Composite

Alternate, toothed
190 Robin's-plantain

182 SPRING BEAUTY (Claytonia virginica)†   Purslane family (Portulacaceae)

Height: 6″-12″ (15-30cm). **Flower:** 1/2″ (1cm) diameter; regular, with 2 sepals, 5 petals, 5 or more stamens, 1 pistil; several, in loose raceme; commonly white with pink stripes or pink with deeper pink stripes. **Leaves:** Linear, tapering at each end; entire; opposite. **In bloom:** March-May. **Habitat-Range:** Rich woods, thickets, clearings and riverbanks; throughout.

These delicate harbingers of spring sometimes grow in such masses they look like patches of unmelted snow. The flowers close at night and on cloudy or stormy days (when pollinating insects are not flying), thus protecting their nectar and pollen from rain or dew. The plant grows from a rootlike tuber resembling small potatoes but with a sweetish, chestnut-like taste. They were used extensively in soups, stews and salads by Indians and early settlers. The generic name honors John Clayton, early American botanist. The Carolina Spring Beauty, *C. caroliniana*, is similar to *C. virginica* but has broadly oblong or oval leaves.

183 ROUND-LOBED HEPATICA   Buttercup family (Ranunculaceae)
(*Hepatica americana*)†

Height: 5″-10″ (12-25cm). **Flower:** 3/4″ (2cm) diameter; regular, with 6-10 colored sepals, numerous stamens, central cluster of pistils; solitary, on hairy stalks. **Leaves:** Heart-shaped with three rounded lobes; entire; basal, on long, hairy petioles. **In bloom:** March-May. **Habitat-Range:** Dry woods and ravines; throughout, but mainly in the eastern part.

Each of these delicate flowers has pink petal-like sepals which can also be shades of lavender, blue or white. The leaves persist through the winter and are reddish brown when the spring blooms appear. The new leaves appear after the flowers die. A similar species found in the western part of our area is the Sharp-lobed Hepatica, *H. acutiloba,* whose leaves have pointed lobes. The generic name (from *hepaticus,* the Latin for "liver") and the common name Liverleaf come from the resemblance of the leaf to the three-lobed mammalian liver. This "signature" led herb doctors to use the plant to treat liver ailments.

184 MOSS PINK (Phlox subulata)†   Phlox family (Polemoniaceae)

Height: 2″-6″ (5-15cm). **Flower:** 1/2″ (1cm) diameter; regular, with 5 petals forming tubular corolla having spreading lobes, 5 stamens, 1 pistil with 3-branched style; many, in terminal cymes. **Leaves:** Needle-like; entire; in whorls at joints of stem. **In bloom:** April-June. **Habitat-Range:** Spread from cultivation, waste places; throughout.

This native American plant was cultivated by man because it grows in dense mats and brightens rock ledges and waste places. Its flowers may be white, purple or violet in addition to the common pink.

185 DEPTFORD PINK (Dianthus armeria)   Pink family (Caryophyllaceae)

Height: 6″-24″ (15-60cm). **Flower:** 1/2″ (1cm) diameter; regular, having 5 tooth-edge oval petals with tiny, white spots, 10 stamens, 1 pistil with 2 styles; few, in terminal cluster. **Leaves:** Linear; entire; opposite. **In bloom:** May-July. **Habitat-Range:** Dry fields and roadsides; throughout.

Since *Dianthus* is Greek for "Jupiter's flower," one wonders what Jupiter could have seen in this small unattractive flower. The stiffly erect plant bears few flowers and is covered with fine hair. The common name refers to the fields of Deptford, England (now part of industrial London), where it once was abundant. A similar species is Maiden Pink, *D. deltoides*, but it has only one flower on each stem and the round petals are dark pink, markedly toothed, with a dark circle at their base.

186 WILD GERANIUM *(Geranium maculatum)*†   Geranium family *(Geraniaceae)*

Height: 1'-2' (.3-.6m). **Flower:** 1 1/2" (4cm) diameter; regular, with 5 petals, 10 fertile stamens, 1 pistil with 5 styles; few, in loose corymb. **Leaves:** Palmate, five deep lobes; coarsely toothed; opposite. **In bloom:** April-June. **Habitat-Range:** Woods, thickets and meadows; throughout.

There are several species of wild geranium and all have a long pistil which develops a slender, pointed seed pod. The latter accounts for the common and generic (from *geranos*, Greek for "crane") names since it was thought to resemble the beak of a crane. At the base of each petal is a tuft of hair which protects the nectar in the almost upright flower from rain and dew. The Indians used young leaves as greens. Since all parts of the plant contain tannin, it was long used as an astringent in medicine, and a tea made of the leaves served to treat diarrhea, dysentery and bleeding ulcers. The powdered root was used as a coagulant on wounds.

HERB ROBERT *(Geranium robertianum)*†   Geranium family *(Geraniaceae)*

Height: 6"-18" (15-45cm). **Flower:** 1/2" (1cm) diameter; regular, with 5 petals, 10 stamens, 1 pistil with 5 styles; usually in pairs. **Leaves:** Palmate, 3-5 lobes; coarsely toothed; opposite. **In bloom:** May-October. **Habitat-Range:** Rocky woods and ravines; north of line from Maryland to Illinois.

Similar to *G. maculatum* but has smaller flowers, fernlike leaves and a strong scent. The common and species names honor St. Robert. A similar species but with notched petals and less finely divided leaves is Bicknell's Cranesbill, *G. bicknelli*. In the more southern part of our area the Carolina Cranesbill (*G. carolinianum*) resembles *G. bicknelli* but its leaves are more deeply cleft and its flowers form a dense terminal cluster.

187 FIRE PINK *(Silene virginica)*   Pink family *(Caryophyllaceae)*

Height: 1'-2' (.3-.6m). **Flower:** 2" (5cm) diameter; regular, with 5 wide-spread deeply notched petals, 10 stamens, 1 pistil; several, on slender stalks from upper leaf axils. **Leaves:** Lanceolate, sessile; entire; opposite. **In bloom:** April-September. **Habitat-Range:** Open woods, rocky slopes; south of a line from New Jersey to Wisconsin.

The flowers of many members of the Pink family are called Catchflies because they have a sticky exudation on their stems and tubular parts. It is thought that this sticky material traps crawling insects, preventing them from collecting the flower's nectar. The generic name is derived from the Greek *sialon*, meaning "saliva," an allusion to the viscid excretions of the stem and flower. Fire Pink was once used as a worm medicine by herb doctors. Roundleaf Catchfly (*S. rotundifolia*) is similar to it but its petals are more deeply cleft and its leaves are much rounder and have petioles. Royal Catchfly

(*S. regina*) also resembles *S. virginica* except that the petals of the scarlet flower are not notched.

188 GARDEN PHLOX *(Phlox paniculata)*   Phlox family *(Polemoniaceae)*

Height: 2′-6′ (.6-2m). **Flower:** 1″ (2.5cm) long: regular, with 5 petals united to form a trumpet-shaped corolla and slightly indented at their flared tips, 5 short stamens, 1 pistil with 3 stigmas; many, in pyramidal corymb. **Leaves:** Oblong, lanceolate or ovate; bristling margins; opposite. **In bloom:** July-October. **Habitat-Range:** Open woods, thickets; south of a line from central New York to northern Illinois; often escaped from gardens elsewhere.

The hairy, purplish pink flowers not only gave color to herb gardens but were widely used as a medicinal herb. A cold-water infusion of the roots was used to treat upset stomach and as an eyewash. A boiled-leaf infusion served as a laxative and is still used by country people to treat boils. *P. divaricata,* an earlier blooming species (April-June), has pale violet or light blue flowers, is shorter (10″-20″, 25-50cm), and has opposite, oblong leaves with smooth margins. A southern species, *P. glaberrima,* also blooms early (May-June), is not hairy, and its leaves are narrower and have smooth margins.

WILD SWEET WILLIAM *(Phlox maculata)*   Phlox family *(Polemoniaceae)*

Height: 1′-3′ (.3-1m). **Flower:** 1 1/2″ (4cm) long; regular, with 5 petals united to form a trumpet-shaped corolla and slightly indented at their flared tips, 5 short stamens, 1 pistil with three styles; many, in pyramidal corymb. **Leaves:** Lanceolate to linear, very short petiole or sessile; entire; opposite. **In bloom:** May-August. **Habitat-Range:** Moist woods, streambanks; throughout.

Similar to *P. paniculata* but the flowers are reddish-pink, purple or sometimes white, and the stem has small, purple dots. Sweet William is named after an English nobleman, William, Duke of Cumberland, who defeated the Scots in battle; the grateful English named the striking flower in his honor. In contrast, the defeated Scots named the rank weed *Senecio jacobaea,* Stinking Willie.

189 RED TRILLIUM *(Trillium erectum)*†   Lily family *(Liliaceae)*

Height: 6″-12″ (15-30cm). **Flower:** 2″ (5cm) diameter; regular, with 3 sepals, 3 petals, 6 stamens, 1 pistil with 3 stigmas; solitary, nodding on short pedicel. **Leaves:** Broadly ovate, sessile; entire; three, in a whorl a short distance below flower. **In bloom:** April-June. **Habitat-Range:** Rich woods; mostly throughout northern part of range; in mountains further south.

The common and generic names indicate that the flower parts and leaves come in threes or in multiples of threes. The maroon-red flowers are in bloom when the robins have returned north; hence its other common name, Wake-Robin. Because of its drooping head, the flower is often overlooked in the rich, moist woods in which it grows. But it is easily found and pollinated by carrion flies attracted by its color and carrion odor. Because of the resemblance of the flowers to the color and odor of rotting flesh, its rhizomes were used as a treatment for gangrene by early herb doctors who practiced their art according to the "doctrine of signatures." Indians and early settlers also chewed the dried rhizome as an astringent in treating diarrhea, snakebite and as an anesthetic. The rank odor of the flowers also gained it the other common names of Stinking Benjamin and Wet-Dog Trillium.

SESSILE TRILLIUM *(Trillium sessile)*† Lily family *(Liliaceae)*

Height: 6″-12″ (15-30cm). **Flower:** 1″-2″ (2.5-5cm) long; regular, with 3 sepals, 3 petals, 6 stamens, 1 pistil with 3 stigmas; solitary, sessile, erect. **Leaves:** Broadly ovate, sessile; entire; 3, in a whorl at base of flower. **In bloom:** April-May. **Habitat-Range:** Rich woods; south of a line from southern New York to Illinois.

The single flower looks like a partially opened Red Trillium but it differs in that it is sessile and erect and pleasantly aromatic. Its leaves are often mottled purple-brown. There is also a yellow-green form of this plant. Three species of Sessile Trillium are common in the southern part of our range. *T. cuneatum* resembles *T. sessile* but is larger and has petals up to 3″ (7.5cm) long. *T. recurvatum* also resembles *T. sessile* but the sepals bend downward and its leaves are stalked. A yellow species, *T. luteum*, which also resembles *T. sessile*, has a lemon odor.

190 ROBIN'S-PLANTAIN *(Erigeron pulchellus)* Composite family *(Compositae)*

Height: 6″-16″ (15-35cm). **Flower:** 1″ (2-5cm) diameter; composite, with disc flowers encircled by many ray flowers; solitary or several heads, in flat corymb. **Leaves:** Upper are oblong, toothed, sessile, alternate; lower are wedge-shaped, toothed, alternate. **In bloom:** April-August. **Habitat-Range:** Thickets, shores, springy slopes; throughout.

The generic name combines the Greek words *eri*, meaning "early," and *geron*, meaning "old man," alluding to the white down covering stem and leaves of this early-blooming plant. Indians used it as a diuretic, a tonic and an astringent. Early settlers dried and burned it as an insect repellant. A similar species with more, but smaller flowers is Common Fleabane *(E. philadelphicus)*. Its flowers are pale in color and more numerous.

191 WILD COLUMBINE *(Aquilegia canadensis)* Buttercup family *(Ranunculaceae)*

Height: 1′-2′ (.3-.6m). **Flower:** 1″-2″ (2.5-5cm) length; regular, with 5 funnel-shaped petals with long, knobbed spurs, numerous stamens and 5 pistils projecting beyond petals; solitary, nodding on stalks from upper leaf axils. **Leaves:** Compound, divided and subdivided into 3's; generally 3-lobed; basal and scattered along stem. **In bloom:** April-July. **Habitat-Range:** Woodlands, shaded rocks and cliffs; throughout.

The flowers, which have red tubular sepals with curved, knobbed spurs, yellow petals within, hang from rather long stems and account for the common name Rock Bells. The red color of the flower attracts hummingbirds whose long tongues can reach the nectar at the base of the long spurs. These long spurs also explain the generic and common names for they were said to resemble the talons of an eagle *(aquila* in Latin) or a circle of doves *(columba* in Latin) drinking around a fountain. A group was once formed to make the columbine the national floral emblem of the United States because the common name suggests Columbia, a popular patriotic name for America, and the botanical name symbolizes our national bird, the eagle. The roots of the plant were boiled and eaten as a famine food by the Indians and to stop coughs and stomachache. Some Indian tribes used the pulverized seeds as a love charm, the suitor dusting his palms with the powdered seed and then holding hands with the girl. English settlers mixed the seeds in wine to speed childbirth.

192 SHOOTING STAR *(Dodecatheon meadia)*   Primrose family *(Primulaceae)*

Height: 4″-20″ (10-50cm). **Flower:** 1″ (2.5cm) long; regular, with 5 petals pointed backward, 5 stamens froming a beaklike cone in center, 1 pistil protruding beyond them; several, nodding in umbel, on leafless stalk; also has white and blue forms. **Leaves:** Narrowly elliptical-oblong, often reddish at base; entire; basal rosette. **In bloom:** April-June. **Habitat-Range:** Open woods, meadows, moist slopes and prairies; south of a line from northern Virginia to Wisconsin.

The common name derives from the appearance of the swept-back petals trailing the "star"—a cluster of yellow stamens. A smaller species, *D. amethystinum*, grows no higher than 1′ (.1m), has pale leaves without red bases and deep crimson flowers and is found locally in eastern Pennsylvania and in the Mississippi Valley.

193 WILD BLEEDING HEART *(Dicentra eximia)*   Poppy family *(Papaveraceae)*

Height: 10″-20″ (25-50cm). **Flower:** 1″ (2.5cm) long; irregular, flattened, with 4 petals, the two inner ones adhering at their tips and enclosed by the two outer ones whose tips are inflated and extended backward; many, in drooping racemes. **Leaves:** Dissected, numerous narrow segments; basal. **In bloom:** May-August. **Habitat-Range:** Rocky woods and cliffs; from New York south to West Virginia and Tennessee.

The common name derives from a fancied resemblance of the two outer spurred petals to a heart and the united tips of the two inner petals to a drop of blood. The roots contain an alkaloid, corydalin, which has been used as a tonic. Climbing Fumitory, *Adlumia fungosa*, is similar but is a climbing vine and its flowers are pale pink and not so heart-shaped.

194 PALE CORYDALIS *(Corydalis sempervirens)*   Poppy family *(Papaveraceae)*

Height: 6″-36″ (15-90cm). **Flower:** 1/2″ (1cm) long; irregular, having 4 petals, 2 outer and 2 inner forming a tubular corolla, upper outer one with a round spur; several, in loose panicle. **Leaves:** Dissected, bluntly lobed, upper ones sessile; alternate. **In bloom:** May-September. **Habitat-Range:** Rocky places and recent clearings; throughout.

The pink or purplish petals have yellow tips. There are also a number of species with yellow flowers. The spur on the upper petal is responsible for the common and generic names because it reminded early botanists of the crested lark (*korydalos* in Greek) which has a spur. The flowers of Fumitory, *Fumaria officinalis*, resemble those of *C. sempervirens*, but are tipped with maroon and its leaves are finely cut and grayish-green and the plant looks like a puff of smoke in the distance; hence its other common name, Earth Smoke.

195 FIELD GARLIC *(Allium vineale)*   Lily family *(Liliaceae)*

Height: 1′-4′ (.3-1m). **Flower:** 1/4″ (6mm) long; regular, with 3 sepals and 3 petals of the same size and color, 6 stamens, 1 pistil, flowers sometimes replaced by small bulbs having slender "tails"; many, in a loose umbel. **Leaves:** Flat, linear, hollow; entire;

mostly basal, upright. **In bloom:** May-July. **Habitat-Range:** Grasslands, fallow fields, roadsides; south of a line from Massachusetts to Illinois.

Various species of garlic have been used in various ways since ancient times. The Romans gave it to soldiers to arouse courage. Mohammed advised it for the stings of scorpions and other insects and it was also used thus by American Indians. It was said to stimulate digestion, cure bronchial disorders and rid the bowels of parasites. Garlic bulbs were worn on a string around the neck by early physicians to protect them from the diseases of their patients. The leaves are often chopped and added to salads.

196 WILD GARLIC *(Allium canadense)*   Lily family *(Liliaceae)*

Height: 8″-24″ (20-60cm). **Flower:** 1/4″ (6mm) long; regular, with 3 sepals and 3 petals of the same color and size forming a star-shaped perianth; flowers sometimes replaced by small bulbs with or without slender "tails"; several, in a loose umbel. **Leaves:** Flat, linear; entire; mostly basal, upright. **In bloom:** May-July. **Habitat-Range:** Open woods, thickets and meadows; throughout.

Similar to *A. vineale* but its leaves are not hollow, it has fewer flowers and they are star-shaped. It is preferred to *A. vineale* for eating because of its milder flavor. The top bulbets may be used as cocktail onions. The underground bulbs are added to soups, stews and sweet peas.

197 DRAGON'S-MOUTH *(Arethusa bulbosa)*†   Orchid family *(Orchidaceae)*

Height: 5″-12″ (12-30cm). **Flower:** 2″-3″ (5-7cm) long; irregular, with similar sepals and petals arching over a broad pinkish white lip blotched with purple and with 3 hairy yellow ridges down its surface; solitary, terminal, on scaly stem. **Leaves:** Flat, thin, grasslike; entire; single upright leaf appears after flowering season. **In bloom:** May-August. **Habitat-Range:** Bogs and peaty meadows; throughout northern regions and in mountains in South.

This orchid is locally abundant but is becoming rare. The flower has three erect sepals and two curved petals that arch over a broad, curved lip that is marked with crimson spots and has several rows of yellow or white hairs. The bizarre shape and markings of the flower account for its common name.

SNAKE-MOUTH *(Pogonia ophioglossoides)*†   Orchid family *(Orchidaceae)*

Height: 6″-24″ (15-60cm). **Flower:** 2″ (5cm) long; irregular, with rose-pink petals and sepals of the same shape; the lower lip pink with red veins and fringed; beard of yellow-tipped hairs; solitary, terminal. **Leaves:** Ovate or elliptical; entire; single leaf midway on stem at flowering time. **In bloom:** May-August. **Habitat-Range:** Bogs, wet shores and glades; throughout.

Similar to *A. bulbosa* but the lower lip of the flower is fringed, has a beard of yellow-tipped hairs, which accounts for its generic name (from *pogonias*, Greek for "bearded"). The plant also differs from *A. bulbosa* in having a stem leaf at flowering time.

GRASS PINK *(Calopogon pulchellus)*   Orchid family *(Orchidaceae)*

Height: 12″-18″ (30-45cm). **Flower:** 1″ (2.5cm) long; irregular, having a spoon-shaped lip with a tuft of yellow hairs above the spreading petals and sepals; several, in loose raceme. **Leaves:** Linear, grasslike; entire; single, upright, sheathing base of flower stem. **In bloom:** May-August. **Habitat-Range:** Bogs, wet shores; throughout.

Similar to *Pogonia ophioglossoides* but the bearded lip is uppermost and the single leaf is grasslike. The yellowish white "beard" is so distinctive that it is responsible for the generic name, which combines two Greek words, *calos*, meaning "beautiful," and *pogon*, "beard." A species with a smaller flower and thinner leaves, *C. pallidus*, is called Small-flowered Grass Pink and is found in the southernmost part of our range.

198 FRINGED POLYGALA *(Polygala paucifolia)*   Milkwort family *(Polygalaceae)*

Height: 3"-6" (7-15cm). **Flower:** 3/4" (2cm) long; irregular, with the petals forming a tube with finely fringed crest, 2 winglike pink sepals; one or a few, on long stems from upper leaf axils. **Leaves:** Lower ones are scale-like and alternate; upper ones are oval, entire, crowded near the top. **In bloom:** May-July. **Habitat-Range:** Damp, rich woods; throughout northern part and in mountains in South.

The generic name combines two Greek words, *polys*, meaning "much," and *gala*, "milk." At one time milkworts were eaten by nursing mothers and fed to dairy cattle in the belief that they increased milk production.

199 RED CLOVER *(Trifolium pratense)*   Pea family *(Leguminosae)*

Height: 8"-15" (20-37cm). **Flower:** 3/8" (1cm) long; irregular, pealike, tubular with banner folded over the wings and keel; many, clustered in a round head. **Leaves:** Palmate, three oval leaflets; entire; alternate. **In bloom:** May-September. **Habitat-Range:** Roadsides, clearings and lawns; throughout.

Clovers have palmate leaves with three lobes; hence the generic name meaning "three leaves." Some writers believe that the clover leaf was the original shamrock. The leaf was also thought to resemble the three-knobbed club carried by Hercules; hence the plant was called "clava," the Latin for club, which was corrupted into "clover." This also explains why the club in playing cards is a clover leaf. The green leaves, which often show pale chevron marks, were used in salads or added to soups and stews by Indians. Pioneers used the dried flower heads to make a tea reputedly good for boils and other skin eruptions. When onions and honey were added to the tea, it was prescribed for coughs and hoarseness. Because their root systems harbor nitrogen-fixing bacteria, clovers add nutrients to the soil. A common species with pink or white flowers and elliptical leaflets without chevron marks is Alsike Clover, *T. hybridium.*

200 SWAMP PINK *(Helonias bullata)*†   Lily family *(Liliaceae)*

Height: 1'-2' (.3-.6m). **Flower:** 1/3" (8mm) diameter; regular, with 3 sepals and 3 petals of the same color and size, 6 stamens, 1 pistil; many, in short, dense raceme. **Leaves:** Spatulate; entire; basal rosette. **In bloom:** April-May. **Habitat-Range:** Swamps and bogs; coastal plain from Staten Island to eastern Virginia; also mountains of Pennsylvania south.

The blue anthers contrast with the pink petals. The flower stem is hollow and has scale-like bracts near its base. The short flowering raceme elongates to 8" (20cm) when in fruit. The common and generic names (from Greek *helos* meaning "a swamp") indicate its habitat.

201 PITCHER PLANT *(Sarracenia purpurea)*†   Pitcher-plant family *(Sarraceniaceae)*

Height: 8″-24″ (20-60cm). **Flower:** 2″ (5cm) diameter; regular, with 5 petals forming a globular corolla, numerous stamens, 1 pistil with an umbrella-like end; solitary, nodding, on leafless stalk. **Leaves:** Long (4″-10″, 10-25cm), hollow, pitcher-shaped with wing along one side, hood at opening; several, in a basal tuft. **In bloom:** May-August. **Habitat-Range:** Sphagnum bogs; mostly throughout, mainly along coast in South.

The leaves are responsible for the common name because they are hollow and shaped like a hooded pitcher. The reddish-purple flower is short-lived but the leaves persist and are marked with purple lines and veins. The hood and upper part of the leaf is covered with backward-pointing bristles. Insects unfortunate enough to enter the leaf find it almost impossible to exit because of the bristles. Exhausted, they fall toward the bottom of the "pitcher" which usually contains a fluid that is partly rain water and partly a secretion of the plant. The secretion digests the insect and the plant obtains nitrogen compounds. Thus, these plants can live in bog soils which are poor in nitrogen. The root was regarded by Indians as a specific cure for smallpox not only by shortening the term of the disease but also preventing the formation of pox marks.

202 SHOWY ORCHIS *(Orchis spectabilis)*†   Orchid family *(Orchidaceae)*

Height: 4″-12″ (10-30cm). **Flower:** 1″ (2.5cm) long; irregular, with 3 sepals and two petals forming a hood over a white, spurred lip; 3-12 flowers emerging from the axils of leaflike bracts. **Leaves:** Ovate, blunt-ended, lustrous; entire; two, basal. **In bloom:** April-June. **Habitat-Range:** Woods and moist slopes; throughout the northern regions and in mountains in the South.

With their hood of pink or purple petals and sepals arching over a white lip and spur, the flowers are quite striking. *Orchis* is the Greek for "testicle," an allusion to the appearance of the rounded, fleshy root from which an orchid grows. This was considered a "signature" and the roots were used as a remedy for sexual impotence in the aging.

203 RABBIT-FOOT CLOVER *(Trifolium arvense)*   Pea family *(Leguminosae)*

Height: 6″-24″ (15-60cm). **Flower:** 1/4″ (6mm) long; irregular, pealike, tubular with banner folded over wings and keel, sepals hairy and longer than petals; many, clustered in elongated head. **Leaves:** Palmate, 3 narrow, elliptical leaflets; entire; alternate. **In bloom:** May-October. **Habitat-Range:** Dry roadsides and fields; throughout.

Similar to *T. pratense* but has fuzzy pinkish gray flower heads and very narrow leaflets.

204 INDIAN PAINTBRUSH   Figwort family *(Scrophulariaceae)*
(Castilleja coccinea)†

Height: 1′-2′ (.3-.6m). **Flower:** 1″ (2.5cm) long; irregular, with 5 petals forming a 2-lipped corolla, upper lip long and arched, shorter lower lip 3-lobed, 4 unequal stamens, 1 pistil; in axils of scarlet-tipped bracts on terminal spike. **Leaves:** Basal rosette of oblong leaves with entire edges; sessile stem-leaves cleft into 3-5 sharp lobes. **In bloom:** April-August. **Habitat-Range:** Moist meadows, thickets, roadsides; mostly throughout.

Partially parasitic plants growing on grasses and other plants in sandy meadows and prairies. The pale, greenish-yellow flowers are actually hidden by the larger 3-5 lobed scarlet tipped bracts which make the plant conspicuous and explain why it is put into the red section of this book. The generic name honors Domingo Castillejo, a Spanish botanist. The common name derives from an Indian legend of an Indian brave who was attempting to paint a sunset with war paints and lamented to the Great Spirit his inability to duplicate a sunset. The Great Spirit responded by supplying him with brushes dripping with all the colors of a sunset. As the Indian painted his picture he discarded his brushes. Another common name is Painted-Cup. The blaze of the plant's color was taken as a "signature" by Indian medicine men that the plant could be used to treat burns and the burning bite of the centipede. Women of some Indian tribes drank a tea of the whole plant to "dry up the menstrual flow."

205 WOOD BETONY *(Pedicularis canadensis)* Figwort family *(Scrophulariaceae)*

Height: 6″-12″ (15-30cm). **Flower:** 3/4″ (2cm) long; irregular, with 5 petals forming a 2-lipped corolla, upper lip arched and concave, lower lip 3-lobed, 4 stamens in pairs, 1 pistil; many, on short, dense spikes. **Leaves:** Lanceolate; toothed lobes; many basal, others scattered along stem. **In bloom:** April-June. **Habitat-Range:** Open woods, thickets, clearings; throughout.

This plant catches our eye even before it is in bloom because of the dark green rosette of hairy, fernlike leaves. The flowers may be red or yellow. Farmers once believed that if their cattle grazed on this plant they became infested with lice, which accounts for its other common name Lousewort and for its generic name, which is Latin for "louse." European immigrants used a related species for the aches and pains associated with various illnesses and when Italians wished to praise someone they said, "He has more virtues than betony."

206 PINK LADY SLIPPER *(Cypripedium acaule)*[†] Orchid family *(Orchidaceae)*

Height: 6″-14″ (15-35cm). **Flower:** 2″-3″ (5-7cm) long; irregular, having 3 long, spreading sepals and 2 smaller side petals that are greenish-purple, 1 pink pouchlike lip slit down the middle and folded inward; solitary, nodding on leafless stem. **Leaves:** Oval, parallel ribbing; entire; only two arching basal leaves. **In bloom:** April-July. **Habitat-Range:** Dry, acid soil, woodlands but sometimes in wet woods and bogs; throughout.

This orchid is also called Moccasin Flower. Its generic name combines Greek *cyris*, meaning "Venus," and *pedilon*, "slipper." A later blooming species is the Showy Lady's Slipper, *C. reginae*; its slipper is white marked with rose. The slipper is a saclike petal with a longitudinal cleft. Insects landing on the flower fall through the cleft into the sac and move out through two openings at the rear of the "slipper," brushing against the reproductive structures located there, thus insuring cross-pollination. A tea made from the dried leaves was used by Indians as a tranquilizer and a cure for insomnia. Until the 1930's the roots were used by physicians as a nerve medicine.

207 STEEPLEBUSH *(Spiraea tomentosa)* Rose family *(Rosaceae)*

Height: 1′-4′ (.3-1m). **Flower:** 1/4″ (6mm) diameter; regular, with 5 petals, 10-50 stamens, 5 pistils; many, crowded in steeple-shaped raceme, lower ones emerging from leaf axils. **Leaves:** Ovate or oblong, the underside covered with dense, woolly hairs;

coarsely toothed; alternate. **In bloom:** July-September. **Habitat-Range:** Moist fields and meadows; mostly throughout.

Although it grows from woody stems and therefore should not be included in this book, it is associated with many herbaceous plants and will be seen with them in summer meadows. The flowers at the tip of the inflorescence open first.

208 **PINK PYROLA** *(Pyrola asarifolia)*   Wintergreen family *(Pyrolaceae)*

Height: 6″-15″ (15-37cm). **Flower:** 1/2″ (1cm) diameter; regular, with 5 rounded petals, 10 stamens with hairy filaments, 1 short, conical style with round stigma; several, in raceme. **Leaves:** Kidney-shaped, glossy green; small, rounded teeth; basal rosette. **In bloom:** June-August. **Habitat-Range:** Bogs, rich woods and thickets; throughout northern regions.

These summer flowers bloom in shady woods in summer when most plants bloom in sunny meadows.

209 **BLAZING-STAR** *(Liatris* spp.*)*   Composite family *(Compositae)*

Height: 1′-4′ (.3-1m). **Flower:** Tiny; indistinguishable, having tubular florets with long and slender styles protruding beyond petals; several or many florets forming a head with many heads forming a spike. **Leaves:** Linear; entire; alternate. **In bloom:** July-October. **Habitat-Range:** Most prefer dry, open places; throughout.

The many species of blazing-star are difficult to distinguish without a minute examination of the flower and because the different species hybridize. However, the genus itself is easily recognized because of its distinct, fuzzy flower heads with their distinct bracts which are often colored and beautiful. *L. spicata* illustrates these features. Most species also have purple, resinous dots on the leaves. The plant grows from a corm, which makes it easy to transplant to a cultivated garden. The corms were dug and stored by Indians in the fall and provided them with a nutritious ingredient for winter meals.

210 **CARDINAL FLOWER** *(Lobelia cardinalis)*[†]   Bluebell family *(Campanulaceae)*

Height: 2′-5′ (.6-1.5m). **Flower:** 1 1/2″ (4cm) long; irregular, with 5 petals forming a 2-lipped tubular corolla, lower lip with 3 spreading lobes, upper lip 2-lobed, 5 stamens in a ring around single pistil which projects upward through a slit in upper lip; several, in leaf axils and bracted racemes. **Leaves:** Lanceolate; irregularly toothed; alternate. **In bloom:** July-September. **Habitat-Range:** Damp shores, meadows, swamps; throughout.

These brilliantly colored flowers are found abundantly in wet places at the edges of streams and swamps. Its relative inaccessibility has prevented gross overpicking but it is still on the conservation list of flowers to be protected. The tubular scarlet flower is especially appealing to hummingbirds. The striking color is said to resemble the scarlet finery of the cardinals of the Roman Catholic Church; hence its common name. Its generic name honors Matthias de l'Obel, a Flemish herbalist.

211 **CASTOR BEAN** *(Ricinus communis)*   Spurge family *(Euphorbiaceae)*

Height: 3′-6′ (1-2m). **Flower:** 3/4″ (2cm) long; irregular, monoecious, without petals, pistillate flowers with red, plume-like styles, staminate flowers with numerous yellow filaments; many, on raceme with pistillate above and staminate below. **Leaves:** Broadly palmate, 5-11 clefts; toothed; alternate. **In bloom:** July-September. **Habitat-Range:** Waste ground; locally throughout southern region.

A handsome tropical plant with reddish foliage, it often escapes cultivation and has become a common plant in waste places locally especially in the southern region. The two kinds of flowers are easily distinguished by the color of their reproductive parts. The seeds are often brightly colored and mottled, giving them some resemblance to a tick. Hence, its generic name which is Latin for the Mediterranean sheep tick. The plant is very poisonous if eaten but an oil has been extracted from it which has been used medicinally as a cathartic.

212 FIREWEED *(Epilobium angustifolium)*   Evening-primrose family *(Onagraceae)*

Height: 3'-7' (1-2m). **Flower:** 1"-1 1/2" (2.5-4cm) diameter; regular, with tubular calyx, 4 rounded petals, 8 stamens, 1 pistil; many, in spike-like raceme. **Leaves:** Slender, willow-like; entire; alternate. **In bloom:** July-September. **Habitat-Range:** Dry soils, fields and roadsides; throughout northern regions and in mountains in the South.

The common name alludes to its quick growth in areas devastated by fire, the pink-magenta flowers brightening the fire-blackened land. During World War II the plant grew in large numbers in bombed and burned-over areas of London. Its many long slender leaves account for its other common name, Willow Herb. Flower buds at the top of the spike droop down and the reddish seed pods angle upward. When the pods open, the seeds are seen to have white, silky tufts. Young shoots can be cooked and eaten like asparagus.

213 VIRGINIA MEADOW BEAUTY   Melastoma family *(Melastomataceae)* *(Rhexia virginica)*

Height: 12"-18" (30-45cm). **Flower:** 1"-1 1/2" (2.5-4cm) diameter; regular, having 4 rounded petals, 8 prominent stamens in 2 rows, 1 pistil; few, in cyme. **Leaves:** Oval, sessile; finely toothed; opposite. **In bloom:** July-September. **Habitat-Range:** Wet, sandy and gravelly soil; mostly throughout.

The stem is 4-angled, slightly winged and bristly. These attractive plants often grow in large clusters and are a favorite browse of deer; hence another common name, Deer Grass. Another very similar Meadow Beauty, *R. aristosa*, is found only in sandy bogs and wet pine barrens from New Jersey to Georgia. Unlike *R. virginica* it lacks winged stems, has narrow lanceolate leaves, and petals that taper to narrow points. Maryland Meadow Beauty, *R. mariana*, grows from a horizontal runner, the flower is a pale pink, and its leaves have petioles.

214 SEASHORE MALLOW   Mallow family *(Malavaceae)* *(Kosteletzkya virginica)*

Height: 1'-3' (.3-1m). **Flower:** 1"-2" (2.5-5cm) diameter; regular, having 5 petals, numerous stamens forming a collar around the style with anthers on outside, 1 pistil with 5-knobbed stigma; few, terminal. **Leaves:** Resemble maple leaf with 3 or 5 pointed lobes; toothed; alternate. **In bloom:** July-September. **Habitat-Range:** Brackish and nearly fresh marshes and shores; along the coast from Long Island south.

Mallows are characterized by the peculiar arrangement of their stamens. Numerous stamens form a cylinder around the style, making it appear to be covered with yellow bristles. Mallows were used in various herbal medicines. An infusion of dried leaves was said to be good for coughs, and bruised, fresh leaves "laid on the eyes with a little honey" was said "to take inflammation from them." Parts of the plant were also used to treat constipation, bee stings, dandruff and even loss of hair. One of the economically important members of the mallow family is the cotton plant. The Swamp Rose Mallow, *Hibiscus palustris*, is taller, has a larger flower (4"-7" (10-18cm) diameter), and its leaves are oval with pointed lobes.

MARSH MALLOW *(Althaea officinalis)*   Mallow family *(Malvaceae)*

Height: 2'-4' (.6-1m). **Flower:** 1"-1 1/2" (2.5-4cm) diameter; regular, having 5 petals, numerous stamens forming a collar around the style, with anthers on the outside, 1 pistil with 5-knobbed stigma; several, clustered in leaf axils. **Leaves:** Oval or heart-shaped; coarsely toothed or lobed; alternate. **In bloom:** August-October. **Habitat-Range:** Marsh edges; coastal; south to Virginia and locally inland.

Similar to *K. virginica* but the leaves are oval or heart-shaped, and it looks gray-green and is velvety to the touch. It was once cultivated for its roots, which was the original source of a mucilaginous material used to make the favorite campfire confection, marshmallows. Musk Mallow, *Malva moschata*, is similar to *A. officinalis* but the petals are notched, the leaves are deeply lobed and the flowers may be lavender or white.

215 ROSE PINK *(Sabatia angularis)*†   Gentian family *(Gentianaceae)*

Height: 6"-36" (15-90cm). **Flower:** 1"-1 1/2" (2.5-4cm) diameter; regular, with 5 petals, 5 stamens, 1 pistil with two-cleft style; single, on branched stems. **Leaves:** Oval, sessile, clasping; entire; opposite. **In bloom:** July-September. **Habitat-Range:** Rich soils, meadows and thickets; throughout, excepting northern New York and New England.

The flowers are identified by a yellow or yellowish green center with a dark red border. The stem is sharply 4-angled. It is also called Bitter-bloom because of its use as a bitter tonic. The generic name honors Liberato Sabbati, an 18th-century Italian botanist. The Marsh Pink or Sea Pink, *S. stellaris*, is found in marshes along the seacoast and has narrow, elliptical leaves.

216 HAIRY BEARDTONGUE   Snapdragon family *(Scrophularaceae)*
(Penstemon cobaea)

Height: 8"-36" (20-90cm). **Flower:** 1" (2.5cm) long; irregular, tubular corolla with mouth having 2-lobed upper lip and 3-lobed lower lip, 4 anther-bearing stamens and one sterile hairy stamen; on long stems from axils of upper leaves. **Leaves:** Ovate or broadly lanceolate, sessile; toothed; opposite. **In bloom:** May-July. **Habitat-Range:** Plains, prairies, bluffs, rocky openings; mainly western part, spreading from cultivation in the East.

Found mainly in the West, it is one of 16 almost indistinguishable species of beard-tongue in our range. The common name derives from the resemblance of the fuzzy stamen to a hairy, yellow tongue on the lower lip of the flower. Indians considered all beardtongues a priceless medicine. The juice, or a solution of the boiled stems, was applied to the genitals to prevent gonorrhea. A tea from the leaves served as a laxative and an infusion from the flowers was used for chest colds.

217 RAGGED-ROBIN *(Lychnis flos-cuculi)* Pink family *(Caryophyllaceae)*

Height: 1'-3' (.3-1m). **Flower:** 1" (2.5cm) diameter; regular, with 5 deeply cleft Y-shaped petals, 1 pistil with 5 styles; several, in cyme. **Leaves:** Lanceolate; entire; opposite. **In bloom:** June-July. **Habitat-Range:** Fields and meadows; locally in northeastern regions.

The deeply cleft pink, blue or white petals give this flower a ragged appearance. It is a garden escape now found in fields and meadows. The latter part of its species name accounts for another of its common names, Cuckoo Flower.

218 BEEBALM *(Monarda didyma)* Mint family *(Labiatae)*

Height: 1'-4' (.3-1m). **Flower:** 1 1/2"-2" (4-5cm) long; irregular, with 5 petals forming tubular corolla with 2 lips, upper lip arched, lower one 3-lobed and drooping, 2 protruding stamens, 1 pistil; many, in solitary, terminal clusters. **Leaves:** Oval to lanceolate; sharply toothed; opposite. **In bloom:** June-September. **Habitat-Range:** Rich, moist woods, bottomlands; south of a line from New York to Michigan.

The stem is square in cross-section (a characteristic of most mints) and hairy at the nodes. The scarlet flowers are further complemented by the red-tinged bracts and the red tinge of the leaves just below them. This red color and the long tubular flowers make them attractive to hummingbirds and butterflies but not bees as the common name suggests. Another common name is Oswego-Tea, a reference to the use of its leaves by patriots in their boycott against the use of China tea because of the English import taxes. The Oswego Indians, who lived in an area now known as Oswego, New York, also used the herb to flavor meats and other foods. Herb doctors found this plant a useful remedy for flatulence and nervous stomach. The generic name dedicates the plant to Nicholas Monardes, author of many publications on medicinal and other useful plants in America.

219 WILD BERGAMOT *(Monarda fistulosa)* Mint family *(Labiatae)*

Height: 1'-5' (.3-2m). **Flower:** 1" (2.5cm) long; irregular, with 2-lipped corolla, upper lip erect, hairy and toothed, lower lip 3-lobed, spreading, 2 stamens, 1 pistil with two-lobed style; many, in terminal heads. **Leaves:** Lanceolate; toothed; opposite. **In bloom:** July-August. **Habitat-Range:** Open woods and roadsides; throughout, and in mountains in the South.

As with many members of the mint family, the leaves were used to make a mint-flavored tea. The Indians also boiled the leaves along with their meat to enhance flavor. The oil from boiled leaves was inhaled to relieve bronchial complaints, was applied to pimples, and was used by Indians to dress their hair.

220 KNAPWEED *(Centaurea* spp.*)* Composite family *(Compositae)*

Height: 1'-3' (.3-1m). **Flower:** Tiny; indistinguishable; many, forming a head made up of clusters of small, tubular flowers, the outermost resembling ray flowers. **Leaves:** Lanceolate; pinnately lobed or toothed; alternate. **In bloom:** June-August. **Habitat-Range:** Fields, roadsides, waste places; mostly throughout.

The knapweeds, also called Star-thistles, are European imports that escaped from cultivation. Although the flower heads resemble those of the thistle, most of these plants have no spines. The shape and color of the scale-like bracts that form the base of the head helps the botanist to distinguish between species. Another common name is Bachelor's Button, a reference to the practice of English maidens who wore the flower as a sign they were eligible for marriage. North Africans eat the leaves and young stems of some species in salads and feed the plant to camels.

221 WILD ONION (*Allium stellatum*)   Lily family (*Liliaceae*)

Height: 1'-2' (.3-.6m). **Flower:** 1/4" (6mm) long; regular, with 3 petals and 3 sepals of the same color and size, 6 stamens, 1 pistil; many, in dome-shaped umbel. **Leaves:** Grasslike; entire; upright, from base. **In bloom:** July-August. **Habitat-Range:** Rocky prairies, slopes, ridges; throughout the western parts of our range.

Wild onion bulbs were used by Indians and early settlers in raw or cooked form. The onions also played many roles in pioneer life: onion juice was used to open nostrils during colds; boiled onion water and honey was taken for asthma and coughs; men ate onions to increase their sperm; and raw onions were rubbed on the body as an insect repellant. Their hot taste and burning effect on the eyes was seen as a "signature" by herb doctors, who applied sliced onions to the soles of the feet to "draw out" the fever of pneumonia and used onion juice and salt on scalds and burns. The Nodding Onion, *A. cernuum*, has a crook near the top of the flower stem, causing the flower head to nod.

222 SCARLET LYCHNIS (*Lychnis chalcedonica*)   Pink family (*Caryophyllaceae*)

Height: 2'-3' (.6-1m). **Flower:** 3/4" (2cm) diameter; regular, with 5-cleft, Y-shaped petals, 1 pistil with 5 styles; many, in cyme. **Leaves:** Ovate or cordate; entire; opposite. **In bloom:** June-August. **Habitat-Range:** Thickets, roadsides, open woods; locally in northern regions.

Similar to *L. flos-cuculi* but has smaller flowers less deeply cleft and are found in a congested flower head. The flowers may be pink or white but are usually red; hence its common name.

223 NODDING THISTLE (*Carduus nutans*)   Composite family (*Compositae*)

Height: 1'-4' (.3-1m). **Flower:** Tiny; indistingusihable, slender and tubular; many, in dome-shaped, nodding head. **Leaves:** Pinnate; spiny lobes; alternate. **In bloom:** June-October. **Habitat-Range:** Fields and waste places; north of a line from Maryland to Illinois.

The base of the flower head is encircled with many backward-curved purple bracts. The spiny stem has interrupted prickly "wings."

224 TEASEL (*Dipsacus sylvestris*)   Teasel family (*Dipsacaceae*)

Height: 2'-6' (.6-2m). **Flower:** 1/2" (1cm) long; irregular, having 4-lobed, tubular corolla, 4 stamens, 1 pistil; many crowded in oval heads 2″-5″ (5-13cm) long. **Leaves:** Lanceolate, sessile; toothed; opposite. **In bloom:** July-October. **Habitat-Range:** Roadsides, fields, old pastures; throughout.

Many spines emerge between the small flowers and several large spines surround the head. The stem is covered with prickles. It was cultivated in Europe and manufacturers of woolen goods found the dried flower heads ideal for raising the nap on cloth because the head breaks at any firm obstruction where a metal device would tear the material. The common name alludes to "teasing" the nap of wool. The generic name derives from the Greek *dipsa*, meaning "thirst," because some species (e.g. *D. laciniatus*) have coarsely lobed leaves whose bases unite around the stem to form a cup that may hold rainwater. Country folk used to say that water from this cup would cure warts.

225 PINK WILD BEAN *(Strophostyles umbellata)*   Pea family *(Leguminosae)*

Height: Trailing vine. **Flower:** 1/2″ (1cm) long; irregular, pealike, having 5 petals the two lower ones forming a keel that curves upward; several, in raceme on long, upright stalk. **Leaves:** Palmate, 3 lanceolate leaflets; entire; alternate. **In bloom:** July-October. **Habitat-Range:** Sandy woods, clearings and fields; throughout the area south of a line from Illinois to Long Island.

The flowers of this vine are on stalks that protrude beyond the leaves. The seed pods produced by the plant were used by early settlers in a concoction to treat fever and inflammation of the skin. The leaves of Trailing Wild Bean, *S. helvola*, are bluntly lobed and the flower stalk is much shorter. Wild Bean, *Phaseolus polystachios*, is similar to *S. umbellata* but its leaflets are round and the flowers are loosely arranged along the flower stalk. The flowers may also appear to be more purple than pink. Seed pods of this species are curved, whereas in *S. umbellata* they are usually straight.

226 FIELD MILKWORT *(Polygala sanguinea)*   Milkwort family *(Polygalaceae)*

Height: 6″-15″ (15-37cm). **Flower:** 1/4″ (6mm) long; indistinguishable; overlapping in oblong head. **Leaves:** Linear, with short, abrupt tips; entire; alternate. **In bloom:** June-October. **Habitat-Range:** Poor meadows and moist, open, acid soils; throughout.

The flower color ranges from rose-pink to white and is often mistaken for clover because of the shape of the flower head. Milkworts were at one time fed to nursing mothers and dairy cattle in the belief that they helped produce milk. The generic name is derived from Greek *polys*, meaning "much," and *gala*, "milk." It is also called Candyroot because the crushed root has a wintergreen flavor.

CROSS-LEAVED MILKWORT   Milkwort family *(Polygalaceae)*
(Polygala cruciata)

Height: 4″-12″ (10-30cm). **Flower:** 1/4″ (6mm) long; indistinguishable; dense cluster forming a head. **Leaves:** Linear-oblong; entire; mostly in whorls of 4 along the stem. **In bloom:** July-October. **Habitat-Range:** Wet pinelands, savannas and sands; along the coastal plains and inland south of a line from Ohio to Minnesota.

Similar to *P. sanguinea* but the leaves come in whorls of four and form a cross; hence the common and species names, derived from the Latin *crucis*, meaning "cross."

The Whorled Milkwort, *P. verticullata*, has 3 to 5 leaves in each whorl and the flower head is a tapering cluster of usually whitish flowers.

227 CROWN VETCH *(Coronilla varia)*   Pea family *(Leguminosae)*

Height: Creeping stems. **Flower:** 1/2″ (1cm) long; irregular, pealike with a circular banner and incurved keel; 10-15 flowers in umbel at the end of a long stem from leaf axil. **Leaves:** Pinnate, 5-12 pairs of leaflets; entire; alternate. **In bloom:** June-August. **Habitat-Range:** Cultivated fields, roadsides; throughout.

The common and generic names refer to the circular cluster of bicolored (pink and white) flowers, *Coronilla* being the Latin for "little crown." These plants are often planted on the banks of new highways to prevent erosion.

228 PIPSISSEWA *(Chimaphila umbellata)*[†]   Wintergreen family *(Pyrolaceae)*

Height: 8″-12″ (20-30cm). **Flower:** 1/2″ (1cm) diameter; regular, having 5 concave, rounded petals, 10 stamens, 1 conical style with round stigma; several, nodding in loose umbel. **Leaves:** Lanceolate; toothed; opposite or whorled in tiers. **In bloom:** July-August. **Habitat-Range:** Dry woods; throughout.

This flower can be seen in woods in midsummer. The small, waxy, flesh-colored or pink flowers are inconspicuous but the shiny, dark green leaves catch the eye. These leaves stay green throughout the winter and account for the generic name, which combines the Greek *cheima*, meaning "winter," and *phelein*, "to love." This also explains why it is often called Wintergreen. The leaves are refreshing when chewed and have been used in making root beer. Tea from the leaves was used by both Indians and early settlers to induce sweating. It was also a favorite of the medical profession in the early 1800's for treating aches and pains. Its beneficial effects were apparently due to salicylates (aspirin) in the plant.

229 TICK-TREFOIL *(Desmodium* spp.*)*   Pea family *(Leguminosae)*

Height: 6″-48″ (.2-1m). **Flower:** 1/2″ (1cm) long; irregular, pealike; many or few in raceme. **Leaves:** Palmate, clover-like, divided into three leaflets; entire; alternate. **In bloom:** July-August. **Habitat-Range:** Open woods; throughout.

Many species are found throughout our range. This weedy plant is not very showy except when in large numbers, but most people are familiar with it because its seed pods are covered with minute hooks and consist of a number of roughly triangular joints; hence its generic name, which is derived from the Greek *desmos*, meaning "chain." Most species have pink flowers but there are also white and lavender forms. They differ from one another mainly in the shape of their leaflets and seed pods but identification of all species is beyond the scope of this book. The early settlers used tick-trefoils as fodder for cattle and horses.

230 ROSEBUD ORCHID *(Cleistes divaricata)*[†]   Orchid family *(Orchidaceae)*

Height: 1′-2′ (.3-.6m). **Flower:** 2″ (5cm) long; irregular, with 3 long, narrow, brown sepals and a tubular shape formed by a troughlike greenish lip and the two other petals; single, nodding on stem. **Leaves:** Linear, with short, abrupt tips; entire; alternate. **In bloom:** June-October. **Habitat-Range:** In pine barrens and peaty thickets; on southern coastal plain to New Jersey and inland to Kentucky and Tennessee.

This orchid is unusual because the three petals form a tube rather than a spreading, open flower, the two upper petals fusing and joining with the lower troughlike lip. The generic name reflects this since it derives from Greek *cleistos*, meaning "closed."

231 SMARTWEED *(Polygonum* spp.*)*   Buckwheat family *(Polygonaceae)*

Height: 1'-5' (.3-1.5m). **Flower:** Tiny; indistinguishable; many, on long or short spike. **Leaves:** Mostly lanceolate; entire; alternate. **In bloom:** June-September. **Habitat-Range:** Damp shores, thickets, margins of ponds or streams; mostly throughout.

There are many species of this ubiquitous plant. They have a swelling at each leaf joint, which is usually sheathed. The swollen leaf joints are responsible for the generic name (from *poly*, Latin for "many," and *gonu*, Latin for "joint"). Herb doctors saw these swollen joints as the plant's "signature" and prescribed smartweed in treating arthritis, rheumatism and gout. The many small flowers produce an abundance of seeds which provide food for many kinds of game birds. Early settlers gathered the seeds and ground them into meal as a substitute for buckwheat. The leaves vary in shape depending on whether the plant grows in water or on land, thus making it difficult to distinguish species. Pale Smartweed, *P. lapathifolium*, is the species illustrated here. Lady's Thumb, *P. persicaria*, has reddish stems and a purple blotch in the middle of the leaf blade. Swamp Smartweed, *P. coccineum*, is usually found floating or sprawling in water and has many flowers on a long, slender spike.

ARROW-LEAVED TEARTHUMB   Buckwheat family *(Polygonaceae)*
(Polygonum sagittatum)

Height: 2'-6' (.6-2m). **Flower:** Tiny; indistinguishable; few, in terminal heads. **Leaves:** Narrow, arrow-shaped; entire; alternate. **In bloom:** June-October. **Habitat-Range:** Marshes and wet places; throughout.

This species of *Polygonum* has curved prickles on the stem and on the underside of the midrib of the leaf, which accounts for the "tearthumb" in its name. The Halberd-leaved Tearthumb, *P. arifolium*, has arrow-shaped leaves with flaring bases and is found in coastal marshes from Delaware south.

232 THREE-BIRDS ORCHIS *(Triphora trianthophora)*†   Orchid family *(Orchidaceae)*

Height: 3"-10" (7-25cm). **Flower:** 3/4" (2m) long; irregular, having 2 lateral and one erect sepal which are pink and larger than petals, 2 upper petals form a hood over lower petal (lip), which is marked with 3 green lines; usually three, nodding on curved stalks. **Leaves:** Ovate, clasping; entire; alternate. **In bloom:** July-September. **Habitat-Range:** Rich, damp woods; locally throughout northern regions and in mountains in the South.

This orchid, which blooms in the woods during the summer, grows from a tuber underground and because it is relatively short, one often has to brush aside leaf litter to see the plant fully. The common and generic names (from *treis*, Greek for "three," and *phoros*, meaning "bearing") refer to the three flowers the plant usually bears. The small, ovate, clasping leaves distinguish it from other earlier blooming pink orchids.

Blue-Violet

Key

	SPRING (March-early May)	SUMMER (late May-early August)	FALL (late August-October)
Indistinguishable			

Leafless, when blooming
234 Skunk Cabbage

Alternate, entire
271 Common Burdock
Alternate, pinnate
273 Bull Thistle
    Pasture Thistle
Alternate, lobed
272 Canada Thistle
Alternate, toothed
269 New York Ironweed
Opposite, toothed
268 Mistflower
Whorls, toothed
267 Hollow Joe-Pye Weed
    Sweet Joe-Pye Weed
    Spotted Joe-Pye Weed

Regular

Basal, entire
233 Large Blue Flag
    Slender Blue Flag
Opposite, entire
247 Bluets
Alternate, entire
239 Virginia Bluebells
237 Wild Comfrey
235 Forget-me-not
    Smaller Forget-me-not
    Crested Dwarf Iris
Alternate, toothed
238 Purple Cress
236 Venus' Looking-glass
248 Slender Speedwell
Alternate, lobed and toothed
281 Passion Flower
Alternate, pinnate
    Long-plumed Purple
    Avens

Opposite, entire
255 Spiderwort
262 Purple Loosestrife
275 Purple Gerardia
    Seaside Gerardia
290 Common Milkweed
    Purple Milkweed
Opposite, toothed
260 Blue Vervain
    Hoary Vervain
    Narrow-leaved Vervain
Opposite, pinnate
265 Leather Flower
Alternate, entire
261 Pickerelweed
280 Blue-eyed Grass
264 Bittersweet Nightshade
286 Harebell
    Clustered Bellflower
278 Flax
    Common Morning
    Glory
Alternate, toothed
263 Jimson Weed
    Creeping Bellflower
    Southern Harebell
288 Tall Bellflower

Opposite, entire
295 Fringed Gentian
294 Closed Gentian

	SPRING (March-early May)	**SUMMER** (late May-early August)	**FALL** (late August-October)
Regular		*Alternate, pinnate* 279 Jacob's Ladder Greek Valerian 270 Purple Avens *Alternate, palmate* 266 Ivy-leaved Morning Glory	
Irregular	*Basal, entire* 276 Large Twayblade *Basal, toothed* 242 Lyre-leaved Sage 249 Common Blue Violet *Basal, lobed and toothed* 243 Dwarf Larkspur *Basal, palmate* 246 Birdsfoot Violet *Opposite, entire* 241 Heal-all 276 Large Twayblade *Opposite, lobed* 240 Hairy Skullcap Common Skullcap *Opposite, toothed* 244 Blue-eyed Mary Mad-dog Skullcap *Alternate, palmate* 253 Wild Lupine 252 Blue False Indigo *Alternate, pinnate* 251 Cow Vetch 250 Beach Pea Marsh Pea *Alternate, entire* 245 Blue Toadflax *Alternate, toothed* American Dog Violet Tall Larkspur	*Opposite, entire* 259 Water Willow 256 Bluecurls *Opposite, toothed* 277 Square-stemmed Monkey Flower Sharp-winged Monkey Flower 292 Woundwort Basil 291 Motherwort *Alternate, entire* 254 Asiatic Dayflower Slender Dayflower 285 Viper's Bugloss 284 Purple Fringed Orchis *Alternate, toothed* 274 Downy Lobelia Indian Tobacco 287 Monkshood *Alternate, pinnate* 257 Groundnut *Alternate, palmate* 289 Bush Clover 258 Butterfly Pea	*Alternate, entire* 293 Great Lobelia
Composite		*Alternate, entire* 283 Chicory *Alternate, lobed* 282 Blue Lettuce	*Alternate, toothed or entire* 296 Wild Aster

233 LARGE BLUE FLAG (*Iris versicolor*)   Iris family (*Iridaceae*)

Height: 2'-3' (.6-1m). **Flower:** 3" (8cm) diameter; regular, having 3 petal-like sepals that curve downward and outward; base is whitish with a yellow spot and purple veins, 3 smaller upright petals, 3 petal-like styles that arch over the sepals, 3 stamens hidden under the styles; solitary, on branched stem. **Leaves:** Flat, swordlike; entire; upright, rising from basal cluster. **In bloom:** May-August. **Habitat-Range:** Marshes and wet meadows; in northern part of range.

This common, large, showy iris is found in the northern part of our range. A similar species common in the South is the Southern Blue Flag, *I. virginica*. The yellow spot on its sepals is usually brighter and downy. There are also yellow, white or copper-colored species. Because of their spectacular colors, these lovely flowers were named *iris*, the Greek for "rainbow." "Flag" is derived from Middle English *flagge*, meaning "rush" or "reed." The flower was also the model for the emblem chosen by King Louis VII of France; hence the name *fleur-de-lis*, a corruption of "flower of Louis." The Iris was also one of the most popular of Indian medicinal plants. It grows from a rhizome which was cultivated and used as a cathartic and, in pulverized form, as a poultice for sores and bruises.

SLENDER BLUE FLAG (*Iris prismatica*)   Iris family (*Iridaceae*)

Height: 1'-3' (.3-1m). **Flower:** 3" (8cm) diameter; regular, having 3 petal-like sepals that curve downward and outward, 3 smaller upright petals, 3 petal-like styles that arch over the sepals, 3 stamens hidden under the styles; solitary, on branched stem. **Leaves:** Thin, grasslike; entire; upright, rising from basal cluster. **In bloom:** May-July. **Habitat-Range:** Marsh, swamps and wet meadows; along the seacoast.

It is similar to *I. versicolor* but has grasslike leaves and is found only near coastal areas.

CRESTED DWARF IRIS (*Iris cristata*)   Iris family (*Iridaceae*)

Height: 3"-5" (8-13cm). **Flower:** 2" (5cm) diameter; regular, with 3 petal-like sepals that curve downward and outward and have fringed orange and white crests, 3 smaller upright petals, 3 petal-like styles that arch over the sepals, 3 stamens hidden under the styles; solitary, on branched stem. **Leaves:** Flat, lanceolate; entire; overlapping on flower stem, alternate. **In bloom:** April-May. **Habitat-Range:** Rich woods and ravines or bluffs; south of a line from Maryland to Indiana.

It is similar to *I. versicolor* but is very short, has short leaves that overlap on the stem, and has sepals with bearded crests. The Dwarf Iris, *I. verna*, is similar to *I. cristata* but the flower has no crests and the leaves are much narrower and longer. Its rhizome is usually exposed.

234 SKUNK CABBAGE (*Symplocarpus foetidus*)   Arum family (*Araceae*)

Height: 3"-6" (7-15cm). **Flower:** Tiny; indistinguishable; many on a knoblike spadix enclosed within a dark-purple, hoodlike spathe which is often dappled with green or yellow. **Leaves:** Large (1'-2', .3-.6m long), broadly ovate; entire; basal, upright. **In bloom:** February-May. **Habitat-Range:** Wet meadows, swampy woods; throughout northern regions, in mountains in South.

As the common and species names suggest (*foetidus* in Latin means "foul smelling"), the plant has an unpleasant odor. However, the odor and color attract carrion flies which are necessary for cross pollination. The plant produces heat as it grows and this helps to volatilize the odor. The leaves are initially rolled into compact cones but they unfurl and become huge in summer. The young leaves were boiled several times by Indians to remove the offensive taste and then eaten like spinach. Some Indians crushed the leaves and inhaled the odor as a treatment for headache. The roots become edible after roasting and may be ground into a starchy flour. A decoction of the root was drunk for venereal disease and if taken three times a day for three weeks was supposed to produce sterility.

235 FORGET-ME-NOT *(Myosotis scorpioides)*   Forget-me-not family *(Boraginaceae)*

Height: Initially erect, 12″-28″ (30-70cm), then trailing. **Flower:** 1/3″ (1cm) diameter; regular, having 5 blue petals with central yellow "eye," 5 stamens; many, in coiled, one-sided raceme. **Leaves:** Linear-oblong, sessile; entire; alternate. **In bloom:** May-October. **Habitat-Range:** Wet soil, especially along streams; mostly throughout.

Since part of the raceme with young flower buds is tightly coiled, it reminded early botanists of the tail of a scorpion; hence the species name. This "signature" also led early herbalists to use it in treating the stings of scorpions and insects. Innumerable legends are associated with its common name and it is the favorite flower of lovers the world over. The classical legend on which most of the stories are based concerns a lover who tried to gather some of the blossoms for his sweetheart and tumbled into a deep pool. As he sank, he threw a handful of flowers on the bank and called out, "Forget-me-not."

SMALLER FORGET-ME-NOT   Forget-me-not family *(Boraginaceae)*
(Myosotis laxa)

Height: 6″-20″ (15-50cm). **Flower:** 1/4″ (6mm) diameter; regular, having 5 blue petals with central yellow "eye," 5 stamens; many, in coiled, one-sided raceme. **Leaves:** Lanceolate-oblong, sessile; entire; alternate. **In bloom:** May-August. **Habitat-Range:** In water and wet ground; mostly throughout, and in mountains in South.

Similar to *M. scorpioides* but the flowers are smaller and usually have some leaves on the inflorescence. A species with small 1/8″ (4mm) diameter, cup-shaped, blue or white flowers without yellow eyes is the Field Forget-me-not, *M. arvensis.*

236 VENUS' LOOKING-GLASS   Bluebell family *(Campanulaceae)*
(Specularia perfoliata)

Height: 6″-36″ (15-90cm). **Flower:** 3/4″ (2cm) diameter; regular, with 5 petals forming star-shaped corolla, 5 stamens, 1 pistil with 3 stigmas; one or two at leaf axils. **Leaves:** Round to ovate, clasping base; toothed; alternate. **In bloom:** May-August. **Habitat-Range:** Sterile open ground; throughout.

Its five-petalled flowers are distributed along a slender stem and are tucked into the clasping bases of the leaves. The upper flowers are large and attractive, but in many instances the lower ones never open although they do produce seeds. The generic name derives from *speculum*, Latin for "mirror," an allusion to the plant's flattish, polished mirror-like seeds. A southern species, the Small Venus' Looking-glass (*S. biflora*), bears only one or two showy flowers and its leaves do not clasp the stem.

237 **WILD COMFREY**   Forget-me-not family *(Boraginaceae)*
(Cynoglossum virginianum)

Height: 1'-2' (.3-.6m). **Flower:** 3/8″ (1cm) diameter; regular, having 5 petals forming a funnel-shaped corolla, 5 stamens, 1 pistil; several, in panicle. **Leaves:** Oval; entire; many large basal leaves, few smaller, clasping, alternate stem leaves. **In bloom:** May-June. **Habitat-Range:** Open deciduous woods; south of a line from southwestern Connecticut to southern Illinois.

The inflorescence is spirally coiled, straightening out as the flower buds open. The shape and rough texture of the leaves explains the generic name, derived from Greek *cynos*, meaning "of a dog," and *glossa*, meaning "tongue," and its other common name, Hound's-tongue. A species with dull, reddish-purple flowers, *C. officinale*, has a disagreeable, mousey odor. It was used as an anesthetic by herb doctors, the bruised leaves being applied to hemorrhoids.

238 **PURPLE CRESS** *(Cardamine douglassii)*   Mustard family *(Cruciferae)*

Height: 4″-12″ (10-30cm). **Flower:** 1/2″ (1cm) diameter; regular, with 4 petals in form of cross; 6 stamens; 1 pistil; several, in terminal raceme. **Leaves:** Basal leaves rounded on long petioles, entire; stem leaves lance-shaped, toothed, sessile. **In bloom:** March-May. **Habitat-Range:** Wet woods, swamps, around springs; south of a line from Connecticut to Wisconsin.

The stem of this early-blooming plant is hairy. The leaves have been used as a substitute for water cress in salads.

239 **VIRGINIA BLUEBELLS**   Forget-me-not family *(Boraginaceae)*
(Mertensia virginica)†

Height: 8″-28″ (20-70cm). **Flower:** 1″ (2.5cm) long; regular, with 5 petals forming a trumpet-shaped corolla, 5 stamens, 1 pistil; several, nodding in panicles. **Leaves:** Oval, lower ones with petioles, upper ones sessile; entire; alternate. **In bloom:** March-May. **Habitat-Range:** Rich woods, floodplains; mostly throughout, except New England.

The buds and immature flowers are pink, but the mature flowers, growing in mass profusion, bathe the floor of woods in a sky-blue color, especially in Virginia; hence their common and specific names. The generic name honors Karl Mertens, a distinguished German botanist. It is also commonly called Oysterleaf because its fleshy leaves taste of oyster when chewed. Another species found growing on sandy beaches from Massachusetts northward is *M. maritima*. Its flowers are only 1/3″ (1cm) long and the plant has a whitish bloom.

240 **HAIRY SKULLCAP** *(Scutellaria elliptica)*   Mint family *(Labiatae)*

Height: 6″-24″ (15-60cm). **Flower:** 3/4″ (2cm) long; irregular, having 2-lipped calyx, the upper lip with a hump, 2-lipped corolla, the upper lip hoodlike, the lower lip flat and 3-lobed, 2 pairs of stamens, 1 pistil; 6-20 flowers in terminal racemes. **Leaves:**

Ovate; scalloped; opposite. **In bloom:** May-August. **Habitat-Range:** Dry, sandy woods and fields; south of a line from New Jersey to Ohio.

As the common name suggests, the leaves and stems are covered with soft hairs. A similar species, Showy Skullcap (*S. serrata*), is not hairy but its leaves have serrated edges. About a dozen species of skullcaps occur in our area. Their flowers are blue or violet, and in rare instances pink or white. Each flower has two upper lips with the uppermost arched and humped, reminding early botanists of the skullcap worn by the Romans; hence the common name. The humped lip was also likened to a rounded platter, called *scutella* in Latin; hence the generic name. Although all skullcaps are members of the mint family, they are not aromatic. They are bitter to the taste and were used by herbalists to treat fevers.

COMMON SKULLCAP *(Scutellaria epilobiifolia)* Mint family *(Labiatae)*

Height: 4″-40″ (10-100cm). **Flower:** 3/4″ (2cm) long; irregular, having 2-lipped calyx, the upper lip with a hump; a 2-lipped corolla, the upper lip hoodlike, the lower lip flat and 3-lobed; 2 pairs of stamens, 1 pistil; single, in leaf axils. **Leaves:** Lanceolate or ovate, with short petiole or sessile; rounded teeth; opposite. **In bloom:** June-September. **Habitat-Range:** Swampy shores, meadows and thickets; north of a line from Delaware to Illinois.

This blue-violet flower with a white throat is also called Marsh Skullcap because of its preferred habitat. It is similar to *S. elliptica* but its flowers occur singly in leaf axils.

MAD-DOG SKULLCAP *(Scutellaria lateriflora)*† Mint family *(Labiatae)*

Height: 4″-40″ (10-100cm). **Flower:** 1/2″ (1cm) long; irregular, having 2-lipped calyx, the upper lip with a hump; a 2-lipped corolla, the upper lip hoodlike, the lower lip flat and 3-lobed; 2 pairs of stamens, 1 pistil; many, in one-sided racemes emerging from leaf axils. **Leaves:** Ovate to lanceolate; coarsely serrated; opposite. **In bloom:** June-September. **Habitat-Range:** Wet woods and thickets; throughout.

It is similar to *S. elliptica* but it is not hairy and the racemes emerge from the leaf axils. The common name derives from the fact that early settlers used the powdered herb in treating rabies as well as hysteria and convulsions, and the Indians used it for nervousness. Its curative powers are now known to have a scientific basis. Modern science has extracted an antispasmodic substance from the dried flowers and named it scutellaine.

241 HEAL-ALL *(Prunella vulgaris)* Mint family *(Labiatae)*

Height: 3″-12″ (8-30cm). **Flower:** 1/2″ (1cm) long; irregular, with 2-lipped corolla, upper lip arched, lower lip spreading and 3-lobed; many, in axils of large, bristle-fringed bracts, forming cylindrical head. **Leaves:** Ovate; entire or slightly toothed; opposite. **In bloom:** May-September. **Habitat-Range:** Grasslands, roadsides, waste ground; throughout.

The plant was brought from Europe by early herb doctors because of its outstanding reputation as a medicinal herb. It was applied to all kinds of wounds; hence its other common name, Selfheal. Since each flower consists of a "mouth and throat," the herb was used for inflammation of the mouth and throat. It is well adapted to living in lawns because when mowed it becomes densely matted and small leaved.

242 LYRE-LEAVED SAGE *(Salvia lyrata)*   Mint family *(Labiatae)*

Height: 1'-2' (.3-.6m). **Flower:** 1" (2.5cm) long; irregular, with 2-lipped corolla, upper lip upright, lower lip 3-lobed and spreading; 2 stamens; 1 pistil; many, in several whorls along upper part of stem; may also be bright blue. **Leaves:** Lanceolate; wavy, toothed margins or pinnately lobed; most in basal rosette. **In bloom:** April-June. **Habitat-Range:** Sandy, open woods and clearings; south of a line from southwestern Connecticut to Illinois.

A salve used to be made from the astringent roots and applied to sores. The seeds have been made into refreshing drinks and teas and ground into a flour for baking bread.

243 DWARF LARKSPUR *(Delphinium tricorne)*   Buttercup family *(Ranunculaceae)*

Height: 12"-30" (30-75cm). **Flower:** 1"-1 1/2" (2.5-4cm) long; irregular, having 5 large, petal-like sepals, the uppermost forming an erect spur; 4 small petals, the upper pair forming spurs enclosed in the spur of the calyx; several, in loose raceme. **Leaves:** Palmate, 5-7 leaflets; cleft and toothed; mostly basal. **In bloom:** April-May. **Habitat-Range:** Rich woods, rocky slopes; south from western Pennsylvania to Wisconsin.

The conspicuous spur reminded early botanists of the long spur on the foot of a lark; hence, the common name. The generic name from the Greek *delphinus,* meaning "dolphin" is based on a fancied resemblance to that animal. All parts of the plant are poisonous but the Indians used it as a narcotic to induce sleep.

TALL LARKSPUR *(Delphinium exaltatum)*   Buttercup family *(Ranunculaceae)*

Height: 2'-6' (.6-2m). **Flower:** 3/4" (2cm) long; irregular, having 5 large petal-like sepals, the uppermost forming an erect spur; 4 small petals, the upper pair forming spurs which are enclosed in the spur of the calyx; many, in dense raceme. **Leaves:** Palmate, 3-5 leaflets; cleft and toothed; alternate. **In bloom:** July-August. **Habitat-Range:** Rich woods, thickets, rocky slopes; south of a line from central Pennsylvania through Ohio.

This late-blooming species is similar to *D. tricorne* but is much taller and has a densely packed raceme, and its palmate leaves have fewer and thinner leaflets.

244 BLUE-EYED MARY   Figwort family *(Scrophulariaceae)*
(Collinsia heterophylla)

Height: 8"-24" (20-60cm). **Flower:** 1/2" (1cm) long; irregular, having a globular 2-lipped corolla, upper lip 2-lobed, lower lip 3-lobed; several, in whorls in upper leaf axils. **Leaves:** Lanceolate, lower ones with petioles, upper ones clasping; sparsely toothed; opposite. **In bloom:** April-June. **Habitat-Range:** Rich, moist woods especially on banks; in the western and southern part of our range.

These flowers are characterized by white upper lobes and bright blue lower lobes. The generic name honors Zaccheus Collins, a 19th-century Philadelphia botanist.

245 BLUE TOADFLAX *(Linaria canadensis)*   Figwort family *(Scrophulariaceae)*

Height: 4″-32″ (10-80cm). **Flower:** 1/2″ (1cm) diameter; irregular, with 5 petals forming a 2-lipped corolla, upper lip 2-lobed and erect, lower lip 3-lobed with long, thin spur; several, on loose, terminal raceme. **Leaves:** Linear; entire; basal rosette, stem leaves sessile and alternate. **In bloom:** April-September. **Habitat-Range:** Dry, sandy and poor soil; throughout.

The country people of England often used such terms as "toad" to convey an idea of unworthiness and they applied it to this rank weed with pale blue flowers having white swellings on its lower lips and a very long spur. It was also said to resemble the true flax, *Linum* spp.; hence its common and generic names.

246 BIRDSFOOT VIOLET *(Viola pedata)*   Violet family *(Violaceae)*

Height: 4″-10″ (10-25cm). **Flower:** 3/4″ (2cm) diameter; irregular, with 5 petals, side ones beardless, lower one spurred; 5 stamens that are a bright orange-yellow; 1 pistil; solitary, on leafless stalk. **Leaves:** Palmate, cleft into 9-15 slender lobes; entire; basal, upright. **In bloom:** March-June. **Habitat-Range:** Dry, sunny openings in sandy fields or rocky banks; throughout, except upper New England.

Easily distinguishable because, as the common name suggests, its leaves are cleft into segments resembling a bird's foot. All petals may be lavender or the two upper ones may be purple. The leaves and flowers occur on separate stems.

247 BLUETS *(Houstonia* spp.*)*†   Bedstraw family *(Rubiaceae)*

Height: 2″-8″ (5-20cm). **Flower:** 1/2″ (1cm) diameter; regular, having 4 petals forming funnel-shaped corolla, 4 stamens, 1 pistil with 2 stigmas; solitary, on branching stems. **Leaves:** Oblong to elliptical; entire; basal rosette and stem leaves opposite. **In bloom:** April-July. **Habitat-Range:** Turfy slopes and fields; throughout.

In fields in early spring one may be attracted to what appears to be a lingering patch of snow. Close inspection reveals that it is densely packed light blue or white flowers with yellow eyes. These flowers were much loved by the early settlers who also called them Quaker Ladies, Quaker Bonnets and Innocence. Their generic name honors Dr. William Houston, an English botanist. There are various species of bluets but the minor differences between them are of concern only to specialists.

248 SLENDER SPEEDWELL   Snapdragon family *(Scrophulariaceae)*
(Veronica filiformis)

Height: Low, creeping. **Flower:** 1/2″ (1cm) diameter; regular, having 4 petals, the lower one smaller and narrower than the other three; 2 stamens, 1 pistil with knoblike stigma; single, on long, slender stems from leaf axils. **Leaves:** Roundish or kidney-shaped; rounded teeth; alternate. **In bloom:** May-September. **Habitat-Range:** Lawns, waste places; locally throughout.

This large-flowered plant, one of more than 20 species of speedwells in our range, trails on the ground and forms mats. The blossoms of most speedwells are not very large, but they usually grow in large clusters. The generic name is derived from a supposed resemblance to the image that legend says was left on a towel that a maiden (canonized as St. Veronica) used to wipe Christ's face as he passed toward Calvary. Special healing virtues were transferred to the plant; hence the common name. One ancient herbalist wrote, "The decoction of *Veronica* drunk, sootheth and healeth all flesh and old wounds, cleanseth the blood of all corruption, is good to be drunk for the kidneys and against foul and consuming sores."

249 COMMON BLUE VIOLET (*Viola papilionaceae*)   Violet family (*Violaceae*)

Height: 3″-8″ (7-20cm). **Flower:** 3/4″ (2cm) diameter; irregular, with 5 purple petals whitish toward the center, side ones bearded, lower ones spurred; 5 stamens; 1 pistil; solitary, on leafless stalk. **Leaves:** Broadly heart-shaped; toothed; basal, upright. **In bloom:** March-June. **Habitat-Range:** Damp woods, meadows and roadsides; throughout.

This is the commonest of the many species of purple ("blue") violets with flowers and leaves on separate stalks. A white variety with purple veins is common in the South and is called Confederate Violet. The flowers are high in vitamin C and make a nutritious garnish on a salad. The leaves and seeds were made into poultices for swellings and inflamed eyes by early settlers. A mild syrup of violets and honey was given to children as a laxative. The odor is said to result in a temporary loss of smell.

AMERICAN DOG VIOLET (*Viola conspersa*)   Violet family (*Violaceae*)

Height: 2″-6″ (5-15cm). **Flower:** 1/2″ (1cm) diameter; irregular, with 5 lavender petals, 3 lower ones dark-veined, side ones bearded and lower one spurred; 5 stamens; 1 pistil; nodding on long stems from leaf axils. **Leaves:** Heart-shaped; toothed; alternate. **In bloom:** April-June. **Habitat-Range:** Low woods, meadows; throughout northern regions; in mountains in South.

This is one of the commonest species of purple ("blue") violet with leaves and flowers on the same stalk. There are toothed stipules in the leaf axils. A similar species whose flower has an exceptionally long spur is the Long-spurred Violet, *V. rostrata*.

250 BEACH PEA (*Lathyrus japonicus*)   Pea family (*Leguminosae*)

Height: Vinelike, climbing on other plants. **Flower:** 3/4″ (2cm) long; irregular, pealike; several, on loose raceme from leaf axils. **Leaves:** Pinnate, 8-12 pairs of oval leaflets; entire; alternate. **In bloom:** May-August. **Habitat-Range:** Sandy shores; along northern coast south to New Jersey and on the shores of northern lakes.

This plant is an example of a vetchling, that is, similar to vetch but having larger flowers and leaflets and with fewer flowers in the raceme. Large arrow-shaped stipules clasp the leaf stalks. The seed pods are edible when cooked and its seeds have been roasted and used as a substitute for coffee.

MARSH PEA (*Lathyrus palustris*)   Pea family (*Leguminosae*)

Height: Vinelike, climbing on other plants. **Flower:** 1/2″-1″ (1-2.5cm) long; irregular, pealike; few, in raceme from leaf axils. **Leaves:** Pinnate, 2-5 pairs of ovate leaflets; entire; alternate. **In bloom:** June-September. **Habitat-Range:** Shores, damp thickets and meadows; north of a line from Kentucky to Long Island; in mountains in the South.

Similar to *L. japonicus* but the stems are winged and the narrow stipules are sharp-pointed at both ends. Another species with winged stems, Everlasting Pea (*L. latifolius*), is a local garden escape throughout most of our range. It has very large (1 1/2″, 4cm long) dark pink or blue flowers and a single pair of leaflets.

251 COW VETCH (*Vicia cracca*)   Pea family (*Leguminosae*)

Height: Vinelike, climbing on other plants. **Flower:** 1/2″ (1cm) long; irregular, pealike; many, growing downward and crowded on one-sided raceme. **Leaves:** Pinnate, 8-12 pairs of narrow, oblong, blunt-ended leaflets and two terminal tendrils; alternate. **In bloom:** May-August. **Habitat-Range:** Fields, thickets; north of a line from Virginia to Illinois.

The flowers appear dark purple when fresh but may turn pink as they wither. The plant was brought from Europe as a forage crop for cattle. It has often been plowed under as a "green manure" since its roots contain nitrogen-fixing bacteria which synthesize nitrates, a valuable plant food. Indians boiled and ate the roots and used the tender stems as spring greens. The seeds were added to soups and used in seasoning. A hairy species with bicolored blue and white flowers is Hairy Vetch, *V. villosa*. A species with 4-9 pairs of leaflets and few flowers is Purple Vetch, *V. americana*. It is one of our few native vetches; hence its other common name, American Vetch. The seeds of Spring Vetch (*V. sativa*), which has notched leaflets, were sown in autumn and cattle were fed the spring sprouts; hence the common name.

252 BLUE FALSE INDIGO (*Baptisia australis*)   Pea family (*Leguminosae*)

Height: 3′-5′ (1-1.5m). **Flower:** 1″ (2.5cm) long; irregular, pealike; several, in raceme. **Leaves:** Palmate, 3 spatulate leaflets; entire; alternate. **In bloom:** May-June. **Habitat-Range:** Rich woods, thickets, stream banks; south of a line from Pennsylvania to southern Indiana.

This is our only species of *Baptisia* with blue flowers, the others being yellow or white. It is often cultivated because of its beauty.

253 WILD LUPINE (*Lupinus perennis*)   Pea family (*Leguminosae*)

Height: 8″-24″ (20-60cm). **Flower:** 1″ (2.5cm) long; irregular, pealike; many, in tall raceme; usually blue but there are also pink and white forms. **Leaves:** Palmate, 7-11 oblanceolate leaflets; entire; alternate. **In bloom:** April-July. **Habitat-Range:** Sandy soil, dry clearings; throughout.

A member of the pea family, the species produces a flat, constricted seed pod that is very hairy and contains 4 or 5 seeds. The common and generic names are derived from the Latin *lupus* meaning "wolf," an allusion to the ancient belief that these plants robbed the soil of minerals. We now know that just the opposite is the case: these plants have nitrogen-fixing bacteria in their root nodules that convert free nitrogen in the air into compounds necessary for plant growth. Indians used the plant for treating sterility and believed it helped in childbirth.

254 ASIATIC DAYFLOWER   Spiderwort family *(Commelinaceae)*
(Commelina communis)

Height: Creeping, reclining. **Flower:** 1/2″-1″ (1-2.5cm) diameter; irregular, having 3 round petals, 2 lateral ones which are large and showy and a lower one which is small and inconspicuous, 6 stamens, three of which are long and incurved, 1 pistil; emerging from folded, heart-shaped spathes. **Leaves:** Lanceolate-ovate, clasping; entire; alternate. **In bloom:** June-October. **Habitat-Range:** Ditches, roadsides; throughout, except upper New England.

This native of Asia is called a dayflower because each blossom lasts only one day. In this species one of the three petals is small, white and almost inconspicuous. The flower reminded Linnaeus, the famous Swedish plant taxonomist, of three brothers in a family, the Commelyns, with which he was acquainted. Two of them published splendid works on botany, but the third published nothing; hence the generic name. A similar species with three blue petals and long hairs at the base of clasping leaves is the Diffuse Dayflower, *C. diffusa.* The tender leaves and stems were gathered in the spring by early settlers and added to green salads or prepared like spinach. Aged men and women drank an infusion of the flowers to increase sexual potency and some even fed the plant to their stud animals.

SLENDER DAYFLOWER   Spiderwort family *(Commelinaceae)*
(Commelina erecta)

Height: 15″-40″ (.4-1m). **Flower:** 1/2″-1″ (1-2.5cm) diameter; irregular, having 3 round petals, 2 lateral ones that are large and showy and a lower one that is small and inconspicuous; 6 stamens, three of which are long and incurved; 1 pistil; emerging from folded, heart-shaped spathe. **Leaves:** Lanceolate to ovate, clasping; entire; alternate. **In bloom:** June-October. **Habitat-Range:** In clearing, on rocky and sandy slopes; throughout, except New England.

Similar to *C. communis* but, as the species name indicates, it is erect and not reclining. A similar erect species with all blue flowers is the Virginia Dayflower, *C. virginica.*

255 SPIDERWORT *(Tradescantia virginiana)*   Spiderwort family *(Commelinaceae)*

Height: 1′-2′ (.3-.6m). **Flower:** 1″ (2.5cm) diameter; regular, having 3 rounded petals, 6 hairy stamens, 1 pistil; few, in cyme. **Leaves:** Linear-lanceolate; entire; opposite. **In bloom:** April-July. **Habitat-Range:** Woods, thickets, meadows, roadsides; south of a line from Connecticut to Wisconsin.

The common name derives from the angular growth of the leaves, which suggests a squatting spider. The generic name honors John Tradescant, botanist and gardener to Charles I of England. The flower is open only in the morning; early in the afternoon its petals wither and it becomes fluid jelly; hence its other common name, Widow's Tears. The stem and leaves are good in salads and the flower can be candied and used to decorate cakes. This species has a hairy stem and leaves whereas a more western species, Ohio Spiderwort (*T. ohiensis*), is smooth, and a common southern species, Zigzag Spiderwort (*T. subaspera*), has more of a zigzag-shaped stem.

256 BLUECURLS *(Trichostema dichotomum)*   Mint family *(Labiatae)*

Height: 4″-30″ (10-75cm). **Flower:** 1/2″ (1cm) long; irregular, having a 2-lipped tubular corolla, upper lip with 4 lobes; single-lobed lower lip; 4 curled stamens extending beyond corolla; 1 pistil; single, or in pairs in slender stalks. **Leaves:** Lanceolate, sessile; entire; opposite. **In bloom:** August-October. **Habitat-Range:** Dry, open soil; throughout.

The common and generic names allude to the very long, hairlike, curved blue-stalked stamens protruding from the flower. *Trichostema* combines two Greek words meaning "hairy stamens." The plant is sticky and hairy and the leaves, when crushed, give off an odor of balsam. A less common, more southern species, *T. setaceum*, is smaller (4″-12″, 10-30cm high) and has a more slender stem with linear leaves.

257 GROUNDNUT *(Apios americana)*   Pea family *(Leguminosae)*

Height: Climbing vine. **Flower:** 1/2″ (1cm) long; irregular, pealike, with strongly upturned keel; many, in compact racemes from leaf axils. **Leaves:** Pinnate, 5 or 7 egg-shaped leaflets; entire; alternate. **In bloom:** June-August. **Habitat-Range:** Moist thickets; throughout.

The flowers are brownish purple and very fragrant. The common name refers to enlargements along the rootstock, which were dug in the fall and eaten by Indians and early settlers. Cut into thin slices, they were used in soups and stews. It is said that the Pilgrims could not have survived the first hard winter in America had not the Indians introduced them to the groundnuts growing near Plymouth Rock.

258 BUTTERFLY PEA *(Clitoria mariana)*   Pea family *(Leguminosae)*

Height: Trailing vine 1′-3′ (.3-1m) long. **Flower:** 2″ (5cm) long; irregular, pealike, having butterfly-shaped corolla with a very large erect standard petal notched at its rounded apex, 2 winglike petals and a short keel-like petal; 1-3 on long stalks from leaf axils. **Leaves:** Palmate, 3 egg-shaped leaflets; entire; alternate. **In bloom:** June-August. **Habitat-Range:** Dry, open woods, thickets, pine barrens; south of a line from southeastern New York to southern Illinois.

This flower owes its showiness to the large, bright blue standard petal. The generic name is derived from the resemblance of the small keel to the mammalian clitoris.

259 WATER WILLOW *(Justica americana)*   Acanthus family *(Acanthaceae)*

Height: 1′-3′ (.3-1m). **Flower:** 3/4″ (2cm) long; irregular, having 5 petals forming a 2-lipped corolla, upper lip curving backward, lower lip with 3 purple-spotted lobes, 2 stamens, 1 pistil; several, in dense heads on long stalks from leaf axils. **Leaves:** Narrowly lanceolate; entire; opposite. **In bloom:** May-August. **Habitat-Range:** Shallow waters and shores of lakes and ponds; throughout, with exception of northeastern New England.

Most members of this genus are tropical. The willow-like shape of the leaves is responsible for its common name. The generic name honors James Justice, 18th-century horticulturist.

260 BLUE VERVAIN *(Verbena hastata)*   Vervain family *(Verbenaceae)*

Height: 1′-5′ (.3-1.5m). **Flower:** 1/8″ (4mm) diameter; regular, having 5 petals forming a slender tube with 5 flaring lobes; 2 pairs of stamens of different lengths; 1 pistil; many, on spikes. **Leaves:** Lanceolate to narrowly ovate; coarsely toothed; opposite. **In bloom:** July-September. **Habitat-Range:** Damp thickets and shores; throughout.

The narrow flower spikes are never in full bloom because the bluish violet flowers open a few at a time, starting at the bottom of the spike. Its rough, hairy leaves grow from a grooved, square stem. Most species are blue or purple but there is a white species (*V. urticifolia*) in our range. The generic name *Verbena* is the Latin for a sacred herb, and according to old herbal writings there was nothing this plant couldn't cure. Its reputation followed it to America, one early American medical book recommending it for "paines of the mother, wounds, tumors, sores, fevers, falling hair, headache, sore throats and toothache." Even its common name derives from two Celtic words, *fer*, meaning "drive away," and *faen*, meaning "stone," an allusion to its supposed ability to cure kidney stones. Because it brought a rich reward to gatherers of herbs (who were called "simplers"), its other common name is Simpler's Joy.

HOARY VERVAIN (*Verbena stricta*) Vervain family (*Verbenaceae*)

Height: 2'-4' (.6-1m). **Flower:** 1/2" (1cm) diameter; regular, having 5 petals forming a slender tube with 5 flaring lobes; 2 pairs of stamens of different lengths; 1 pistil; many, on spikes. **Leaves:** Broadly oval; coarsely toothed; opposite. **In bloom:** June-September. **Habitat-Range:** Dry soils and roadsides; throughout western part of range, with some localization in eastern part.

It is similar to *V. hastata* but the flowers are larger and more purple or even rosy in color, the plant is very hairy, and the leaves are downy underneath and rounder in shape.

NARROW-LEAVED VERVAIN (*Verbena simplex*) Vervain family (*Verbenaceae*)

Height: 1'-2' (.3-.6m). **Flower:** 1/4" (6mm) diameter; regular, having 5 petals forming a slender tube with 5 flaring lobes; 2 pairs of stamens of different lengths; 1 pistil; many, on a solitary spike. **Leaves:** Lanceolate; finely toothed; opposite. **In bloom:** May-September. **Habitat-Range:** Dry and sandy soils; throughout.

Similar to *V. hastata* but flowers are more purple, occur on solitary spikes, and the stems and leaves are not hairy.

261 PICKERELWEED (*Pontederia cordata*) Pickerelweed family (*Pontederiaceae*)

Height: 1'-4' (.3-1m). **Flower:** 1/2" (1cm) long; regular, with 2-lipped tubular corolla, three lobes on both lips, 6 stamens, 1 pistil; many, crowded on dense spike. **Leaves:** Heart-shaped; entire; some basal and upright, stem leaf sessile and clasping. **In bloom:** June-November. **Habitat-Range:** Muddy shores, shallow water; throughout.

The plant grows in the quiet waters of lakes and ponds favored by pickerel; hence its common name. Because the seed pods grow downward into the water when ripe, the seeds serve as food for wild ducks, who strain them from the muddy bottom. Indians roasted the seeds and added them to cereals and breads or ground them into flour.

262 PURPLE LOOSESTRIFE (*Lythrum salicaria*) Loosestrife family (*Lythraceae*)

Height: 2'-6' (.6-2m). **Flower:** 1/2"-3/4" (1-2cm) diameter; regular, with 5-7 somewhat wrinkled petals, 12 stamens, 1 pistil; many, crowded and whorled in a spike. **Leaves:** Lanceolate with wide base, downy, sessile; entire; opposite, sometimes in whorl of three. **In bloom:** June-September. **Habitat-Range:** Swamps, wet meadows, river flood-plains; north of a line from Virginia to Illinois.

A European immigrant, this plant settled in the wetlands and crowded out many other plants that provided more food for waterfowl. Hence, our wetlands are less productive than they once were. There are three types of flowers. In one, the pistils and stamens are on the same level. In another, the pistils are short and the stamens tall. The third has tall pistils and short stamens. These arrangements favor cross pollination. The plant was recommended by Indians as an emergency food, the young leafy shoots being used as a vegetable. Its astringent qualities served in treating chronic diarrhea and in tanning leather. A similar species, *L. virgatum*, found locally in New England, is smooth and has narrow leaves with tapered bases.

NARROW-LEAVED LOOSESTRIFE Loosestrife family *(Lythraceae)*
(Lythrum lineare)

Height: 1'-3' (.3-1m). **Flower:** 1/4" (6mm) regular, with 6 petals, 12 stamens, 1 pistil; single, on very short stalk from leaf axils. **Leaves:** Linear; entire; opposite. **In bloom:** July-September. **Habitat-Range:** Brackish to saline marshes; along the Atlantic coast from Long Island south.

The tiny pale-lilac flowers are tucked into the leaf axils. A similar species, Hyssop-leaved Loosestrife (*L. hyssopifolia*), has alternate leaves.

263 JIMSON WEED *(Datura stramonium)* Nightshade family *(Solanaceae)*

Height: 2'-5' (.6-1.5m). **Flower:** 3"-4" (7.5-10cm) long; regular, with 5 petals forming trumpet-shaped corolla with 5 pointed lobes, 5 stamens, 1 pistil; solitary, in forks of branches. **Leaves:** Ovate; irregularly toothed; alternate. **In bloom:** July-October. **Habitat-Range:** Waste ground; mostly throughout, but mainly in South.

The common name is said to be a corruption of Jamestown weed because, the story goes, some soldiers, sent to that early settlement to put down a rebellion, cooked and ate the young shoots. The hallucinogenic effect of the plant was "a very pleasant comedy for they turned natural fools upon it for several days...returned themselves again, not remembering anything that had passed." Its other common name, Thorn-apple, alludes to its spiny seedpods. The whole plant is considered poisonous but it was used in moderate amounts by Indians as a narcotic to produce hypnotic states presumably to unravel mysteries and as an aphrodisiac. America's first medical men used the leaves in a tobacco that was smoked as a treatment for asthma.

264 BITTERSWEET NIGHTSHADE Nightshade family *(Solanaceae)*
(Solanum dulcamara)

Height: Climbing or twining vine. **Flower:** 1/2" (1cm) diameter; regular, with 5 pointed petals bent backward, 5 stamens whose anthers form a "beak," 1 pistil; few, nodding in cyme. **Leaves:** Oval; sometimes with two conspicuous lobes at base; entire; alternate. **In bloom:** June-September. **Habitat-Range:** Thickets and clearings; throughout.

The flowers quickly develop green berries which then turn bright red. These berries cause nausea if eaten but Indians used them in moderation to treat nervousness and diarrhea. Dried stems were used as a sedative, diuretic and hypnotic. The common name is attributable to a report by early botanists that the chewed root first tasted bitter, then sweet.

265 LEATHER FLOWER (*Clematis viorna*)   Buttercup family (*Ranunculaceae*)

Height: Climbing vine. **Flower:** 1″ (2.5cm) long; regular, with 4 thick, fleshy sepals that curve outward at their tips; many stamens and pistils; nodding, on long stalks from leaf axils. **Leaves:** Pinnate, 3-7 eggshaped leaflets; entire; opposite. **In bloom:** May-August. **Habitat-Range:** Rich woods and thickets; south of a line from Pennsylvania to Illinois.

The silky fruit clusters are more conspicuous than the nodding, bell-shaped flowers. The thick, dull purple, petal-like sepals with the curved tips account for the common name.

266 IVY-LEAVED MORNING GLORY   Morning-glory family (*Convolvulaceae*)
(*Ipomoea hederacea*)

Height: Twining vine. **Flower:** 2″ (5cm) diameter; regular, with 5 petals united to form a funnel-shaped corolla, 5 stamens, 1 pistil; solitary, on very long, twining stalks; bluish but it rapidly turns rose-purple; there are also white-flowered forms. **Leaves:** Palmate, with three lobes; entire; alternate. **In bloom:** June-October. **Habitat-Range:** Fields, roadsides; throughout.

The many species of morning glories get their generic name from Greek *ips*, meaning "worm" and *homoios*, "resembling") from their twining habit. The common name alludes to the fact that they are fully open in the morning and may be closed by mid-afternoon. These plants are a nuisance to corn growers because they invade fields and entangle cornstalks. Another group of similar plants, the Bindweeds (*Convolvulus* spp.), have two stigmas whereas morning glories have only one stigma with two or three lobes.

COMMON MORNING GLORY   Morning-glory family (*Convolvulaceae*)
(*Ipomoea purpurea*)

Height: Twining vine. **Flower:** 2″ (5cm) diameter; regular, with 5 petals united to form a funnel-shaped corolla; 5 stamens; 1 pistil; one or several on long stalks from leaf axils; may also be red, bluish or white. **Leaves:** Broadly heart-shaped; entire; alternate. **In bloom:** July-October. **Habitat-Range:** Roadsides, borders of fields; mostly throughout.

This is a garden plant that easily escapes cultivation. A similar species with small (1″, 2.5cm diameter) white flowers is the Small White Morning Glory (*I. lacunosa*) found mainly in the western and southern parts of our area.

267 HOLLOW JOE-PYE WEED   Composite family (*Compositae*)
(*Eupatorium fistulosum*)

Height: 2′-7′ (.6-2m). **Flower:** indistinguishable, tubular; many, in terminal, dome-shaped cyme. **Leaves:** Lanceolate; coarsely toothed; 4 to 7 (usually 6), in whorls along stem. **In bloom:** July-September. **Habitat-Range:** Moist meadows, thickets; mostly throughout except in northernmost areas.

The stem is hollow and may be tinged with purple. The reputed healing power of this plant is legendary. The generic name honors a biblical herb doctor, Eupator. In colonial New England an Indian herb doctor named Joe Pye was said to have used it to stop a typhus epidemic in Massachusetts; hence its common name. It has also been used to treat gout, dropsy and kidney stones.

SWEET JOY-PYE WEED   Composite family *(Compositae)*
(Eupatorium purpureum)

Height: 2'-6' (.6-2m). **Flower:** Tiny indistinguishable, tubular; many, in terminal dome-shaped cyme; pale lilac or creamy white. **Leaves:** Lanceolate, coarsely toothed; 3 or 4, in whorls along stem. **In bloom:** July-September. **Habitat-Range:** Thickets, woods; south of a line from southern New Hampshire to Wisconsin.

Similar to *E. fistulosum* but stem is not hollow and is marked purple or black at the leaf joints. A vanilla-like odor is emitted when the plant is bruised or crushed.

SPOTTED JOE-PYE WEED   Composite family *(Compositae)*
(Eupatorium maculatum)

Height: 2'-7' (.6-2m). **Flower:** Tiny; indistinguishable, tubular; many, in terminal flat-topped cyme. **Leaves:** Lanceolate; coarsely toothed; 4 or 5 in whorls along stem. **In bloom:** July-September. **Habitat-Range:** Wet thickets, meadows; throughout; only in mountains in the South.

Similar to *E. fistulosum* but its flower cluster is more flat-topped and deeper in color, it has whorls of 4 or 5 leaves, and its stem is deep purple or purple-spotted; hence its common name.

268 MISTFLOWER *(Eupatorium coelestinum)*   Composite family *(Compositae)*

Height: 1'-3' (.3-1m). **Flower:** Tiny; indistinguishable, tubular; many, in crowded, flat-topped corymb. **Leaves:** Triangular; blunt teeth; opposite. **In bloom:** July-October. **Habitat-Range:** Low woods, damp thickets and borders of streams; south of a line from New Jersey to Illinois.

In our range this is the only *Eupatorium* with bluish flowers and is often called Blue Boneset. Because the fuzzy flower is thought to resemble the cultivated *Ageratum*, it is also commonly called Wild Ageratum.

269 NEW YORK IRONWEED   Composite family *(Compositae)*
(Vernonia noveboracensis)

Height: 3'-7' (1-2m). **Flower:** Tiny; indistinguishable, tubular; many, in a thistle-like head, many heads in a flat-topped cyme. **Leaves:** Lanceolate; toothed; alternate. **In bloom:** August-October. **Habitat-Range:** Low grounds, margins of streams; south of a line from southern Massachusetts to southern Ohio.

The flower heads have purplish bracts tipped with bristles. A similar but smaller species, *V. altissima*, lacks these bristly bracts. Various species have been used to treat stomach complaints. The common name comes from the coarse, hard stems noted by farmers who tried to get rid of what they considered a rank weed. The generic name honors William Vernon, an English botanist who collected plants in North America.

270 PURPLE AVENS *(Geum rivale)*   Rose family *(Rosaceae)*

Height: 1'-3' (.3-1m). **Flower:** 1" (2.5cm) diameter; regular, with 5 petals forming a cup-shaped corolla, indefinite number of stamens and pistils; solitary, terminal, nodding. **Leaves:** Basal leaves pinnate with the end leaflet the largest, toothed; stem leaves pinnate, with 3 leaflets, toothed, alternate. **Habitat-Range:** Wet meadows, bogs; north of a line from northern Illinois through West Virginia to northern New Jersey.

The plant is also known as Indian Chocolate because the boiled root was mixed with sugar and milk as a chocolate substitute. It was valued as a home remedy for dysentery and upset stomach. Its astringent action was also used to stop uterine hemorrhage.

LONG-PLUMED PURPLE AVENS   Rose family *(Rosaceae)*
(Geum triflorum)

Height: 6"-16" (15-40cm). **Flower:** 1" (2.5cm) diameter; regular, with 5 petals forming cup-shaped corolla, indefinite number of stamens and pistils; usually three, in nodding cluster. **Leaves:** Pinnate, with largest leaflets near tip; unevenly toothed; alternate. **In bloom:** April-June. **Habitat-Range:** Rocky soil, prairies; Great Lakes area and westernmost part of range.

Similar to *G. rivale* but flowers usually occur in threes; hence the species name. The long feathery hairs of the fruiting head resemble a feather-duster and account for the common name.

271 COMMON BURDOCK *(Arctium mimus)*   Composite family *(Compositae)*

Height: 3'-5' (1-1.5m). **Flower:** Tiny; indistinguishable, tubular; many, forming a head atop a globular collection of hooked bracts, on short stalks from leaf axils. **Leaves:** Ovate-oblong, tapering to a point; entire; alternate. **In bloom:** July-October. **Habitat-Range:** Waste places; mostly throughout.

It was introduced from Europe and the early settlers taught the Indians its food value. The young leaves, stems and roots are edible and very nutritious. A tea made from the roots was a well-known blood purifier, ridding the skin of eruptions and boils. The hooked seed pods attach easily to animal fur or clothing and are thus effectively dispersed. These burrs, which account for its common name, were considered a "signature" by Indian medicine men, who prepared a concoction to aid in remembering, i.e. "sticking in the mind." The inventor of a mechanical fastener got his inspiration from these hooked pods. A species with larger flower heads and roundly ovate leaves is Great Burdock, *A. lappa*.

272 CANADA THISTLE *(Cirsium arvense)*   Composite family *(Compositae)*

Height: 1'-5' (.3-1.5m). **Flower:** Tiny; indistinguishable, slender and tubular; many, in small, dome-shaped heads, several heads in cyme. **Leaves:** Lanceolate; lobes with prickles, wavy edges; alternate. **In bloom:** July-September. **Habitat-Range:** Cultivated and waste places, roadsides; throughout.

Our most common thistle. Similar to *C. vulgare*, but flowers are smaller and there are no prickles on bracts or stem.

273 BULL THISTLE *(Cirsium vulgare)*   Composite family *(Compositae)*

Height: 3'-6' (1-2m). **Flower:** Tiny; indistinguishable, slender and tubular; many, in dome-shaped terminal head. **Leaves:** Pinnate; leaflets and tips armed with prickles; alternate. **In bloom:** June-September. **Habitat-Range:** Clearings, pastures, roadsides; throughout.

The stems are winged. Prickles are the hallmark of the thistle; stems, leaves, bracts are covered with them. A biennial, it produces a basal rosette of leaves the first year and the flower stalk the second year. On the underside of the leaf the vein in the midline is fat and swollen. This was read as a "signature" by herb doctors, who used the plant to treat varicose veins. This practice is reflected in its generic name, *cirsos*, which is Greek for "swollen vein." Warm juice from mashed roots was used to relieve earache and toothache. A decoction of the flowers was taken three times a day to treat gonorrhea. The nutritious roots were also eaten raw, boiled or roasted.

PASTURE THISTLE *(Cirsium pumilum)*   Composite family *(Compositae)*

Height: 1'-3' (.3-1m). **Flower:** Tiny; indistinguishable, slender and tubular; many, in large, dome-shaped head. **Leaves:** Pinnate; leaflets and tips armed with long prickles; alternate. **In bloom:** June-September. **Habitat-Range:** Dry soils, pastures; north of a line from Delaware to Ohio.

This largest flowered thistle is pale reddish-purple. It is similar to *C. vulgaris* but the flower is broader and the stem is hairy and not winged.

274 DOWNY LOBELIA *(Lobelia puberula)*   Bluebell family *(Campanulaceae)*

Height: 1'-4' (.3-1m). **Flower:** 1/2"-1" (1-2.5cm) long; irregular, having 2-lipped corolla, upper lip split into two upright pointed lobes between which is a curved, rodlike structure made up of combined stamens and pistils; lower lip is spreading and 3-lobed; many, on one side of spike. **Leaves:** Narrowly oval; toothed; alternate. **In bloom:** August-October. **Habitat-Range:** Woods and clearings; along coastal plains.

As its common name suggests, this lobelia is covered with a fine down. Lobelias are named in honor of Matthias de l'Obel, Flemish botanist-herbalist who became physician to James I of England. Pale Spike Lobelia, *L. spicata*, is similar to *L. puberula* but downy only at the base and smooth above and with flowers scattered along the upper part of the stem. A species found along the coast from Delaware south is Longleaf Lobelia, *L. elongata*. It is similar to *L. spicata* but its leaves have sharp teeth and the flowers are not as crowded on the spike.

INDIAN TOBACCO *(Lobelia inflata)*   Bluebell family *(Campanulaceae)*

Height: 6"-36" (15-90cm). **Flower:** 1/4" (6mm) long; irregular, having 2-lipped corolla with upper lip split into two upright pointed lobes between which is a curved, rodlike structure made up of combined stamens and pistils; lower lip is 3-lobed and spreading; several, in leafy racemes. **Leaves:** Oval; toothed; alternate. **In bloom:** June-October. **Habitat-Range:** Fields, roadsides and waste places; throughout.

This commonest of all lobelias is distinguished from other blue lobelias by the fact that the base of its flowers become swollen seed pods resembling small inflated balloons; hence its species name. Its common name reflects the American Indian habit of smoking and chewing its bitter leaves. The stems and leaves contain acrid alkaloids that cause nausea and other violent reactions. Thus, the plant found use in many quack medicines in the days when a drug that set one's insides "on fire" was regarded as especially beneficial. The violent reactions to the plant were also used by certain religious groups to "drive the devils out of the body." Now the alkaloid is being used in a number of anti-smoking preparations. Nuttal's Lobelia, *L. nuttallii,* is similar to *L. inflata* but it lacks the swollen seed pods, its leaves are linear, and its flowers are blue with a white center. A similar species that has almost threadlike leaves and lives in a wet habitat is Brook Lobelia, *L. kalmii.*

275 PURPLE GERARDIA *(Gerardia purpurea)*   Figwort family *(Scrophulariaceae)*

Height: 8″-30″ (20-75cm). **Flower:** 1″ (2.5cm) long; regular, with bell-shaped corolla having 5 spreading, unequal lobes, 4 stamens, 1 pistil; few, on short stalks in upper leaf axils. **Leaves:** Linear; entire; opposite. **In bloom:** July-September. **Habitat-Range:** Damp, mostly acid soils; south of a line from Massachusetts to southern Illinois.

The downy flowers are rose-purple with dark spots within the throat. There are a number of species of this plant, which was named for John Gerard, a renowned 16th century herbalist. A more northern species similar to *G. purpurea* is Small-flowered Gerardia, *G. paupercula.* It has smaller flowers on very short stalks and very narrow leaves.

SEASIDE GERARDIA   Figwort family *(Scrophulariaceae)*
(Gerardia maritima)

Height: 2″-12″ (5-30cm). **Flower:** 3/4″ (2cm) long; regular, with bell-shaped corolla having 5 spreading, unequal lobes, 4 stamens, 1 pistil; several, from upper leaf axils. **Leaves:** Linear with blunt tips; entire; opposite. **In bloom:** July-September. **Habitat-Range:** Coastal marshes; along eastern coast.

Similar to *G. purpurea* but flower is not downy and leaves are very narrow, blunt-tipped and succulent. Common in mountainous regions is Slender Gerardia, *G. tenuifolia,* a species with long-stalked, smaller flowers (1/2″, 1cm long).

276 LARGE TWAYBLADE *(Liparis lilifolia)*†   Orchid family *(Orchidaceae)*

Height: 4″-10″ (10-25cm). **Flower:** 3/4″ (2cm) long; irregular, having 3 narrow green sepals, 2 threadlike maroon petals and one large maroon, liplike petal; several, in raceme. **Leaves:** Oval, lustrous; entire; 2 basal ones. **In bloom:** May-July. **Habitat-Range:** Rich or sandy woods and clearings; south of a line from southern New Hampshire to southern Wisconsin.

The common name derives from the two large, shiny leaves. The greasy sheen of the leaves is responsible for the generic name, derived from the Greek *liparos*, meaning "fat."

HEARTLEAF TWAYBLADE *(Listera cordata)*†   Orchid family *(Orchidaceae)*

Height: 3″-10″ (7.5-25cm). **Flower:** 1/4″ (6mm) long; irregular, with 3 green sepals and 2 dull purple petals the same size and shape, and 1 long, forked, liplike petal; several, in raceme. **Leaves:** Small, heart-shaped, sessile; entire; 1 pair midway on stem. **In bloom:** May-August. **Habitat-Range:** Mossy woods; mostly throughout; in mountains in South.

Similar to *Liparis lilifolia* but has smaller flowers, forked lower lip and a pair of heart-shaped leaves on stem. A more southern species, the Southern Twayblade (*L. australis*), has egg-shaped, sessile leaves.

277   SQUARE-STEMMED MONKEY FLOWER   Figwort family *(Scrophulariaceae)* *(Mimulus ringens)*

Height: 1′-3′ (.3-1m). **Flower:** 1″ (2.5cm) long; irregular, having 2-lipped corolla, upper lip erect and 2-lobed, lower lip spreading and 3-lobed; 4 stamens; 1 pistil with 2-lobed stigma; several, on long slender stalks from leaf axils. **Leaves:** Elliptical to obovate, sessile; coarsely toothed; opposite. **In bloom:** June-September. **Habitat-Range:** Shores, meadows and wet places; throughout.

As the common name suggests, this plant has a square stem. The flowers reminded early taxonomists of a grinning, flop-eared head of a monkey, a natural buffoon, which explains its common and its generic name (from *mimulus*, diminutive of the Latin word for "buffoon"). The Indians and early pioneers used its leaves as a wild lettuce and in poultices for wounds.

SHARP-WINGED MONKEY FLOWER   Figwort family *(Scrophulariaceae)* *(Mimulus alatus)*

Height: 1′-3′ (.3-1m). **Flower:** 1″ (2.5cm) long; irregular, having 2-lipped corolla, upper lip erect and 2-lobed, and lower lip spreading and 3-lobed; 4 stamens; 1 pistil with 2-lobed stigma; several, on short stalks from leaf axils. **Leaves:** Lanceolate to ovate; coarsely toothed; opposite. **In bloom:** June-September. **Habitat-Range:** Swamps and low ground; throughout, except most of New England.

It is similar to *M. ringens* but the flowers have short stalks as they emerge from the leaf axils, and the leaves have petioles. In addition, the square stems have thin flanges (wings) along the angles; hence its common name.

278   FLAX *(Linum usitatissimum)*   Flax family *(Linaceae)*

Height: 1′-3′ (.3-1m). **Flower:** 1/2″ (1cm) diameter; regular, with 5 slightly overlapping roundish petals; 5 stamens; 1 pistil; several, in panicle. **Leaves:** Linear-lanceolate, sharply tipped; entire; alternate. **In bloom:** June-September. **Habitat-Range:** Railroad yards and waste places; throughout.

The most common species are pale blue but a number of species are yellow or white. Flax was brought from Europe where it was the source of linseed oil and fibers for linen. The Indians learned to make fishing lines from the fibers. The seeds were used to cure coughs, colds, congested lungs and earache. Its stems were steeped in hot water and taken for stomachache. Pioneer doctors mixed the seed with corn meal, forming a paste, and applied it to the swelling of mumps.

279 JACOB'S LADDER

Phlox family *(Polemoniaceae)*

(Polemonium van-bruntiae)

Height: 1'-3' (.3-1m). **Flower:** 3/4" (2cm) long; regular, having 5 petals united to form a bell-shaped corolla with 5 flared lobes, 5 stamens extending well beyond corolla, 1 pistil; several, in corymb. **Leaves:** Pinnate, 15-21 ovate leaflets; entire; alternate. **In bloom:** June-July. **Habitat-Range:** Wooded swamps, bogs, mossy glades; mainly in mountains from New York and Vermont south to West Virginia and Maryland.

The stamens project well beyond the bell-shaped flowers. The "ladder" in the common name is an allusion to the runglike arrangement of the leaflets in the large, compound leaves. The Indians used a decoction from these leaves as a hair rinse.

GREEK VALERIAN *(Polemonium reptans)*

Phlox family *(Polemoniaceae)*

Height: 5"-20" (13-50cm). **Flower:** 3/4" (2cm) long; regular, having 5 petals united to form a bell-shaped corolla, 5 stamens, 1 pistil; few, in corymb. **Leaves:** Pinnate, 9-17 leaflets; entire; alternate. **In bloom:** April-June. **Habitat-Range:** Rich woodlands and thickets; throughout, except New England.

Similar to *P. van-bruntiae* but the leaves have fewer leaflets and the stamens do not project beyond the flower. The combination of white stamens and blue petals suggests the colors of the Greek flag; hence the common name.

280 BLUE-EYED GRASS *(Sisyrinchium* spp.*)*

Iris family *(Iridaceae)*

Height: 6"-24" (15-60cm). **Flower:** 1/2" (1cm) diameter; regular, having 3 petals and 3 sepals of the same shape and color, tipped with a small, bristly point, perianth parts blue with yellow "eye"; 3 stamens, 1 pistil; solitary or few in terminal cluster. **Leaves:** Grasslike; entire; upright, mostly from base. **In bloom:** April-July. **Habitat-Range:** Some species found in fields and meadows, others in wet places; throughout.

The flowers have a 6-part, blue perianth with a yellow "eye" and grasslike leaves. Determination of species is very difficult, even technical manuals containing conflicting information. To make matters even more confusing, many blue-eyed grasses are yellow, white or purple and are members of the iris family and not a grass family. But the study of the data and the photograph shown here should help you to recognize them. Flowers bloom only for one day and only in the morning providing it is sunny. Upon being picked they close immediately.

281 PASSION FLOWER

Passion-flower family *(Passifloraceae)*

(Passiflora incarnata)

Height: Climbing vine. **Flower:** 2"-3" (5-7.5cm) diameter; regular, having 5 petals and 5 sepals of the same size and color, a fringed throat, 5 stamens, 1 pistil with 3 styles and knoblike stigmas; solitary, from leaf axils. **Leaves:** Palmate, tri-lobed, finely tooth-ed; alternate. **In bloom:** May-August. **Habitat-Range:** Open woods, thickets, dry fields; south of a line from Maryland to Illinois.

The common and generic names refer to a fancied resemblance of the flower parts to aspects of the crucifixion of Christ. The 5 sepals and 5 petals represent the 10 faithful disciples, excluding Judas who betrayed Christ and Peter who denied him. The reddish fringes within the perianth were said to resemble the bloodstained crown of thorns. The stamens represent the 5 wounds he suffered and the three knobbed stigmas represent the 3 nails used to nail him to the cross. A fruit is formed which is yellow and edible when ripe; hence another common name, Wild Apricot. The pulverized roots were used by both Indians and colonists in sedatives and to relieve insomnia.

282 BLUE LETTUCE *(Lactuca floridana)*   Composite family *(Compositae)*

Height: 3′-7′ (1-2m). **Flower:** 1/2″ (1cm) diameter; composite, only with ray flowers; many, in loose panicle. **Leaves:** Large, dandelion-like; deeply lobed; alternate. **In bloom:** August-October. **Habitat-Range:** Moist thickets and woods; throughout, except upper New England.

Although the flowers of this plant are fairly small, its height and mass of fuzzy seeds usually attract attention. Its generic name derives from the Latin *lactus*, meaning "milk," referring to the milky juice of the plant. Some Indians used the juice to cure skin blister of poison ivy. Less common blue-flowered lettuces which are similar to *L. floridana* are Tall Blue Lettuce *(L. biennis)* which grows to 15 feet (4.5m) and has a more crowded inflorescence, and *L. puchella* (also commonly called Blue Lettuce) which grows only in the western part of our range, is only about 3 feet (1m) tall, and has large blue flowers.

283 CHICORY *(Cichorium intybus)*   Composite family *(Compositae)*

Height: 1′-5′ (.3-1.5m). **Flower:** 1 1/2″ (4cm) diameter; composite, of ray flowers only, each with 5 teeth on upper edge; terminal or in leaf axils. **Leaves:** Oblong or lanceolate and clasping stem leaves, entire, sparsely alternate; basal rosette of dandelion-like leaves. **In bloom:** June-October. **Habitat-Range:** Fields, roadsides; throughout.

Only a few flowers are open on a plant at one time. They last only one day, new flowers appearing the next day. They usually close in the heat of the day. This plant grows from a stout root that can be roasted, ground and used as a substitute for coffee. Brought from Europe for this purpose, it is still used by country people. The young basal leaves are also gathered in the spring and used in salads or as cooked greens. The common and generic names derive from *chicourey*, the Arabic name of the plant, which was used by Arabian physicians to treat intestinal disorders. Another common name, Blue Sailors, comes from an old legend about a sailor who went to sea, leaving his beloved waiting day after day along the highway for his return. The gods took pity on her and changed her into a chicory plant that wears sailor blue in its blossoms and still haunts roadsides.

284 PURPLE FRINGED ORCHIS   Orchid family *(Orchidaceae)*
(Habenaria fimbriata)†

Height: 1′-4′ (.3-1m). **Flower:** 1″ (2.5cm) long; irregular, having 3 petals and 3 sepals of the same color, with upper sepal and 2 lateral petals erect, and lower lip with 3 fan-shaped fringed lobes and projecting backward with a downward-pointing spur; many, in dense spike. **Leaves:** Lower ones oval, entire, sheathing base; upper ones small, lanceolate, entire, alternate. **In bloom:** June-August. **Habitat-Range:** Cool, moist woods and meadows; mostly throughout; in mountains in South.

Indians consumed the root tubers of these orchids during times of want. A similar species, Small Purple Fringed Orchis (*H. psycodes*), is a shorter plant whose flowers have lips with very short fringes.

285 VIPER'S BUGLOSS *(Echium vulgare)* Forget-me-not family *(Boraginaceae)*

Height: 1′-3′ (.3-1m). **Flower:** 1″ (2.5cm) long; irregular, having 5 petals forming a 2-lipped, funnel-shaped corolla, upper lip exceeds the lower; 5 stamens extending beyond corolla, 1 pistil with 2 stigmas; many, on short, curved false racemes in upper leaf axils. **Leaves:** Linear-lanceolate, sessile; entire, but wavy margins; alternate. **In bloom:** June-September. **Habitat-Range:** Fields, roadsides, dry places; throughout.

A group of these plants is a startling sight because the buds are pink, the long stamens projecting from the bluish purple flowers are bright red and the older flowers are reddish purple. The plant is rough with spiny bristles and is a pest to dairy farmers, who call them Bluedevils. The stem and its branches have purple spots. Herb doctors saw in the purple mottling a "signature" against the bite of venomous snakes and in the seeds, which resemble the head of a snake (hence the first part of its common name), a plant clearly marked for its medicinal value. This also explains its generic name, *echis* being Greek for "viper." Thus all parts were made into a decoction to cure or prevent snakebite.

286 HAREBELL *(Campanula rotundifolia)*† Bluebell family *(Campanulaceae)*

Height: 6″-20″ (15-50cm). **Flower:** 3/4″ (2cm) long; regular, with 5 petals forming a bell-shaped corolla. 5 stamens, 1 pistil; few, terminal or nodding on long stalks from leaf axils. **Leaves:** Basal leaves round and toothed, stem leaves linear and entire; alternate. **In bloom:** June-September. **Habitat-Range:** Open or rocky banks, meadows, swamps; north of a line from New Jersey to Illinois.

The generic name is a diminutive of the Latin word *campana*, meaning "little bell," an allusion to the shape of the flower. Some of the characteristics of this plant may be altered by the habitat in which it grows. For example, when growing in meadows the leaves are long and thin whereas plants in dry or exposed areas have short, firm leaves. The Bedstraw Bellflower, *C. aparinoides*, has very small pale blue flowers, bristly stems and grows in wet spots. Another species that prefers a wet habitat. Marsh Bellflower, *(C. uliginosa)*. has small dark blue flowers and smooth stems.

CREEPING BLUEBELL Bluebell family *(Campanulaceae)*
(Campanula rapunculoides)

Height: 1′-4′ (.3-1m). **Flower:** 1″-1 1/2″ (2.5-4cm) long; regular, with 5 petals forming a bell-shaped corolla, 5 stamens, 1 straight, white style; several, drooping on one-sided raceme. **Leaves:** Lanceolate-ovate, mostly sessile; irregularly toothed; alternate. **In bloom:** July-September. **Habitat-Range:** Roadsides, fields and thickets; north of a line from Delaware to Illionois.

This garden escape spreads by creeping runners; hence its common name. It differs from *C. rotundifolia* in the shape of its leaves and the arrangement of its flowers.

SOUTHERN HAREBELL
(Campanula divaricata)

Bluebell family *(Campanulaceae)*

Height: 1'-3' (.3-1m). **Flower:** 1/2" (1cm) long; regular, with 5 petals forming a bell-shaped corolla, 5 stamens, 1 pistil extending well beyond corolla; several, dangling from horizontal branchlets of compound panicle. **Leaves:** Lanceolate to ovate, pointed at both ends; coarsely toothed; alternate. **In bloom:** July-September. **Habitat-Range:** Dry woods and rocky slopes; south of a line from western Maryland to Kentucky.

Similar to *C. rapunculoides* but has much smaller flowers on horizontal branchlets.

CLUSTERED BELLFLOWER
(Campanula glomerata)

Bluebell family *(Campanulaceae)*

Height: 1'-2' (.3-.6m). **Flower:** 1" (2.5cm) long; regular, with 5 petals forming a bell-shaped corolla, 5 stamens, 1 pistil; many, clustered in upper leaf axils. **Leaves:** Basal leaves lanceolate, entire with petiole; stem leaves lanceolate, sessile, with clasping bases, entire, alternate. **In bloom:** June-July. **Habitat-Range:** Roadsides, old fields and pastures; north of a line from Massachusetts to Wisconsin.

Similar to *C. rapunculoides* but its flowers are erect and clustered near the top of the stem.

287 MONKSHOOD *(Aconitum uncinatum)*

Buttercup family *(Ranunculaceae)*

Height: 2'-3' (.6-1m). **Flower:** 1" (2.5cm) diameter; irregular, with 5 petal-like sepals, the upper one being large and shaped like a hood; 4 or 6 tiny petals, the upper 2 forming spurs and hidden by hood; several, in panicle. **Leaves:** Palmate, 3-5 deeply cleft lobes; irregularly toothed; alternate. **In bloom:** August-October. **Habitat-Range:** Low woods and damp slopes; south of a line from southern Pennsylvania to southern Indiana.

The stem is weak and the plant often leans against other plants. The common name derives from the hoodlike shape of the large upper sepal. The seeds and roots are very poisonous but early settlers used a dilute solution in a linament to relieve rheumatic pains; first produced a tingling sensation and then numbness.

288 TALL BELLFLOWER *(Campanula americana)*

Bluebell family *(Campanulaceae)*

Height: 2'-6' (.6-2m). **Flower:** 1" (2.5cm) diameter; regular, with 5 pointed petals forming a star-shaped corolla, 5 stamens, 1 pistil with tip curved upward; solitary or clustered in upper leaf axils. **Leaves:** Oblong-lanceolate; toothed; alternate. **In bloom:** June-August. **Habitat-Range:** Rich, moist soil; throughout, except New England.

Although called a bellflower, the blossoms of this plant are open-faced rather than bell-shaped and have a long, conspicuous pistil with its tip curved upward.

289 BUSH CLOVER *(Lespedeza spp.)*

Pea family *(Leguminosae)*

Height: 1'-3' (.3-1m). **Flower:** 1/2"(1cm) long; irregular, pealike, with 5 petals, the two lower ones forming a keel, the two side ones wings, the upper one a banner; many, in loose head. **Leaves:** Palmate, 3 elliptical leaflets; entire; alternate. **In bloom:** July-

September. **Habitat-Range:** Dry woods and clearings; mostly throughout except for northernmost areas.

The bush clovers differ from true clovers in that the flowers are not found in tightly clustered heads but are much more loosely distributed on the flower stalk. The individual flowers are, however, typical of the pea family. The generic name honors Vincente Manuel de Cespedes, Spanish governor of East Florida in the 18th century; his name was later misspelled Lespedes and this misspelling has persisted. Species of bush clover have been planted as pasturage for cattle. It is also especially suitable for erosion control.

290 COMMON MILKWEED *(Asclepias syriaca)*   Milkweed family *(Asclepiadaceae)*

Height: 3'-5' (1-2m). **Flower:** 1/2" (1cm) diameter; regular, with 5 curved-back petals forming a cup that supports 5 little horns curving into a central structure of 5 united stamens and a column of 5 pistils; many, in umbels. **Leaves:** Lanceolate to broadly oval; entire; opposite. **In bloom:** June-August. **Habitat-Range:** Thickets, dry fields, roadsides; mostly throughout.

The dull purple flowers contain much nectar, and Indians sweetened wild strawberries with the dew from the blossoms. When bruised, the stem exudes a milky juice; hence the common name. This was considered a "signature" by Indians who used the juice to treat faulty lactation in nursing squaws. The juice is sticky and served the early settlers as a glue. The young shoots, unopened flower clusters and unripe seed pods were cooked and eaten. Milkweed was also used in the treatment of dropsy and it has now been found that the plant contains the cardiac glycosides used in modern medicine to treat dropsy. The long silky hair on the seeds was used by early settlers to stuff pillows and mattresses, and in World War I children were paid a penny a pound for the "silk," which was used to stuff life preservers. Blunt-leaved Milkweed (*A. amplexicaulis*) has similar flowers but its leaves have wavy margins and are sessile. The Swamp Milkweed, *A. incarnata*, is found in swamps and in wet ground. Its flowers are dull pink and its leaves are narrowly lanceolate.

PURPLE MILKWEED *(Asclepias purpurascens)* Milkweed family *(Asclepiadaceae)*

Height: 2'-3' (.6-1m). **Flower:** 1/2" (1cm) diameter; regular, with 5 curved-back petals that form a cup supporting 5 little horns curving onto a central structure of 5 united stamens and a column of 5 pistils; many, in umbels. **Leaves:** Narrowly elliptical; entire; opposite. **In bloom:** June-July. **Habitat-Range:** Woods, thickets, openings; mostly throughout except for upper New England.

Similar to Common Milkweed (*A. syrica*) but leaves are more narrow and flowers are deep reddish purple. Another reddish purple flower is that of Red Milkweed, *A. rubra*, found in swamps and bogs along the eastern coastal plain. Its flower clusters are small and its leaves taper to long points.

291 MOTHERWORT *(Leonurus cardiaca)*   Mint family *(Labiatae)*

Height: 2'-4' (.6-1m). **Flower:** 1/4"-1/2" (6-12mm) long; irregular, with 2-lipped corolla, upper lip arched, lower lip 3-lobed; many, in whorls at leaf axils. **Leaves:** Narrowly elliptical; deeply cut into three long points, some smaller teeth; opposite. **In bloom:**

June-August. **Habitat-Range:** Waste places; mostly throughout.

The flowers are small but what catches the eye are the leaves which are usually held stiffly in a horizontal position. This herb was often used by women for headaches, menstrual pain and amenorrhea; hence its common name. A dark olive-green dye was also extracted from the plant.

292 WOUNDWORT *(Stachys palustris)*   Mint family *(Labiatae)*

Height: 20″-40″ (.5-1m). **Flower:** 1/2″ (1cm) long; irregular, with two-lipped corolla, upper lip arched, lower lip 3-lobed with the middle lobe largest, 4 stamens, 1 pistil; many, in whorls at leaf axils. **Leaves:** Lanceolate, sessile or nearly so; slightly toothed; opposite. **In bloom:** June-September. **Habitat-Range:** Ditches, low meadows, waste places; throughout northern regions.

The plant is very hairy and smells rank. The calyx of each flower is downy, making the inflorescence seem fuzzy. The young shoots may be eaten like asparagus although they do give off an unpleasant smell. The hairy leaves were once used as dressing for bleeding wounds; hence the common name.

BASIL *(Satureja vulgaris)*   Mint family *(Labiatae)*

Height: 9″-18″ (22-45cm). **Flower:** 1/4″ (6mm) long; irregular, with tubular two-lipped corolla, upper lip erect and notched, lower lip spreading and 3-lobed, 4 stamens, 1 pistil; many, in whorls at leaf axils. **Leaves:** Elliptical; entire or slightly toothed; opposite. **In bloom:** June-September. **Habitat-Range:** Woods, thickets, rocky shores; mostly throughout, in uplands to North Carolina.

Similar to Woundwort *(Stachys palustris)* but plant is smaller, leaves are usually smooth and upper lip of pink-purple flower does not arch. Settlers used the leaves like chervil, especially with scrambled eggs and tomato dishes. A tea made from the leaves was used for relief from sore throat and kidney ailments.

293 GREAT LOBELIA *(Lobelia siphilitica)*   Bluebell family *(Campanulaceae)*

Height: 1′-3′ (.3-1m). **Flower:** 1″ (2.5cm) long; irregular, with 5 petals forming two-lipped tubular corolla, lower lip 3-lobed, upper lip 2-lobed, 5 stamens in a ring around single pistil which projects upward through a slit in upper lip; many, in axils of bracts on crowded raceme. **Leaves:** Lanceolate; untoothed or irregularly toothed; alternate. **In bloom:** August-September. **Habitat-Range:** Rich, low-lying woods, swamps; mostly throughout except for eastern New England.

Since it is closely related to the Cardinal Flower *(L. cardinalis)*, it is sometimes called the Blue Cardinal Flower. The plant is considered poisonous but its leaves were used in a tobacco that was smoked as a treatment for asthma, tonsillitis and bronchial disorders. The species name is due to the belief that the roots could be used to treat syphilis. It was exported to Europe for this purpose but the reactions were often violent and it fell into disrepute.

294 CLOSED GENTIAN *(Gentiana andrewsii)*[†]   Gentian family *(Gentianaceae)*

Height: 1′-3′ (.3-1m). **Flower:** 1 1/2″ (4cm) long; regular, having a cylindrical corolla nearly or tightly closed at summit; sessile, in terminal clusters. **Leaves:** Lanceolate, sessile; entire; opposite. **In bloom:** August-October. **Habitat-Range:** Meadows, low thickets, roadside banks; throughout, with the exception of Maine and New Hampshire.

This gentian differs from many others in that its flowers stay closed or nearly so; hence its common name. The species name honors Henry Andrews, a 19th-century English botanical artist. Another similar, closed-flowered species, Narrow-leaved Gentian (*G. linearis*), found only in the northern part of our range and in the mountains in the South, has narrow, linear leaves. Stiff Gentian, *G. quinquefolia*, has a pale violet-blue or lilac flower which is smaller (3/4", 2cm long) than that of other gentians. The almost closed flowers are clustered on a stem so sharply angled that it has four ridges.

295 FRINGED GENTIAN *(Gentiana crinita)*† Gentian family *(Gentianaceae)*

Height: 6"-36" (15-90cm). **Flower:** 1 1/2" (4cm) long; regular, with 4 conspicuously fringed petals forming a bell-shaped corolla, 4 stamens, 1 pistil; solitary, on long stalk. **Leaves:** Oval or lanceolate, sessile; entire; opposite. **In bloom:** August-November. **Habitat-Range:** Meadows, wet thickets and woods, brooksides; throughout northern part of range; in mountains in South.

Gentians are among the last flowers to bloom in the year, their bluish purple blossoms often popping up among the fallen leaves of autumn. A smaller, similar species with narrower leaves and short, blunt fringes found in northern bogs and swamps is the Smaller Fringed Gentian, *G. procera*. The fringes serve as a deterrent to crawling insects. When an ant tries to crawl into the flower, these delicate fingers collapse and the ant falls to the ground. Flying insects that aid in pollination do not have this problem. The common and generic names derive from Gentius, King of Illyria (in ancient times a country on the Adriatic Sea), who supposedly discovered its medicinal value. An infusion of roots made a bitter drink, called "spring bitter," that was used by early settlers as a spring tonic to "purify" the blood. The Indians applied the same infusion to back pains. White settlers added brandy or gin to the infusion and claimed that it increased appetite and promoted digestion. Today, in Europe, many aperitifs contain extracts of Gentian.

296 WILD ASTER *(Aster* spp.*)* Composite family *(Compositae)*

Height: 1'-5' (.3-1.5m). **Flower:** Species variable in size; composite, with circular cluster of disk flowers surrounded by ray flowers; usually many, in cymes. **Leaves:** Species variable in shape but usually arranged alternately. **In bloom:** August-October. **Habitat-Range:** Species variable; mostly throughout.

There are 54 species of wild aster in northeastern America and they are conspicuous when they bloom (in the late summer and fall). Although many are white, some have lavender, blue, pink or purple ray flowers and the disk flowers are yellow but often change to red or purple. The starlike flowerheads account for the common and generic names, *aster* being Greek for "star." The aster illustrated here, *A. azureus*, will help in identifying the genus but not the species. Indians ate the young leaves of many asters as a pot herb. Sufferers from rheumatism would soak in a bath containing the stems and flowers of fall Asters.

▲Brown▲

Key

	SPRING (March-early May)	**SUMMER** (late May-early August)	**FALL** (late August-October)

Indistinguishable

Basal, entire
301 Narrow-leaved Cattail

Regular

Basal, entire
297 Wild Ginger
Basal, lobed
299 Blue Cohosh
Alternate, entire
300 Dutchman's-pipe
   Virginia Snakeroot

Alternate, scale-like
304 Pinesap

Irregular

Densely crowded, scale-like
298 Squawroot

Alternate, scale-like
303 Beechdrops
302 Autumn Coralroot

297 WILD GINGER *(Asarum canadense)*   Birthwort family *(Aristolochiaceae)*

Height: 6″-12″ (15-30cm). **Flower:** 1″ (2.5cm) diameter; regular, with 3 sepals forming a cup-shaped calyx having 3 pointed, curved, spreading lobes, no corolla, 12 stamens, one 6-lobed pistil; solitary, on short stalk in the crotch formed by the two leaves. **Leaves:** Broadly heart-shaped; entire; single pair, upright. **In bloom:** April-May. **Habitat-Range:** Rich, moist woods, hillsides; throughout.

The low-growing purplish brown flower is often covered by forest litter but the pair of upright leaves on hairy stems is conspicuous early in the spring. This species is very common but there are other species differing mainly in the shape of leaves and flowers. When bruised, the underground stem has a strong ginger-like odor and was used by colonists as a substitute for the tropical spice. Indians added the root to many foods and it was also used in medicines to treat fevers, colds, coughs and stomach disorders.

298 SQUAWROOT *(Conopholis americana)*   Broom-rape family *(Orobanchaceae)*

Height: 3″-10″ (8-25cm). **Flower:** 1/2″ (1cm) long; irregular, with two-lipped corolla, upper lip forming a narrow hood, lower lip 3-lobed and spreading, 4 stamens, 1 pistil; several, in upper scale axils. **Leaves:** Scale-like; crowded on stem. **In bloom:** May-July. **Habitat-Range:** Woods, mostly oak; throughout.

Although the small flowers are yellow, the light brown or tan color of this unusual plant catches the eye. It lacks chlorophyll and it is parasitic on the roots of trees, mainly oak. Because its color and scale-like leaves are thought to resemble those of a pine cone, its generic name combines Greek *conos*, "cone" and *pholis*, "scale." The name Squaw-root was applied to any plant that Indian medicine men used to treat menstrual disorders.

299 BLUE COHOSH *(Caulophyllum thalictroides)*   Barberry family *(Berberidaceae)*

Height: 1′-3′ (.3-1m). **Flower:** 1/2″ (1cm) diameter; regular, having 6 pointed sepals, 6 glandlike petals, 6 stamens, 1 pistil; several, on branched raceme; sometimes purplish or greenish. **Leaves:** Compound, many wedge-shaped leaflets, sessile; lobed; single, upright. **In bloom:** April-June. **Habitat-Range:** Rich woods; throughout; in mountains in South.

The flowers usually appear before the leaf is fully open. At this early stage in its development the plant also has a bluish white appearance. When the single leaf finally opens it is so large and divided into so many leaflets that it resembles a plant with many leaves. The flowers eventually give way to deep blue berry-like seeds. When roasted the seeds were said to be an excellent substitute for coffee. Another common name, Papoose Root, refers to the fact that expectant women among the Indians and early settlers drank a tea made of the root as an aid to childbirth.

300 DUTCHMAN'S-PIPE *(Aristolochia durior)*   Birthwort family *(Aristolochiaceae)*

Height: Climbing vine. **Flower:** 1″-1 1/2″ (2.5-4cm) long; regular, with S-shaped calyx which broadens into 3 flat, brown-purple lobes, 6 stamens, 1 pistil; solitary, or in pairs from leaf axils. **Leaves:** Broadly heart-shaped, 6″-15″ (15-38cm) across; entire; alternate. **In bloom:** May-June. **Habitat-Range:** Rich, moist woods and banks of streams;

southwestern Pennsylvania and West Virginia; in mountains in the South.

The flower varies from brownish purple to yellowish green. Its shape accounts for the common names Dutchman's Pipe and Pipe Vine. It was also thought to resemble the human fetus and this "signature" recommended it as an aid in childbirth; in fact, all members of the Birthwort family were used for this purpose. Hence its generic name, combining Greek *aristos*, "best," and *lochia*, "delivery." A very downy species with smaller leaves, *A. tomentosa*, is found in the western part of our range.

VIRGINIA SNAKEROOT   Birthroot family *(Aristolochiaceae)*
(Aristolochia serpentaria)

Height: 8″-24″ (20-60cm). **Flower:** 1/2″ (1cm) long; regular, with S-shaped calyx which broadens into 3 flat, brownish purple lobes, 6 stamens, 1 pistil; few, on short, slender basal branches. **Leaves:** Narrowly heartshaped with pointed tip; entire; alternate. **In bloom:** May-July. **Habitat-Range:** Rich, limy woods; south of a line from southwestern Connecticut to southern Illinois.

Its flowers are similar to *A. durior* but this plant is not a vine and its leaves are narrowly heart-shaped. As its common and species names suggest, the plant was used to treat snakebite. The Indians chewed the aromatic root and applied the paste to the bite. This remedy was utilized by the English as early as 1650, and early pioneers carried the roots in their packs.

301 NARROW-LEAVED CATTAIL *(Typha angustifolia)*   Cattail family *(Typhaceae)*

Height: 2 1/2′-5′ (.7-1.5m). **Flower:** Tiny; indistinguishable, with densely packed yellow staminate flowers on upper part of flower spike narrowly separated from densely packed brown pistillate flowers on the lower part of spike. **Leaves:** Long, very narrow, grass-like; entire; upright, with sheathing base. **In bloom:** May-July. **Habitat-Range:** Fresh and brackish marshes; throughout, but most abundant near seacoast.

The Common Cattail, *T. latifolia*, is similar but has wider, swordlike leaves and has no gap between the staminate and pistillate flowers on the spike. Indians ate the tender, green shoots of cattails in the spring. The rootstock was eaten raw or roasted or was dried and ground into a flour. The pollen from staminate flowers was gathered and utilized as a nutritious additive to bread and pancakes and as a dusting powder. After the staminate flowers die, the pistillate flowers develop a brown, cylindrical seed mass that bursts into a downy cluster at winter's end. Dipped in fat, the seed heads were used as torches. The down was used as stuffing in quilts and pillows and as a lining for diapers. Indians wove the leaves into mats and rush seats.

302 AUTUMN CORALROOT   Orchid family *(Orchidaceae)*
(Corallorhiza odontorhiza)†

Height: 4″-12″ (10-30cm). **Flower:** 1/2″ (1cm) long; irregular, having 3 purple or green sepals, 3 petals, the 2 lateral ones forming wings, the lower white one forming a wide purple-spotted and crinkled lip; several, in raceme. **Leaves:** Scale-like; alternate. **In bloom:** August-October. **Habitat-Range:** Dry woodlands; throughout.

Although the small flowers of the coralroots may be pink or purple, they have here been classified as brown because the stems and scales are a conspicuous brown or brownish yellow. As the common name suggests, this is a late-blooming species. The Striped Coralroot, *C. striata*, blooms in the spring and its petals and sepals are purple-striped. The lateral petals and upper sepal of the Northern Coralroot, *C. trifida*, come together to form a hood. The lip of the Spotted Coralroot, *C. maculata*, is spotted with red. The common name is derived from the shape of the underground stem, or rhizome, which is branched and pink, resembling a coral-like mass. This is also reflected in the generic name which combines Greek *corallion*, "coral", and *rhiza*, "root."

303 BEECHDROPS *(Epifagus virginiana)*   Broom-rape family *(Orobanchaceae)*

Height: 6″-18″ (15-45cm). **Flower:** 1/4″ (6mm) long; irregular, with the upper larger ones tubular and the lower smaller ones remaining closed; several, in loose spike. **Leaves:** Scale-like; alternate. **In bloom:** August-October. **Habitat-Range:** Beech woods; throughout.

As its common name suggests, this plant is found under beech trees and feeds on beech roots. Its parasitism was recognized by early botanists and they gave it the generic name *Epifagus*, combining Greek *epi*, "upon" and *phagos*, "beech." Two kinds of flowers are found on the plant: the upper ones are tubular with purple or brown stripes but are sterile; the lower ones remain closed but are self-pollinating and produce many seeds.

304 PINESAP *(Monotropa hypopithys)*   Wintergreen family *(Pyrolaceae)*

Height: 4″-16″ (10-40cm). **Flower:** 1/2″ (1cm) long; regular, with varying but equal number of sepals and petals forming bell-shaped perianth; several, in drooping raceme. **Leaves:** Scale-like; alternate. **In bloom:** June-October. **Habitat-Range:** Woodland humus; throughout.

Lacking chlorophyll, Pinesap is a saprophyte deriving its nourishment from decaying matter in the soil. Although most flowers are tawny, bright red specimens occur. The drooping raceme becomes erect as the flowers develop seeds. The common name and species name (from Greek *hypo*, "under" and *pitys*, "pine") suggest that the plant may be found under pine trees, but it occurs in the humus of most hardwood forests. A similar southern species, Sweet Pinesap or Pigmy Pipes (*M. odorata*) is found chiefly under pines but it is much smaller and has light rose or purple flowers and the fragrance of violets.

Color
Illustrations

Note:

The following color illustrations have been divided into five color groups. Within each color group, they have been arranged by their blooming season, and within each season, according to general visual similarities.

The plate number corresponds to the respective species description in the text.

1 Painted Trillium

2 White Trillium   **3** Field Pussytoes

4 Trailing Arbutus

5 Pyxie

6 Lance-leaved Violet

7 Star Chickweed
8 Green Violet

9 Golden Seal
10 Dwarf Ginseng

11 Bladder Campion

12 Fringed Phacelia

13 Starry Campion

WHITE·GREEN SPRING

14 Cut-leaved Toothwort

15 Garlic Mustard

16 Foamflower

17 Pennywort

19 Early Saxifrage

18 Sicklepod

20 One-flowered Cancer Root

WHITE·GREEN SPRING

21 Japanese Honeysuckle

22 Bloodroot

23 Rue Anemone

25 Dutchman's Breeches

24 Mayapple

26 Jack-in-the-Pulpit

WHITE·GREEN SUMMER

27 Arrow Arum

28 Wild Calla

WHITE·GREEN SPRING

29 Colicroot   **30** Culver's-Root   **31** Galax

WHITE·GREEN SUMMER

33 Bugbane

32 Flypoison

34 White Sweet Clover

35 Downy Rattlesnake Plantain

37 Devil's-bit

WHITE·GREEN   SUMMER

38 Soapwort

39 Wild Lily-of-the-Valley   **40** Catnip

*

42 White Fringed Orchis

41 Helleborine

43 Meadowsweet

44 Yarrow

45 White Clover   **46** Bog Twayblade

47 Featherbells

48 Goatsbeard

49 False Hellebore

50 Water Plantain

WHITE·GREEN SUMMER

51 Pokeweed

52 White Clintonia

53 Round-leaved Pyrola

WHITE·GREEN   SUMMER

55 False Nettle

54 Branching Bur-reed

56 Curled Dock

WHITE·GREEN SUMMER

57 Bugleweed

58 Foxglove Beardtongue

59 Turtlehead

60 Hedge Bindweed **61** Swamp Rose Mallow

62 Flowering Spurge **63** Spreading Dogbane

WHITE·GREEN SUMMER

64 False Solomon's Seal

65 Wild Leek

66 Poke Milkweed

68 Bedstraw

67 Dodder

69 Goldthread

*

70 Ox-eye Daisy

71 Mountain Sandwort

72 Daisy Fleabane

WHITE·GREEN   SUMMER

73 Virginia Waterleaf

74 Tall Meadow-Rue

75 Virgin's-bower

76 Checkerberry

WHITE·GREEN   SUMMER

77 Indian Cucumber Root

78 Partridgeberry

79 Hairy Solomon's Seal

WHITE·GREEN   SUMMER

*

80 Sweet Cicely

81 White Baneberry

82 White Snakeroot

WHITE·GREEN SUMMER

83 Queen Anne's Lace

84 Water Hemlock   **85** Fool's Parsley

*

86 Sundew

87 Green Dragon

88 Cow Parsnip

89 Fragrant Water Lily

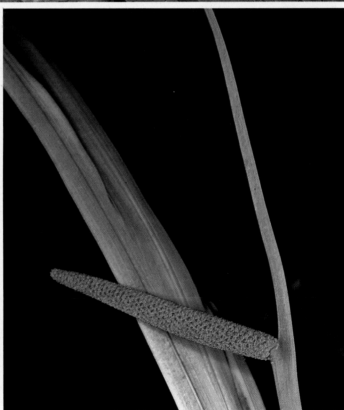

90 Broad-leaved Arrowhead

91 Sweetflag

*

92 White Avens

93 Indian Pipe

94 Bunchberry

95 Spotted Wintergreen

WHITE·GREEN SUMMER

96 Grass-of-Parnassus

97 Bowman's-root

98 Maystar

99 Horse-nettle

100 Wild Strawberry

101 Common Wood Sorrel

WHITE·GREEN SUMMER

102 Great Ragweed

103 Nodding Ladies' Tresses

104 Silverrod

105 White Wood Aster

106 Rattlesnake Root

107 Boneset

WHITE·GREEN   FALL

109 Whorled Pogonia

110 Golden Club

★

111 Trumpet Honeysuckle   **112** Round-leaved Yellow Violet

113 Trout Lily   **114** Hairy Puccoon

YELLOW·ORANGE   SPRING

115 Common Cinquefoil   **116** Sessile Bellwort

117 Celandine

★

118 Celandine Poppy

119 Frostweed   **120** Marsh Marigold

YELLOW·ORANGE   SPRING

121 Coltsfoot

122 Common Dandelion

123 Winter Cress

124 Golden Alexanders

125 Common Day-Lily

126 Blackberry Lily

YELLOW·ORANGE   SUMMER

127 Turk's-Cap Lily

128 Wood Lily

129 Canada Lily

YELLOW·ORANGE   SUMMER

★

130 St. Andrew's Cross

131 Corn Lily

132 Butterfly-Weed

YELLOW·ORANGE   SUMMER

133 Hawkweed

134 Yellow Fringed Orchis

135 Horsemint

136 Spotted Touch-me-not

137 Nodding Mandarin

138 Trumpet-Creeper

139 Wild Indigo

140 Birdsfoot Trefoil

141 Wild Radish

142 Yellow Stargrass

143 Common Buttercup

144 Yellow Wood-Sorrel

145 Yellow Avens

YELLOW·ORANGE SUMMER

★

146 Common Sunflower

147 Black-eyed Susan

148 Gray-headed Coneflower

YELLOW·ORANGE   SUMMER

★

149 Purple-headed Sneezeweed

150 Woolly Ragwort

151 Elecampane

YELLOW·ORANGE   SUMMER

152 Tickseed Coreopsis

153 Bullhead-lily

154 Bladderwort

156 Yellow Lady Slipper

155 Yellow Iris

157 Partridge-Pea

★

158 Common Tansy

159 Wild Senna

160 Common Mullein

YELLOW·ORANGE   SUMMER

★

161 Agrimony

163 Yellow Sweet Clover

164 Common St. Johnswort

165 Velvet Leaf

166 Butter-and-Eggs

YELLOW·ORANGE   SUMMER

★

167 Flower-of-an-Hour

168 Moth Mullein   **169** Evening Primrose

YELLOW·ORANGE   SUMMER

170 Wild Lettuce

171 Yellow False Foxglove

172 Gumweed

173 Yellow Goatsbeard

174 Field Sow-Thistle

175 King Devil

YELLOW·ORANGE SUMMER

176 Canada Goldenrod

177 Elm-leaved Goldenrod   **178** Orange Coneflower

180 Hard-leaved Goldenrod

179 Blue-stemmed Goldenrod

181 Showy Goldenrod

YELLOW·ORANGE   FALL

182 Spring Beauty

183 Round-lobed Hepatica

184 Moss Pink

185 Deptford Pink

187 Fire Pink

189 Red Trillium

190 Robin's-plantain

191 Wild Columbine

192 Shooting Star

193 Wild Bleeding Heart

194 Pale Corydalis

196 Wild Garlic

198 Fringed Polygala

197 Dragon's-mouth

199 Red Clover

RED·PINK   SPRING

200 Swamp Pink

201 Pitcher Plant

202 Showy Orchis

203 Rabbit-foot Clover

204 Indian Paintbrush

205 Wood Betony

206 Pink Lady Slipper

RED·PINK   SPRING

207 Steeplebush   **208** Pink Pyrola   **209** Blazing-star

210 Cardinal Flower

211 Castor Bean

212 Fireweed

213 Virginia Meadow Beauty

RED·PINK SUMMER

214 Seashore Mallow

215 Rose Pink

216 Hairy Beardtongue

217 Ragged-Robin

219 Wild Bergamot

221 Wild Onion

222 Scarlet Lychnis

223 Nodding Thistle

224 Teasel

225 Pink Wild Bean

226 Field Milkwort

RED·PINK   SUMMER

227 Crown Vetch

228 Pipsissewa

229 Tick-trefoil

230 Rosebud Orchid

231 Smartweed

232 Three-Birds Orchis

RED·PINK   SUMMER

233 Large Blue Flag

234 Skunk Cabbage

235 Forget-me-not

236 Venus Looking-glass

237 Wild Comfrey

238 Purple Cress

239 Virginia Bluebells

240 Hairy Skullcap

241 Heal-all

242 Lyre-leaved Sage

243 Dwarf Larkspur

244 Blue-eyed Mary   **245** Blue Toadflax

246 Birdsfoot Violet

BLUE·VIOLET   SPRING

247 Bluets

248 Slender Speedwell

249 Common Blue Violet

250 Beach Pea

251 Cow Vetch

252 Blue False Indigo

253 Wild Lupine

BLUE·VIOLET SPRING

255 Spiderwort

256 Bluecurls

257 Groundnut

258 Butterfly Pea

259 Water Willow

261 Pickerelweed

262 Purple Loosestrife

263 Jimson Weed

264 Bittersweet Nightshade

265 Leather Flower

BLUE·VIOLET SUMMER

266 Ivy-leaved Morning Glory

267 Hollow Joe-Pye Weed

268 Mist flower

269 New York Ironweed

270 Purple Avens

271 Common Burdock

272 Canada Thistle

273 Bull Thistle

274 Downy Lobelia

BLUE·VIOLET SUMMER

275 Purple Gerardia

277 Square-Stemmed Monkey Flower

281 Passion Flower

283 Chicory

BLUE·VIOLET SUMMER

285 Viper's Bugloss

286 Harebell

287 Monkshood

288 Tall Bellflower

289 Bush Clover

BLUE·VIOLET SUMMER

290 Common Milkweed

291 Motherwort

292 Woundwort

293 Great Lobelia

294 Closed Gentian

295 Fringed Gentian

296 Wild Aster

BROWN   SUMMER

297 Wild Ginger

298 Squawroot

299 Blue Cohosh

300 Dutchman's-pipe

BROWN   SPRING

302 Autumn Coralroot

303 Beechdrops

301 Narrow-leaved Cattail

304 Pinesap

BLUE·VIOLET   FALL

Families of Eastern Flowers

Acanthus family *(Acanthaceae)*. *Habit*. Mostly herbs or shrubs. *Leaves*. Simple, opposite. *Flowers*. Cyme, perfect, calyx 4-5 parts, corolla 4-5 parts, 2-lipped, stamens 4, ovary superior. Resembles Snapdragon flowers. Numerous species and varieties grown for ornamental purposes. Only about 3 common species in our area. E.g. Water Willow.

Arrowhead(Water Plantain) family *(Alimataceae)*. *Habit*. Aquatic or marsh perennial herbs. *Leaves*. Simple, long-petioled, arrow-shaped, lance-shaped or oval, mostly basal. *Flowers*. Showy, in whorls of three, regular, perfect or unisexual, 3 sepals, 3 white petals, 6 or more stamens. Genera in our area include *Alisma* (Water Plantains),2 species; and *Saggittaria* (Arrowheads), 5 common species. E.g. Arrowhead and Water Plantain.

Arum family *(Araceae)*. *Habit*. Terrestrial or, rarely, aquatic herbs, varied, sap often acrid because of its calcium oxalate. *Leaves*. Usually large, mostly basal, with sheathing petioles. *Flowers*. Inflorescence usually a spike of many small flowers surrounded by a colored bract. Seven common species in our area: Arrow Arum, Golden Club, Green Dragon, Jack-in-the-Pulpit, Skunk Cabbage, Sweetflag, and Wild Calla.

Barberry family *(Berberidaceae)*. *Habit*. Perennial herbs and shrubs. *Leaves*. Simple, deeply divided or compound with lobed leaflets, alternate or basal, deciduous or evergreen. *Flowers*. 6-9 waxy petals with twice as many sepals, perfect, stamens 4-18, ovary superior. Three common herbaceous species in our area. All are spring flowers. E.g. Mayapple and Blue Cohosh.

Bedstraw (Madder) family *(Rubiaceae)*. *Habit*. Herbs, shrubs, trees. *Leaves*. Simple, entire, opposite or whorled. *Flowers*. Cyme, small, 4-petaled, with funnel-shaped corolla in our area, stamens 4, ovary superior. Important ornamental and economic species: gardenia, coffee, and Quinine (a tree). Herbaceous genera in our area include *Galium* (Bedstraws), 10 common species; *Houstonia* (Bluets), 3 common species; *Mitchella*, 1 species. E.g. Bedstraw, Bluets, and Partridgeberry.

Bignonia family *(Bignoniaceae)*. *Habit*. Woody vines, shrubs, trees. *Leaves*. Opposite, simple or compound. *Flower*. Showy, tubular, perfect, 5-parted calyx, 5-parted corolla, 4 stamens, ovary superior. Only 2 genera grow wild in Northeastern United States: *Campsis* (Trumpet-Creeper) and *Bignonia* (Cross-Vine). *Catalpa*, often cultivated for shade, is a relative. E.g. Trumpet-Creeper.

Birthwort family *(Aristolochiaceae)*. *Habit*. Low herbs, climbing shrubs. *Leaves*. Alternate, simple, entire, large and heart-shaped in our area. *Flowers*. Bisexual, 3 petal-like sepals, no petals, 6-36 stamens, ovary inferior. Two genera in our area: *Aristolochia*, 2 species, and *Asarum*, 2 species. E.g. Dutchman's-pipe and Wild Ginger.

Bladderwort family *(Lentibulariaceae)*. *Habit*. Mostly aquatic, insectivorous herbs. *Leaves*. Submerged, threadlike, bear bladder-like traps, alternate, or in rosettes. *Flowers*. Perfect. Corolla 2-lipped, lower lip large and 3-lobed with a conspicuous spur, 2 stamens, superior ovary. Two genera in our area: *Utricularia*, 6 common species, and *Pinguicula*, 1 species. E.g. Bladderwort.

Bluebell (Bellflower) family *(Campanulaceae)*. *Habit*. Herbs, shrubs, trees, usually with milky sap. *Leaves*. Simple, alternate. *Flowers*. Bluebells are regular bell-shaped with a 5-lobed corolla, bisexual, 5 stamens, inferior ovary. Lobelias have irregular flowers with a 2-lobed upper lip and a 3-lobed lower lip, ovary is superior. Two major genera in our area: *Campanula* (Bluebells) and *Lobelia* (Lobelias). About 18 common species, all blue except for the Cardinal Flower. E.g. Cardinal Flower, Downy Lobelia, Great Lobelia, Harebell, Tall Bellflower, Venus' Looking-glass, Virginia Bluebell.

Broom-rape family *(Orobanchaceae)*. *Habit*. Fleshy root parasites, lacking chlorophyll. *Leaves*. Alternate, scale-like. *Flowers*. Perfect, corolla 5-parted with upper and lower lip similar to snapdragon's, 4 stamens in 2 pairs, superior ovary. Five common species in our area. E.g. Beechdrops, One-flowered Cancer Root, and Squawroot.

Buckwheat family *(Polygonaceae)*. *Habit*. Herbs, with sour juice in our area, stems with swollen nodes. *Leaves*. Alternate, simple, entire, stipules sheathe swollen joints of the stem. *Flowers*. Numerous, tiny, lack petals, 3-6 sepals, 6-9 stamens, ovary superior. The fruit is an achene resembling tiny beechnuts. The common rhubarb is in this family. The major genera in our area are *Polygonum* (Smartweeds and Knotweeds), over 60 Dock species, and *Rumex* (Docks), with 5 common species. E.g. Pale Smartweed and Curled.

Bur-reed family *(Sparganiaceae)*. *Habit*. Reedlike marsh plants, perennial with creeping rootstock. *Leaves*. Alternate, linear, sheathing, erect or floating. *Flowers*. Monoecious, flowers in spherical heads, staminate uppermost, 3-6 sepal-like parts, lacks petal. About 10 species in our area. E.g. Bur-reed.

Buttercup family *(Ranunculaceae)*. *Habit*. Annual or perennial herbs, sometimes vines. *Leaves*. Alternate or basal, usually palmately compound. *Flowers*. Solitary, racemes, or panicles. The 5-7 glossy petals are replaced by 6-10 showy sepals in many species. Numerous stamens form bushy cluster. Medicinal plants include Aconite, Snakeroot and Golden Seal. Over 40 common species in this area. Important genera include *Ranunculus* (Buttercups), 11 common species, and *Anemone* (Anemones), 7 common species. E.g. Black Cohosh, Early Buttercup, Golden Seal, Goldthread, Leather Flower, Marsh Marigold, Monkshood, Round-lobed Hepatica, Rue Anemone, Spring Larkspur, Tall Meadow-Rue, Virgin's-bower, White Baneberry, Wild Columbine.

Cattail family *(Typhaceae)*. *Habit*. Perennial herbs with creeping rootstocks, erect stems. *Leaves*. Erect, long sheathing portion with long narrow blade. *Flowers*. Brown cylindrical heads of tiny flowers; pistillate female flowers located below staminate male flowers with 2-5 stamens. Flowers naked, but surrounded by hairs. *Typha*, 4 species, is the only genus in Northeastern United States. E.g. Fruiting Cattail.

Daffodil family *(Amaryllidaceae)*. *Habit*. Perennial herbs from bulbs or rootstalks. *Leaves*. Narrow, grasslike, straight-veined, mostly basal. *Flowers*. Perfect, regular, 6 petal-like parts, stamens 6, ovary inferior. Includes many ornamentals such as the narcissuses. American Aloe (Century Plant) is widely cultivated in warm countries for sisal hemp and to make mescal or pulque, popular Mexican drinks. There are two common genera: *Hypoxis* (Yellow Stargrass) and *Zephyranthes* (Atamasco Lily) in our area. E.g. Goldstar Grass.

Diapensia family *(Diapensiaceae)*. *Habit*. Low perennial evergreen herbs. *Leaves*. Simple, basal rosettes. *Flowers*. Perfect, regular, all parts in 5's, inferior ovary. The leaves of *Galax* are used for ornament by florists. Three species in our area. E.g. Beetle-weed and Pyxie.

Dogbane family *(Apocynaceae)*. *Habit.* Perennial herbs with milky juice, fibrous stems from horizontal rootstocks related to Milkweeds. *Leaves.* Simple, usually opposite, entire. *Flowers.* Perfect, regular, 5 united sepals, 5 united petals, bell-shaped, 5 stamens, ovary superior. Most species are tropical, acrid, and poisonous. Periwinkle often escapes to moist places. The most common genus in our area is *Apocynum* (Dogbanes), 4 common species. E.g. Spreading Dogbane.

Dogwood family *(Cornaceae)*. *Habit.* Trees, shrubs, and, rarely, low perennial herbs such as bunchberry. *Leaves.* Simple, mostly opposite, or whorled, entire. *Flowers.* Tiny, tightly packed, greenish, inconspicuous, regular, 4-5 parts, ovary inferior. The 4 white bracts outshine the flowers. Only 1 herbaceous species in Northeastern United States: Bunchberry.

Evening-primrose family *(Onagraceae)*. *Habit.* Herbs, shrubs, trees. *Leaves.* Simple, alternate or opposite. *Flowers.* Large, showy, regular, perfect, may be axillary or in terminal racemes. Usually 4 petals, 8 stamens, ovary inferior. About 15 common species in our area. E.g. Cut-leaved Evening Primrose and Fireweed.

Flax family *(Linaceae)*. *Habit.* Herbs and shrubs. *Leaves.* Simple, entire, alternate. *Flowers.* Cyme, perfect, regular, 5 sepals, 5 petals, 5 stamens united at the base. Flax plants supply fibers for linen, and seeds for linseed oil. There is one genus, *Linum* (Flax), 2 common species, in our area, a yellow native species, and a blue introduced species. E.g. Flax.

Forget-me-not family *(Boraginaceae)*. *Habit.* Mostly coarse herbs. *Leaves.* Hairy, simple, alternate, entire. *Flowers.* Perfect, in cymes or racemes, often blue or white, 5 united petals, tubular corolla, superior ovary. About 16 common species in our area. E.g. Forget-me-not, Hairy Puccoon, Viper's Bugloss, Wild Comfrey.

Gentian family *(Gentianaceae)*. *Habit.* Mostly herbs. *Leaves.* Opposite, entire, simple. *Flowers.* Cyme, regular, perfect, 5 united sepals, 5 united petals, 5 stamens, ovary superior. Genera in this area include the mostly blue *Gentiana*, about 10 species, and the mostly pink *Sabatia*, about 5 species. E.g. Closed Gentian, Fringed Gentian, Penny-work, and Rose Pink.

Gentian family *(Geraniaceae)*. *Habit.* Mostly herbs. *Leaves.* Opposite, entire, simple. *Leaves.* Deeply dissected and may be palmate or fernlike. *Flowers.* Cyme or umbel, pink or lavender with 5 sepals, 5 petals, 5-15 stamens, ovary superior. A long erect beaked pistil or "cranesbill" remains after the petals fall. The cultivated "geranium" is a native of South Africa and belongs in the genus *Pelargonium*.The most important genus in our area, *Geranium*, has about 8 common species. E.g. Wild Geranium.

Ginseng family *(Araliaceae)*. *Habit.* Herbs, shrubs, trees. *Leaves.* Alternate, compound usually. *Flowers.* Small, regular, 5 minute sepals, usually with 5 petals, 5 stamens, ovary inferior. Inflorescence an umbel. Two herbaceous genera in our area, *Panax* (Ginseng), 2 species, and *Aralia* (Sarsaparilla), 3 species. E.g. Dwarf Ginseng.

Heath (Heather) family *(Ericaceae)*. *Habit.* Shrubs and trees, rarely trailing. *Flower.* Solitary or raceme, perfect, regular, usually united in a bell shape, 8-10 stamens. Includes heather, cranberries, blueberries, huckleberries, rhododendrons, and azaleas.

Four common herbaceous species in our area. E.g. Trailing Arbutus and Checkerberry.

Honeysuckle family *(Caprifoliaceae). Habit.* Trees or shrubs. *Leaves.* Opposite, simple or compound. *Flowers.* Bell-shaped flowers often in cymes, perfect, flaring corolla composed of 5 united petals, 5 stamens, ovary inferior. Many species are grown as ornamentals. Elderberry fruit is used for wine and preserves. The most important genus, *Lonicerca,* contains 6 common species in our area. E.g. Trumpet Honeysuckle and Japanese Honeysuckle.

Iris family *(Iridaceae). Habit.* Perennial herbs from rhizomes or corms. *Leaves.* Mostly basal, long, narrow, toothless. *Flowers.* Showy, perfect, in 3's, 3 stamens. Orris root, a violet perfume from a species of *Iris,* and saffron, the source of a yellow dye from a species of *Crocus,* come from this family. Many cultivated species. About 11 common species in our area. Important genera: *Iris* (Irises) 6 species; *Sisyrinchium* (Blue-eyed Grasses), 4 species; *Belamcanda* (Blackberry Lily), 1 species. E.g. Larger Blue Flag, Yellow Iris, Blue-eyed Grass, Blackberry Lily.

Lily family *(Liliaceae). Habit.* Perennial herbs from rhizome, bulb corm, or tuber. *Leaves.* Parallel-veined, may be basal, alternate or in whorls. *Flowers.* Perfect, symmetrical, usually 3 sepals, 3 petals, 6 stamens, often large and showy. Over 50 common species in our area, including such vegetables as onions and asparagus. Some important genera include *Lilium* (Lilies), 6 species; *Trillium,* 8 species and *Allium* (Wild Onions), 5 species. E.g. Canada Lily, Colicroot, Day Lily, Devil's-bit, Field Garlic, False Hellebore, False Solomon's Seal, Featherbells, Flypoison, Hairy Solomon's Seal, Indian Cucumber Root, Nodding Mandarin, Merrybells, Painted Trillium, Red Trillium, Trout Lily, Turk's-cap Lily, White Clintonia, Wild Leek, Wild Lily-of-the-Valley, White Trillium, Wood Lily.

Lizard's-tail family *(Saururaceae). Habit.* Perennial herbs, moist situations. *Leaves.* Large heart-shaped leaves in our area. *Flowers.* Tiny, perfect, lack petals and sepals. Only 1 species in our area: Lizard's-tail.

Loosestrife family *(Lythraceae). Habit.* Herbs, shrubs, trees. *Leaves.* Simple, entire, opposite or whorled. *Flowers.* In spikes or leaf axils, perfect, usually 6 petals, stamens twice the number of petals, ovary superior. All true loosestrifes in our area are pink. The Yellow "Loosestrifes" belong in the Primrose family. Seven common species in our area. *Lythrum* (True Loosestrifes) contains 5 species. E.g. Purple Loosestrife.

Mallow family *(Malvaceae). Habit.* Herbs, shrubs, trees. *Leaves.* Simple, alternate, stipulate, usually palmately ribbed. *Flowers.* Showy, 5 sepals, 5 petals, with numerous stamens enveloping the pistils. Includes cotton and hollyhocks. Okra is the green capsules of one species of *Hibiscus.* Important wild genera include *Hibiscus,* 4 common species, and *Malva,* 4 common species. E.g. Swamp Rose Mallow, Seashore Mallow, Flower-of-an-Hour, and Velvet leaf.

Meadow-beauty family *(Melastomataceae). Habit.* Often shrubs or trees in the tropics, but all in Northeastern United States are perennial herbs, somewhat woody at the base and tuber-bearing. *Leaves.* Simple, 3-5 nerves, opposite. *Flowers.* Perfect, regular, 4 sepals, 4 petals, 8 stamens. *Rhexia,* with 2 common species, is the only genus in our area. E.g. Virginia Meadow Beauty.

Milkweed family *(Asclepiadaceae). Habit.* Perennial herbs, shrubs, mostly with milky juice. *Leaves*. Simple, entire, mostly opposite or whorled, stipulate. *Flowers*. Regular, perfect, 5-parted, 5 united stamens, ovary superior, usually in umbels or cymes. Of 13 common species in this area, 12 are in the genus *Asclepias* (Milkweeds). E.g. Common Milkweed, Poke Milkweed, Butterfly-Weed.

Milkwort family *(Polygalaceae)*. *Habit*. Low herbs, shrubs, trees. *Leaves*. Usually alternate, simple, small, linear. *Flowers*. Unisexual, irregular, 2 colored sepals. "wings," and 3 smaller sepals, usually 3 tiny united petals, and often 8 stamens, 1 pistil. Only 1 genus, *Polygala*, with about 10 common species in Northeastern United States. E.g. Fringed Polygala and Field Milkwort.

Mint family *(Labiatae)*. *Habit*. Usually herbs, secretes characteristic aromatic oils, stem square. *Leaves*. Simple, opposite. *Flowers*. Small, perfect, irregular, 2-lobed upper lip, 3-lobed lower lip, 5-parted calyx, conspicuously ribbed, 2 pairs of stamens, ovary superior. The most common seasoning mints include peppermint, spearmint, sage, thyme, and rosemary. Lavender is a source of perfume. Over 60 common species in our area. Some common genera: *Mentha* (Mints), 6 species; *Scutellaria* (Skullcaps), 9 species; and *Monarda* (including Beebalms), 5 species. E.g. Beebalm, Bluecurls, Bugleweed, Catnip, Hairy Skullcap, Heal-all, Horsemint, Motherwort, Lyre-leaved Sage, Wild Bergamot, Woundwort.

Morning-glory family *(Convolvulaceae)*. *Habit*. Herbs, shrubs, trees, often twining, sap may be milky. *Leaves*. Simple, alternate. *Flowers*. Perfect, regular, usually solitary and axillary, 5 sepals, 5-lobed corolla, bell-shaped and showy, 5 stamens, ovary superior. Includes the morning glories, bindweeds, the leafless parasitic dodders, and the sweet potato. Nine common species in our area. *Ipomoea* (Morning glories), and *Convolvulus* (Bindweeds) are the most important genera. E.g. Ivy-leaved Morning glory, Hedge Bindweed, Dodder.

Mustard family *(Cruciferae)*. *Habit*. Pungent herbs, annual, biennial, or perennial. *Leaves*. Simple, lobed alternate. *Flowers*. Small, perfect, regular, in racemes, 4 sepals, 4 petals, 6 stamens, ovary superior. The single pistil often develops into characteristic erect slender seed pod. Includes cabbage, cauliflower, turnips, radish, black mustard, watercress, and Brussels sprouts. Over 40 common species in the area. E.g. Cut-leaved Toothwort, Garlic Mustard, Purple Cress, Sicklepod, Wild Radish, Winter Cress.

Nettle family *(Urticaceae)*. *Habit*. Fibrous herbs, shrubs, small trees. *Leaves*. Simple, stipulate, sometimes with stinging hairs, toothed, opposite. *Flowers*. Tiny, greenish clusters, unisexual, regular, calyx mostly 4-parted, no petals, 4 stamens, ovary superior or inferior. The Chinese silk plant yields a tough silky fiber used in China and Japan. A few species have ornamental value, but most species are weedy. Genera in this area include *Urtica*, 2 species, with stinging hairs; *Boehmeria*, 1 species; *Pilea*, 1 species. E.g. False Nettle.

Orchid family *(Orchidaceae)*. *Habit*. Perennial herbs from rhizomes or fleshy roots. *Leaves*. Parallel-veined, usually alternate, simple. *Flowers*. Perfect, irregular, 3 green or colored sepals, 2 lateral petals, 1 larger petal often of different shape and color which forms a lip, and frequently extended into spur, 1 stamen, sometimes 2, ovary inferior, complex adaptations for pollination. All species are terrestrial in our area, but many tropical orchids cling to branches of trees as epiphytes. Vanilla extract is prepared from the pods of certain epiphytic cultivated orchids. Over 40 species relatively common in Northeastern United States, but more numerous in the South. About half of these species are in the genus *Habeneria*. Other common genera are *Orchis* and *Cypripedium* (Lady Slipers). E.g. Bog Twayblade, Coralroot, Downy Rattlesnake Plantain, Dragon's Mouth, Helleborine, Nodding Ladies' Tresses, Large Twayblade, Pink Lady Slipper, Yellow Lady Slipper, Purple Fringed Orchis, Rosebud Orchid, Three-Birds Orchis, Showy Orchis, White Fringed Orchis, Whorled Pogonia, Yellow Fringed Orchis.

Parsley (Carrot) family *(Umbelliferae)*. *Habit*. Mostly biennial or perennial herbs, stem often stout with hollow internodes, usually aromatic. *Leaves*. Alternate or basal, pinnately or palmately compound, petioles are dilated and sheathing at the node. *Flower*. Numerous, in flat-topped clusters or compound umbels, 5 sepals, 5 petals, 5 stamens, ovary inferior. Useful species include celery, parsley, parsnips, carrot, dill, anise, caraway, and myrrh. Water Hemlock and Poison Hemlock are very poisonous. About 18 common species in our area. E.g. Cow Parsnips, Fool's Parsley, Golden Alexanders, Queen Anne's Lace, Sweet Cicely, Water Hemlock.

Passion-flower family *(Passifloraceae)*. *Habit*. Shrubs, herbs, mostly climbers with tendrils. *Leaves*. Alternate, stipulate, simple or compound, entire. *Flowers*. Inflorescence usually axillary and in pairs, regular, usually 4-5 sepals and petals, sepals often more conspicuous than petals, 5 stamens. Economically important as ornamentals and for edible fruits. *Passiflora* is mainly a South American genus. E.g. Passion Flower.

Pea family *(Leguminosae)*. *Habit*. Herbs, shrubs, trees, some with roots, containing nitrogen-fixing bacteria, many are thorny. *Leaves*. Alternate, usually pinnately compound, stipulate. *Flowers*. Perfect and irregular, 5 petals, 1 larger "banner" petal, 2 lateral "wing" petals, and 2 lower "keel" petals that join each other; 10 stamens, ovary superior. The fruit is a legume. Useful species include peas, beans, peanuts, lentils, alfalfa, clover, hematoxylin (dye), and licorice (drug). Locoweed is poisonous. Over 65 common herbaceous species in our area. E.g. Beach pea, Birdfoot Trefoil, Blue False Indigo, Bush Clover, Butterfly Pea, Cow Vetch, Crown Vetch, Groundnut, Pink Wild Bean, Prostrate Tick-trefoil, Rabbitfoot Clover, Red Clover, White Clover, White Sweet Clover, Yellow Sweet Clover, Wild Indigo, Wild Lupine, Wild Senna.

Phlox family *(Polemoniaceae)*. *Habit*. Mostly annual or perennial herbs. *Leaves*. Simple or pinnately compound, mostly opposite, usually entire. *Flowers*. Showy, commonly in cymes, 5-parted with united petals, 5 stamens, 3-pronged style, superior ovary. Important genera include the pink *Phlox*, 6 common species, and blue *Polemonium*, 2 common species. E.g. Garden Phlox, Jacob's Ladder, Moss Pink.

Pickerelweed family *(Pontederiaceae)*. *Habit*. Aquatic herbs, rooted or floating. *Leaves*. Usually opposite or whorled, long-petioled. *Flowers*. Perfect, perianth in 6 parts, 6 stamens, ovary superior. Two genera in our area are *Pontedria* (Pickerelweed), 1 species, with purplish spikes, and *Heteranthera* (Mud-plantains), 3 species with smaller 6-pointed flowers of white, blue, or yellow. E.g. Pickerelweed.

Pink family *(Caryophyllaceae)*. *Habit*. Annual or perennial herbs, stems with swollen nodes. *Leaves*. Simple, entire, opposite or whorled, mostly narrow. *Flowers*. Cyme or solitary, regular, 5 sepals, 4-5 "pinked" (notched) petals, 10 stamens, ovary superior. The Carnation is a well known cultivated species. Over 30 common species in our area. Common genera include *Silene* (Campions), and *Stellaria* (Chickweeds). E.g. Bladder

Campion, Star Chickweed, Fire Pink, Ragged-Robin, Sandwort, Soapwort, Scarlet Lychnis, Starry Campion, Swamp Pink.

Pitcher-plant family *(Sarraceniaceae)*. *Habit*. Insectivorous, perennial herbs, found in bogs. *Leaves*. Basal, pitcher-like. *Flowers*. Usually solitary on leafless stems, perfect, regular, 5 broad sepals, 5 broad petals, stamens numerous, style has umbrella-like cap, ovary superior. Only 1 genus, *Sarracenia*, 2 species, in our area. E.g. Trumpets.

Pokeweed family *(Phytolaccaceae)*. *Habit*. Tall, strong-smelling perennial. *Leaves*. Simple, toothless, alternate. *Flowers*. Tiny, white, in terminal racemes, regular, usually bisexual, 4-5 sepals, no petals, 10 stamens, fruit a fleshy, dark purple berry. *Phytolacca americana* is the only species in our area. E.g. Pokeweed.

Poppy family *(Fumaraceae)*. *Habit*. Annual or perennial herbs, usually have milky or colored juice. *Leaves*. Alternate, entire or cleft. *Flowers*. Often showy, regular, perfect, usually solitary, 2-3 sepals (falling before flowers open), 4-12 petals with many stamens, ovary superior. Opium and morphine derive from this family. Includes many ornamentals. About 15 common species in our area, 9 of these in the Bleeding-heart Subfamily. E.g. Bloodroot, Celandine, Celandine Poppy, Dutchman's Breeches, Pale Corydalis, Wild Bleeding Heart.

Primrose family *(Primulaceae)*. *Habit*. Usually perennial, sometimes annual. *Leaves*. Simple, undivided, opposite, whorled, or basal. *Flowers*. Sometimes on leafless stalk, perfect, regular, mostly 5 parts (starflower has 6-7 parts), ovary superior. Primulas and Cyclamen are cultivated varieties. About 11 common species in our area. E.g. Whorled Loosestrife, Shooting Star, Starflower.

Purslane family *(Portulacaceae)*. *Habit*. Small succulent, often prostrate, annual or perennial. *Leaves*. Simple, entire, usually opposite, usually stipulate. *Flowers*. Regular, perfect, cyme or solitary, 2 sepals, 5 petals, 4-6 stamens, ovary superior. (An exception to the above is the Fameflower with basal leaves and flowers in cyme.) Well-known members are Purslane, a common weed, and the cultivated Portulaca. Four common species in our area. E.g. Spring Beauty.

Rose family *(Rosaceae)*. *Habit*. Herbs, shrubs, trees. *Leaves*. Simple or compound, alternate, stipulate. *Flowers*. Perfect, regular, 5 sepals united at the base, 5 petals, numerous stamens, ovary nearly or completely inferior. This mostly woody family includes apples, pears, plums, cherries, prunes, apricots, peaches, almonds, strawberries, blackberries, raspberries, and hundreds of other climbers, shrubs, and trees cultivated for their beauty. Over 40 herbaceous species in the Northeast. Herbaceous genera include *Potentilla* (Cinquefoils), 12 common species, and *Geum* (Avens), 7 common species. E.g. Agrimony, Bowman's Root, Common Cinquefoil, Common Strawberry, Goatsbeard, Meadowsweet, Purple Avens, Steeplebush, White Avens, Yellow Avens.

Rock-rose family *(Cistaceae)*. *Habit*. Low herbs or shrubs with volatile oils. *Leaves*. Simple, entire, usually alternate. *Flowers*. Perfect, regular, 5 sepals, 2 outer sepals are smaller, 3-5 petals, lasting one day or less, stamens many, ovary superior. *Helianthemum* is a large genus that includes Frostweed.

Saxifrage family *(Saxifragaceae)*. *Habit*. Herbs, shrubs, small trees. *Leaves*. Alternate or opposite, simple or compound, commonly deciduous. *Flowers*. Perfect, regular, often borne in clusters, 4-5 sepals (often united), 4-5 petals, 5 stamens, ovary inferior to superior. Includes mock-orange, hydrangeas, gooseberries, and currants. About 9 common herbaceous species in our area. E.g. Early Saxifrage, Foamflower and Grass-of-Parnassus.

Snapdragon family *(Scrophulariaceae)*. *Habit.* Mostly herbs, *Leaves.* Simple, sometimes toothed. *Flowers.* Irregular, perfect 2-lobed upper lip, 3-lobed lower lip, usually 4 stamens, in pairs. Foxglove (*Digitalis*) belongs to this family. Over 40 common species. Important genera include *Gerardia* (False Foxgloves), 8 common species, and *Veronica* (Speedwells), 10 common species. E.g. Beardtongue, Blue Toadflax, Blue-eyed Mary, Butter-and-Eggs, Common Mullein, Foxglove Beardtongue, Indian Paintbrush, Moth Mullein, Purple Gerardia, Slender Speedwell, Square-Stemmed Monkey Flower, Turtlehead, Wood Betony, Yellow False Foxglove.

Spiderwort family *(Commelinaceae)*. *Habit.* Stems herbaceous, roots fibrous. *Leaves.* Sheathing, alternate, parallel-veined, entire. *Flowers.* Bisexual, 3 green sepals. Spiderworts have 3 symmetrical petals with golden stamens. Dayflowers have 2 large upper petals and 1 smaller lower one that supports curved stamens. Genera in our area include *Tradescantia* (Spiderworts), and *Commelina* (Dayflowers). E.g. Spidewort, Asiatic Dayflower.

Spurge family *(Euphorbiaceae)*. *Habit.* Herbs, shrubs, trees, usually with milky juice, some succulent. *Leaves.* Usually alternate, stipulate simple, some with glands at base. *Flowers.* Unisexual, regular, 5 sepals or none, 5 petals or usually none, stamens 1 to many, ovary superior. Economically important species provide rubber, tung oil, castor oil and tapioca. Ornamentals include Poinsettia and Crown-of-thorns. The principal genus in our area is *Euphorbia*, 7 species, all with tiny naked unisexual flowers. E.g. Flowering Spurge, Castor Bean.

St. Johnswort family *(Hypericaceae)*. *Habit.* Herbs, shrubs. *Leaves.* Opposite or whorled, entire, covered with dots or pits. *Flowers.* Usually in cymes, usually yellow or orange, 5 petals, numerous bushy stamens. Two genera in our area: *Hypericum* (St. Johnswort), 10 common species; *Ascyrum*, 2 species, low evergreen shrubs. E.g. Common St. Johnswort and St. Andrew's Cross.

Sundew family *(Droseraceae)*. *Habit.* Perennial glandular herbs of bogs, insectivorous. *Leaves.* Basal in rosette, have tentacles that trap insects. *Flowers.* Perfect, regular, 5 sepals, 5 petals, 5-20 stamens, 2-5 styles, ovary superior, flowers on long stems. Four common species in our area, all in the genus *Drosera*. E.g. Thread-leaved Sundew.

Sunflower family *(Compositae)*. *Habit.* Usually herbs, sometimes shrubs. *Leaves.* Alternate or, rarely, opposite or whorled, simple, entire to variously dissected. *Flowers.* Flower heads are clusters of small flowers, typically flat "ray" flowers surround a center disk of small tubelike "disk" flowers, disk flowers with 5 united petals forming small tube, 5 anthers united into tube around pistil, ovary inferior. Largest family of flowering plants, varied in appearance and specialized in insect pollination and seed dispersal. Over 230 common species in our area, including many large groups such as asters, hawkweeds, thistles, sunflowers, coneflowers, and goldenrods. E.g. Black-eyed Susan, Blue Lettuce, Blue-stemmed Goldenrod, Boneset, Bull Thistle, Canada Goldenrod, Canada Thistle, Chicory, Coltsfoot, Common Burdock, Common Dandelion, Common Ragweed, Common Sunflower, Common Tansy, Daisy Fleabane, Dense Blazing-star, Elecampane, Elm-leaved Goldenrod, Field Pussytoes, Field Sow-thistle, Golden

Ragwort, Gray-headed Coneflower, Great Ragweed, Gumweed, Hairy Hawkweed, Hollow Joe-Pye Weed, Tickseed Coreopsis, Mistflower, New York Ironweed, Nodding Thistle, Orange Coneflower, Ox-eye Daisy, Showy Goldenrod, Silverrod, Sneezeweed, Spotted Knapweed, Rattlesnake Root, Robin's-plantain, White Lettuce, White Snakeroot, White Wood Aster, Whorled Coreopsis, Wild Aster, Wild Lettuce, Yarrow, Yellow Goatsbeard.

Teasel family *(Dipsacaceae)*. *Habit.* Mostly herbs. *Leaves.* Opposite or whorled. *Flowers.* Tiny florets in dense bracteate heads, perfect, irregular, small cuplike calyx, 4- or 5-lobed corolla, 4 stamens, ovary inferior. A native of eastern Mediterranean region, these scabrous herbs have been grown for both commercial and ornamental purposes. Genera that have escaped into Northeastern United States include *Knautia* (Field Scabious), 1 species; *Dipsaucus* (Teasel), 2 species. E.g. Teasel.

Tomato (Nightshade) family *(Solanaceae)*. *Habit.* Herbs, shrubs, trees. *Leaves.* Alternate, simple, coarse-toothed. *Flowers.* Trumpet-shaped, sometimes reflexed, perfect, regular, 5-parted calyx, 5 united petals, 5 stamens, ovary superior. Important commercial species: potatoes, tomatoes, eggplant, peppers, chilies, belladonna (Atropine), and tobacco. Petunia is a common garden ornamental. Many species are at least partially poisonous, particularly Jimsonweed and the nightshades. Genera include *Solanum* (Nightshades), 3 species; *Physalis* (Ground cherries), 5 species; *Datura* (Jimsonweed). E.g. Bittersweet Nightshade, Horse-Nettle, and Jimsonweed.

Touch-me-not family *(Balsaminaceae)*. *Habit.* Herbs with watery stems. *Leaves.* Simple, pinnately veined, thin, alternate. *Flowers.* Brightly colored, perfect, irregular, 3-5 sepals, 2 very small, 1 large sepal is petal-like with a curved spur, 5 petals, 2 pairs united, 5 stamens, ovary superior. Ripe pods "pop" when touched. Only 1 genus in North America: *Impatiens*, 2 species. E.g. Spotted Touch-me-not.

Vervain family *(Verbenaceae)*. *Habit.* Herbs, shrubs, trees. *Leaves.* Usually opposite, simple, toothed. *Flowers.* Perfect, small, usually irregular, 5-parted calyx, 5-parted corolla, 4 stamens, in two pairs, ovary superior. Ornamentals include *Verbena* and *Lantana*. Five common wild herbaceous species in our area, all in the genus *Verbena*. E.g. Blue Vervain.

Violet family *(Violaceae)*. *Habit.* Herbs, shrubs, usually perennial. *Leaves.* Simple, usually alternate or basal, with prominent stipules. *Flowers.* Irregular, perfect, 5 sepals, 5 petals, 1 petal usually wider, veined and spurred, 5 stamens, ovary superior, some flowers lack petals and are self-fertilized. Many varieties of violets and pansies are cultivated. Over 40 wild species in our area, all in the genus *Viola*. E.g. Birdsfoot Violet, Common Blue Violet, Green Violet, Lance-leaved Violet, Round-leaved Yellow Violet.

Waterleaf family *(Hydrophyllaceae)*. *Habit.* Herbs, rarely shrubs, often hairy. *Leaves.* Mainly alternate or from base, often 5-7 lobed. *Flowers.* Perfect, regular, 5 sepals, 5 united petals, bell-shaped, 5 stamens, ovary superior. Inflorescence often in cymes. Genera in our area include *Hydrophyllum* (Waterleafs), 4 species; *Phacelia,* 2 common species. E.g. Virginia Waterleaf, Fringed Phacelia.

Water-lily family *(Nymphaeaceae)*. *Habit.* Perennial aquatic herbs, rhizomes. *Leaves.* Alternate, usually long-petioled, often floating, large, simple. *Flowers.* Large, showy, solitary, perfect 3-6 sepals, petals 3-numerous, stamens 3-many, ovary superior. Seven common species in our area. E.g. Bullhead Lily, Fragrant Water Lily.

Wintergreen (Pyrola) family *(Pyrolaceae)*. *Habit*. Small woodland herbs. *Leaves*. Usually evergreen but may lack green pigment and be reduced to scales. *Flowers*. Solitary or in raceme, usually hang downward, perfect, 4-5 sepals, 4-5 petals, 8-10 stamens, ovary superior. Five genera in our area include about 13 species. E.g. Indian Pipe, Pinesap, Pink Pyrola, Pipsissewa, Round-leaved Pyrola, and Spotted Wintergreen.

Wood-sorrel family *(Oxalidaceae)*. *Habit*. Perennial herbs or shrubs, often with rhizomes or tubers. *Leaves*. Alternate, typically compound, trifoliate and heart-shaped in our area. *Flowers*. Perfect, regular, 5 sepals, 5 petals, 10 stamens, 5 styles, ovary superior. Only one genus, *Oxalis*, in our area. These herbs produce a sour juice containing oxalic acid. About 6 common species. E.g. Common Wood Sorrel, Yellow Wood Sorrel.

Wildflower Recipes

Almost anyone can enjoy eating the most natural foods of all—wild edible plants. Aside from the pleasures of eating, the foraging activity is itself healthful and brings one close to the simpler way of life.

Many wild edible plants are considered "weeds" and their removal will be welcomed by property owners, but protected species should not be collected. Enough of the less plentiful species should be left to ensure next year's supply. Plants should not, of course, be collected from areas that have been sprayed with chemicals.

BEFORE-DINNER BEVERAGES

Milkweed Blossom Drink (Summer)
Gather the fresh fully-opened flowers of the common milkweed (*Asclepias syriaca*) after the dew has dried. Rinse clusters in water but not long enough to dilute nectar and fragrance.

> 25 to 30 flower heads
> 1/2 cup lemon juice
> 2 cups water

Put water and lemon juice in blender and liquefy. Drop one or two heads in at a time until all are thoroughly puréed. Heat purée for five minutes at low boil. Strain and press out all juice through paper toweling in a sieve. Add 1/2 cup of sugar and enough water to the extract to make 1/2 gallon. Chill.

Milkweed Blossom Punch (Summer)
To stimulate the appetite even further, add 1 pt. dry vermouth and 1 qt. of pink wine to a punch bowl before adding chilled Milkweed blossom drink. Decorate with fresh Milkweed flower heads, and to add sparkle, consider freezing some fresh Milkweed flower heads in a cake of ice.

Oxalis Lemonade (Spring-Fall)

> 2 lbs. Oxalis leaves
> 4 cups water
> 1 cup sugar
> 1/4 tsp. peppermint extract

Boil 5 minutes, then strain and press out liquid. Dissolve 4 tbsp. of unflavored gelatin in liquid. Add sugar and peppermint extract. Stir and serve chilled. Makes 1/2 gallon.

Beers:
Burdock, Common
Root ale. Boil 1 oz. dried burdock and 1 oz. ginger root in water. Strain, add sugar and yeast. Allow to work 12 hours at room temperature.
Dandelion, Common
Boil blossoms in water, strain, add brown sugar, lemon juice, ginger, and yeast. Allow to work 12 hours.

Wines:

(Never use metal containers; stir daily during fermentation. Age 6 months to 1 year for best flavor.)

Clover, Red

Boil flower heads in water; cool and strain. Add sugar, lemon juice, orange juice, yeast. Ferment 1 week, then bottle, leaving cork loose for 1 week.

Coltsfoot

Boil dried flowers in water. Strain and cool, then add sugar and yeast and cut-up oranges and lemons. Let stand 3 months, bottle.

Daisy

Let flowers stand overnight in water, then boil. Strain, cool, add sliced lemons, oranges, raisins, sugar, and yeast. Cover crock with cloth, ferment 3 weeks, bottle.

Marsh Marigold

Pour boiling water over blossoms; add sugar, grated orange and lemon rind; strain, cool, and add yeast; after 1 week, skim, add an equal amount of brandy and bottle.

SOUPS

Cattail Stalk Soup (Spring-Summer)

Pull Cattail stalks (*Typha latifolia*) from the roots found in any pond. Cut off roots at the base and discard. Cut off and discard the top of the stalk about 18 inches from the base. Wash thoroughly and peel off brown or damaged leaf scales. Cut stalks into 1/2-inch lengths — the smaller, the better. About 25 to 30 stalks will make 1/2 gallon of soup stock. Put half of the cut stalks in a large kettle with 6 cups of water. Boil for 30 minutes. Put portions of the boiled stalks in a blender and liquefy until reduced to a pulp. Strain and squeeze out all liquid from the remaining pulp. Return liquid to the kettle and add a second batch of stalks, with 2 cups of water, and repeat the process. Strain resulting extract through paper toweling in a sieve. If necessary, add water to make 1/2 gallon.

> 2 cups Cattail extract
> 1 cup chicken broth with diced chicken
> 1 tsp. minced wild onion or leeks
> 1 tsp. soy sauce
> 1 tsp. sassafras file (finely powdered leaves)
> 1/2 cup quick rice
> Salt and pepper to taste

Prepare rice and add to soup just before removing from heat.

Clover Blossom Bouillon (Summer)

Gather the fresh flowering tops of Red Clover (*Trifolium pratense*) in full bloom, choosing flowers with leafy tips. Dry in shade and cover from the dew at night. Cover 1/2 lb. of dried Clover tops with 2 qts. of water in a large kettle and simmer for 20 minutes. Press off the liquid through paper toweling in sieve. This should give about 3 qts. of extract. Then add:

> 2 tbsp. Worcestershire sauce
> 16 beef bouillon cubes
> 2 envelopes gelatin, dissolved in a little water

Add enough water to make 1 gallon; heat, and serve hot.

SALADS

Winter Cress and Dock (Spring)
Gather equal quantities of tender leafy tips of Winter Cress and Curled Dock. Wash and cut or tear into small pieces. Add finely chopped onion. Mix and serve with an oil and vinegar dressing and, if desired, with wild-herb flavoring. If desired, the leaves may be wilted with bacon grease and served with crumbled bacon and hard-boiled eggs, chopped or sliced. Serve with an herb vinegar or vinegar and oil dressing.

Day-Lily Gelatin (Summer)
Ingredients of Day-Lily extract:
> 35 to 40 fresh flowers
> 1/4 cup lemon juice
> 1/2 cup water

Liquefy in blender and press out liquid through paper toweling in sieve. Dissolve a 6-oz. package of lemon gelatin in 2 cups of boiling water. Add 1 cup of the Day-Lily extract and 1 cup of cold water. Chill in refrigerator to set.

MAIN COURSE

Milkweed Loaf (Early Summer)
Gather tender leafy tips and young flower buds of common Milkweed. Cut young Milkweed tops into 1-inch pieces. Boil for 20 minutes. Drain and purée in blender, adding just enough liquid to cover the material.

2 cups Milkweed top purée	1/4 tsp. pepper
1 cup corn meal	1/2 tsp. thyme
1/2 lb. ground beef	2 tsp. soy sauce
1/2 cup butter or margarine	1/2 cup tomato sauce or catsup
1/2 cup powdered milk	1/4 cup diced green pepper
1/2 cup minced onion	1/4 tsp. garlic powder
1/2 tsp. salt	1/4 cup grated cheddar cheese

Sauté the ground beef and minced onion in butter. Add to the other ingredients and mix well. Form into a loaf or put into an appropriate baking dish, greased. Sprinkle top with grated cheese and bake in preheated oven at 400° for 30-40 minutes. Serves six.

Day-Lily and Macaroni (Summer)
> 50 fresh Day-Lily flowers cut into 1/2- to 1-inch pieces
> 1 medium-sized onion, finely chopped
> 1/4 cup mayonnaise or salad dressing
> 4 strips of bacon, fried crisp, drained, and crumbled
> 2 tsp. lemon juice
> 2 cups of macaroni, cooked and drained

Wash and chop flowers and mix with lemon juice. Prepare macaroni and set aside. Combine onion with mayonnaise in pan and sauté chopped Day-Lily and lemon mixture for a few minutes. Add bacon crumbles and mix in the macaroni. Sprinkle with paprika and garnish with parsley. Serve cold with strips of sharp cheddar cheese.

MUFFINS

Buckwheat Muffins (Fall)

Gather the vines of *Polygonum* spp. in the fall when seeds are ripe. Place in a plastic sack and flail with a stick until the seeds are separated. Lift off the straw as you shake. Winnow the seed in front of an electric fan until it is clean. Put through a coffee or flour mill, or a blender, and reduce to a fine flour. Use 1 cup Buckwheat flour and 1 cup whole wheat flour in basic recipe.

> 3 tsp. baking powder
> 1 tsp. salt
> 1 egg
> 3 tsp. oil
> 1 1/3 cups milk
> 1 cup Buckwheat flour
> 1 cup whole wheat flour

Mix the dry ingredients. Add milk, egg, and oil and mix until smooth. Bake.

Pokeberry Jelly (Late Summer-Fall)

Gather Pokeberry bunches in late summer. Strip berries from the stalks. Put into cloth bag and mash and squeeze out the pulp. Since the juice may irritate the skin, wear rubber gloves. Filter the pulp through paper toweling to get a clear jelly.

> 1/2 cup Pokeberry juice
> 1/2 cup water
> 1 1/2 cups apple juice
> 1/2 cup lemon juice
> 4 1/2 cups sugar
> 1 box "Sure Jel" or equivalent

Add "Sure Jel" to liquids and bring to heavy boil. Add sugar and continue boiling for 1 minute. Remove from heat and skim if necessary. Pour into prepared glasses and seal. Makes about 3 pints. (Note: Pokeberries are toxic if eaten fresh, especially when they contain the seeds, and so are uncooked Poke stalks and leaves.)

DESSERT

Wild-Ginger Pudding (Summer-Fall)

Gather the roots of Wild Ginger in the late summer or fall. Wash and air dry until hard and brittle. Break into small pieces and put into blender or coffee grinder and reduce to powder. Store in air-tight jar.

> 1 tsp. powdered Wild Ginger root
> 6 cups milk
> 1/2 cup lemon juice
> 2 5-oz. packages of vanilla pudding mix

Add pudding mix to liquids. Bring to boil over medium heat, stirring constantly. Add Ginger powder and lemon juice. Continue stirring until mixture comes to a boil. The pudding will thicken on cooling. If a lemon-flavored pudding is used instead of vanilla and lemon juice, a thicker pudding will result.

AFTER-DINNER DRINK

Dandelion Wine (Late Spring)

> 1 gal. Dandelion flower heads
> 1 gal. boiling water
> 4 oranges, finely chopped
> 2 lemons, finely chopped
> 3 lbs. sugar
> 1 cinnamon stick
> 1 oz. yeast

Add flowers to a large crock of boiling water. Cover crock with cheesecloth and let stand for 3 days with occasional stirring. Remove the flowers, squeeze, dry, and discard. Pour remaining liquid into a large pot and add all other ingredients except yeast. Stir the mixture well, boil for 30 minutes and pour into a crock. When the mixture cools, crumble the yeast cake into it. Then cover the crock with cheesecloth and allow to ferment for 3 weeks. Before bottling, the wine should be strained through filter paper or a paper towel. It may be 6 months to a year before the wine loses its cloudy appearance and becomes a clear, golden fluid, but the wait is worthwhile.

Wild Edible Plants

The following wild plants, all of them described elsewhere, can help you develop your own special dishes. An effort has been made to avoid endangered species.

Note: Only the parts of the plants listed below are edible and only when properly prepared.

WILD SALADS

(Use tender young leaves and stems unless otherwise indicated.)

Brooklime, American. Good flavor
Burdock, Common. Tender shoots.
Butter-and-Eggs
Calamus (Sweetflag). Shoots.
Cattail, Common. Sprouts.
Chickweed, Star
Chicory. Leaves and spring roots.
Clintonia, White (Corn Lily)
Clover, Red, and White, White Sweet, and Yellow Sweet
Cress, Winter
Dandelion, Common
Dayflower, Asiatic
Day-Lily. Young crisp tubers; flowers.
Dock, Curled
Evening Primrose, Common
Fireweed
Garlic, Field and Wild
Ginger, Wild. Fresh roots.

Goatsbeard, Yellow. Roots and shoots.
Heal-all (Self-heal)
Indian Cucumber Root. Sliced roots.
Knapweed, Spotted
Leek, Wild
Lettuce, Wild
Mallow, Seashore. Roots boiled in sugar; also tender shoots.
Meadow Beauty
Monkey Flower, Square-stemmed
Mullein, Common. Flowers.
Mustard, Garlic
Onion, Wild. Leaves and bulbs.
Oxalis spp.
Parsnip, Cow
Pickerelweed
Solomon's Seal, Hairy and False. Young leaves and roots.
Spiderwort

Spring Beauty. Boiled tuberous roots; fresh young leaves.
Toadflax, Blue
Thistle, Bull and Canada. Shoots.

Toothwort, Common and Cut-leaved. Raw root.
Venus' Looking-glass
Violet, Birdsfoot. Leaves and flowers.
Waterleaf, Virginia

COOKED GREENS AND POTHERBS

(Use young leaves prepared like spinach unless otherwise indicated.)

Aster, White. Good when boiled with fish.
Beebalm (Oswego Tea)
Bedstraw. Shoots.-
Bergamot, Wild
Burdock, Common. Young leaves and peeled stalks.
Butterfly-Weed. Tender shoots.
Campion, Bladder
Cattail, Common. Peeled young shoots.
Celandine
Chickweed. Boiled.
Chicory
Clover, Red, and White, White Sweet and Yellow Sweet
Coltsfoot
Comfrey (Wild Hound's-tongue)
Cress, Winter. Change waters to remove bitterness.
Dandelion, Common. Boiled leaves good with fatty meats.
Dayflower, Asiatic
Dock, Curled. A superior spinach substitute.
Evening Primrose, Common. Shoots.
Fireweed. Shoots, cooked as asparagus

Geranium, Wild
Goatsbeard, Yellow
Indigo, Wild. Young shoots. Must be cooked.
Jewelweed (Spotted Touch-me-not). Stem prepared like green beans.
Lettuce, Blue and White
Loosestrife, Purple and Whorled. Leafy shoots.
Mallow, Seashore. Good potherb.
Marsh Marigold. Excellent spinach substitute.
Milkweed, Common. Shoots. Cook thoroughly, changing water.
Parsnip, Cow
Pea, Beach. Boiled sprouts.
Pokeweed
Pickerelweed
Saxifrage, Early
Skunk Cabbage. Boil in several waters.
Solomon's Seal, False and Hairy. Shoots.
Spiderwort
Spring Beauty
Thistle. Boil tender shoots and serve with cream sauce.
Waterleaf, Virginia. Shoots.

SOUPS AND STEWS

Bean, Wild. Beans dried and cooked.
Burdock, Common. Dried roots.
Campion, Bladder. Boiled young leaves.
Clover, Red, and Yellow Sweet. Leaves and seeds.
Coltsfoot. Young leaves.
Clintonia, White. Young leaves.
Day-Lily. Dried flowers are good thickeners.
Evening Primrose, Common. Boiled roots.

Fireweed. Gelatinous pith.
Groundnut. Boiled tubers.
Garlic, Wild. Underground bulbs.
Heal-all. Broth.
Indian Cucumber Root. Root.
Ironweed, New York. Young leaves.
Leek, Wild. Underground bulbs.
Mallow, Seashore. Leaves add body.
Onion, Wild. Leaves and underground bulbs.
Parsnip, Cow. Seeds.

Pea, Beach. Seeds.
Pickerelweed. Young leaves.
Queen Anne's Lace. Boiled roots and seeds.

Spring Beauty. Tubers.
Violet, Birdsfoot and Common Blue. Leaves for thickening.
Water Lily. Leaves and roasted seeds.

FLAVORING

Agrimony. Stems and flowers used for flavoring beer.
Avens, Purple, and White. Roots used to flavor beer, ale, liquor. Purple Avens also used as cocoa substitute.
Cicely, Sweet. Use leaves to flavor potatoes.
Clover, Yellow Sweet. Leaves impart vanilla flavor to cookies and puddings.
Coltsfoot. Use leaves and flowers to flavor cough drops.
Garlic. Flavor soups and meats, particularly mutton.
Ginger, Wild. Root used to flavor fruit, chicken, pastries and beverages.
Lily, Tiger. Use fresh or dried buds to flavor chicken or duck soup.
Meadow Rue. Leaves used to flavor brown bread, gravy and stews.
Meadowsweet. To flavor soup.

Mint. Leaves used to flavor salads, potatoes, peas, beans, and beverages.
Motherwort. Flowering tops used to flavor saki and other alcoholic beverages.
Onion, Wild. Salads, soups, meats.
Sage. Good to flavor turkey, ham, and cottage cheese.
Goatsbeard (Salsify). Cook buds with omelets.
Sunflower, Common. Boil seeds in water, strain and use to flavor brandy or gin.
Tansy, Common. Young leaves and flowers for flavoring fish, meat, cookies, cakes, puddings, and as substitute for sage.
Toothwort. Roots cooked with roast beef.
Thistle. Flower heads used to flavor punch.

BEVERAGES

(Non-alcoholic, serve chilled)

Avens, Purple. Root beer with a chocolate-like flavor.
Ginger, Wild. Add ginger, lemon juice, sugar, and yeast. Age 7 days to produce Ginger Pop.
Mayapple. Fruit juice; strain the seeds.
Meadowsweet. Dried herb infusion sweetened with honey.
Milkweed, Common. Juice from flowers.
Oxalis spp. Lemon-flavored drink.

Beers:
Burdock, Common. Root ale. See recipe section.
Dandelion, Common. Blossoms. See recipe section.

Wine:
Clover, Red. Flower heads. See recipe section.
Coltsfoot. Dried flowers. See recipe section.
Daisy. Flower heads. See recipe section.
Dandelion, Common. Flower heads. See recipe section.
Marsh Marigold. Blossoms. See recipe section.
Pokeberry. Use ripe fruit, sugar, yeast. Ferment 1 week and age.

Whisky:
Queen Anne's Lace. Roots are used to make "carrot whisky." First make a beer by boiling roots in water and adding sugar and yeast. Then distill.

Coffee Substitutes:
(The seeds or roots are roasted and ground and used as coffee or mixed with coffee.)

Chicory. Roots.

Dandelion. Roots.

Goatsbeard (Salsify). Roots.

Partridge Pea. Roots.

Sunflower, Common. Seeds.

WILD TEAS

Add 1 tsp. tea (use dried leaves unless otherwise indicated) per cup of water and 1 tsp. to the pot. Pour in boiling water, cover and let steep for 3 minutes. Stir and let steep for another minute, then serve. (Note: A non-metal pot is preferable.) Never boil tea. Some prefer to flavor with lemon, orange, or mint. Sweeten with honey.

Agrimony. A French peasant drink with apricot-like aroma.

Beebalm (Oswego Tea). Good China tea substitute; has a minty flavor.

Boneset. Used for diarrhea.

Bugleweed. This tea with mint flavor is said to have calming effect.

Burdock, Common. Use the dried roots or seeds.

Catnip. For colds, fever, insomnia.

Cinquefoil, Common. Used as gargle for sore throat.

Clover, Red. Use dried flower heads. Rich in iron.

Daisy, Ox-eye. Use dried flowers.

Fireweed. A favorite Russian peasant tea.

Heal-all (Self-heal). Used as gargle.

Mallow. Use dried flowers.

Mullein, Common. Use flowers and leaves, but must be strained.

Sage, Lyre-leaved. Use dried blossoms.

Strawberry, Wild. Potent diuretic. Use dried leaves.

Thistle, Bull and Canada. For fever.

Vervain, Blue. Nerve calming.

Yarrow. Use leaves and flowers; has a pleasant aroma.

Edible Parts of Plants

ROOTS

(Cook like vegetables unless otherwise indicated.)

Arrow Arum. Roasted.
Arrowhead. Roasted like potatoes.
Blazing-star, Dense
Bugleweed
Burdock, Common. Boiled in two
changes of water.
Colic Root
Cattail, Common. Raw, boiled or
roasted. Can be made into flour.
Chicory. Roasted; coffee substitute.
Cinquefoil, Common. Roasted.
Daisy, Ox-eye. Roasted.
Day-Lily
Dandelion, Common. Roasted and
ground, or boiled as vegetables.
Evening Primrose. Boiled.
Goatsbeard, Yellow
Golden Club. Repeated washings
necessary.
Groundnut. Potato substitute.

Leek, Wild
Onion, Wild
Parsnip, Cow. Tastes like celery when
boiled. High in protein.
Plantain, Water
Puccoon, Hairy
Queen Anne's Lace (Wild Carrot). Cook
like carrots.
Shooting Star. Roasted.
Skunk Cabbage. Roasted and ground
into flour.
Solomon's Seal, Hairy or False. Boiled
or baked; as potato substitutes or as a
bread.
Spring Beauty. Roasted.
Thistle, Bull and Canada
Toothwort. Raw or boiled.
Water Lily. Roasted with meat.
Woundwort

FLOWERS

Buttercup, Early. Pickled.
Cattail, Common. Use pollen as pancake
or muffin additive.
Chicory. Pickled; conserves.
Clover, White. Ground into meal.
Dandelion, Common. Buds, boiled or
pickled.
Day-Lily. Buds, fried in egg batter or
cooked with pork or chicken. Use
flowers in salads.

Marsh Marigold. Buds and fresh flowers.
Milkweed, Common. Buds, flowers.
Spiderwort. Candied.
Sunflower, Common. Buds, like
artichokes in taste.
Thistle, Bull and Canada. Use flower
heads to make punch.
Violet, Birdsfoot and Common Blue. Raw
in salads or candied.
Water Lily. Steam flowers with fish.

FRUIT AND PODS

Buckbean. Boil and rinse to remove
bitterness.
Butterfly-Weed. Cooked pods.
Cinquefoil, Common. Fruit.

Evening Primrose. Seed pods.
Honeysuckle, Japanese. Berries; also
delicious as syrup.
Honeysuckle, Trumpet. Berries.

Mayapple (Mandrake). Ripe fruit has lemon flavor, good in preserves.
Milkweed, Common. Pods; cook like green beans.
Pea, Beach. Young pods or peas; boil in salted water.
Solomon's Seal, False. Berries.
Strawberry, Wild. Fruit.
Trefoil, Birdsfoot. Pods; cook like green beans.

SEEDS

Bedstraw. Roasted as coffee substitute.
Bean, Wild. Green or dried, but must be cooked.
Buttercup, Early. Parched and ground into meal.
Cohosh, Blue. Boiled or roasted as coffee substitute.
Evening Primrose, Common. Ground into meal.
Flax. Roasted, or cooked with other foods.
Goldenrod. Seeds of many Solidago species eaten by Indians.
Golden Club. Dry and boil repeatedly.
Lupine, Wild. Must be boiled like domestic peas.
Mustard, Garlic
Pea, Beach. Roasted; coffee substitute.
Pickerelweed. Used in cereals and breads.
Pussytoes, Field
Sage, Lyre-leaved. Ground into flour.
Smartweed. Seeds substituted for buckwheat; used in pancakes.
Sunflower. Raw or roasted.
Velvet Leaf
Water Lily spp. Roasted or popped.
Winter Cress

Poisonous Plants

Baneberry, White. Its toxic essential oil causes severe gastrointestinal upset.
Bleeding Heart. Contains poisonous alkaloid.
Bloodroot. Contains poisonous poppy alkaloids.
Blue Flag Iris. Leaves and rhizomes cause severe digestive upset. Do not confuse with Sweetflag or Cattail.
Devil's-bit. Foliage causes vomiting and dizziness.
Dutchman's Breeches. Contains an alkaloid causing convulsions.
Flypoison. Bulbs and foliage very poisonous. Do not touch.
Hellebore, False or White Hellebore. Leaves particularly poisonous.
Hemlock, Poison. Leaves and seeds contain extremely toxic alkaloid. Foliage resembles the Wild Carrot; be careful!
Hemlock, Water. The most poisonous plant in North America. The roots look and smell like parsnips.
Jimsonweed. Contains powerful narcotic. Beware!
Larkspur. Contains poisonous alkaloids.
Lobelia spp. Contains poisonous alkaloids.
Monkshood. Contains poisonous alkaloids.
Nettle, Horse. All parts contain toxic solanine.
Nightshade, Bittersweet. All parts contain solanine, a powerful toxic agent.
Parsley, Fool's. Has poisoned persons who mistook it for parsley.

Potentially Poisonous Plants

Black-eyed Susan. Not recommended; some species of Rudbeckia have produced toxicity in domestic animals.
Buttercup spp. Root is very purgative. Tender shoots must be cooked.
Butterfly-Weed. Root is very purgative. Tender shoots must be cooked.
Calla, Wild. Contains oxalate crystals when fresh.
Campion, Bladder. Must be cooked.
Celandine. Sap causes severe irritation to digestive tract if ingested raw; but Chinese have eaten the cooked leaves for centuries.
Dogbane, Spreading. Contains bitter toxic glycosides.
Golden Club. Rootstock and seeds require repeated boilings to remove toxic substances.
Indigo, Wild. Must be cooked. Raw Baptisia contains poisonous principles.
Jewelweed (Spotted Touch-me-not). Must be cooked.
Jack-in-the-Pulpit (Indian Turnip). Requires repeated boilings to remove oxalate crystals which penetrate mouth and tongue and cause intense burning.
Lupine, Wild. Leaves and seeds contain a poison and must be cooked.
Marsh Marigold. Must be cooked.
Mayapple (Mandrake). Only ripe fruit is edible; the roots and leaves are poisonous.
Milkweed, Common. Must be cooked.
Pea, Beach. Must be cooked.

Plantain, Water. Contains an acrid resin; must be cooked.

Pokeweed. Mature stem and roots are poisonous, but berries less so. Greens and berries are edible if cooked.

Queen Anne's Lace (Wild Carrot). Mildly toxic; must be cooked.

Skunk Cabbage. Must be cooked several times.

Snakeroot, White. Milk from cows feeding on this plant can cause poisoning called "milksickness."

Soapwort. Contains toxic saponins.

Spurge, Flowering. Sap can burn the skin; it poisons livestock.

St. Johnswort. Contains a heat-resistant principle causing photosensitization.

Trefoil, Birdsfoot. Uncooked leaves in salads not recommended.

Trout Lily. Raw bulb not recommended.

Select Bibliography

Barton, J.G.
1963, *Wild Flowers*, Spring Books, London.
Blanchan, Neltje
1901, *Nature's Garden*, Doubleday, Page & Co., New York.
Campbell, C.C., W. Hutton, H. Macon & A. Sharp
1964, *Great Smokey Mountains Wildflowers*, University of Tennessee Press, Memphis.
Crowhurst, Adrienne
1973, *The Flower Cookbook*, Lancer Books, New York.
1972, *The Weed Cookbook*, Lancer Books, New York.
Dana, Mrs. William Starr
1963, *How to Know the Wildflowers*, revised edition, Dover Publishing Co., New York.
Friend, Rev. Hilderic
1883, *Flowers and Flower Lore*, George Allen & Co., London.
Gibbons, Euell
1966, *Stalking the Healthful Herbs*, David McKay Co., New York.
1964, *Stalking the Wild Asparagus*, David McKay Co., New York.
Gottscho, Samuel
1951, *The Pocket Guide to Wildflowers*, Pocket Books, Inc., New York.
Grimm, William C.
1968, *How To Recognize Flowering Wild Plants*, Castle Books, New York.
Hatfield, Audrey W.
1971, *How to Enjoy Your Wildflowers*, Collier Books, New York.
Hinds, Harold and Wilfred Hathaway
1953, *Wildflowers of Cape Cod*, The Chatham Press, Chatham, Massachusetts.
Justice, William S. and C. Richie Bell
1968, *Wildflowers of North Carolina*, University of North Carolina Press, Chapel Hill.

Klein, Isabelle H.
1970, *Wildflowers of Ohio and Adjacent States*, Cleveland Museum of Natural History, Cleveland.
Leighton, Ann
1970, *Early American Gardens*, Houghton Mifflin Co., Boston.
Moldenke, Harold
1949, *American Wild Flowers*, D. Van Nostrand Co., New York.
Montgomery, F.H.
1962, *Native Wild Plants of Northwestern United States and Eastern Canada*, Frederick Warne & Co., New York.
Newcomb, Lawrence
1963, *Pocket Key to Common Wild Flowers*, The New England Wild Flower Preservation Society, Framingham, Massachusetts.
Peterson, Roger T. and Margaret McKenny
1968, *A Field Guide to Wild Flowers*, Houghton Mifflin Co., Boston.
Rickett, Harold W.
1966, *Wild Flowers of the United States: The Northeastern States*, 2 volumes, McGraw-Hill Book Co., New York.
1963, *The New Field Book of American Wild Flowers*, G.P. Putnam's Sons, New York.
1953, *Wild Flowers of America*, Crown Publishers, Inc., New York.
Stupka, Arthur
1965, *Wildflowers in Color*, Harper & Row Publishers, New York.
Thomas, Mai
1965, *Grannies' Remedies*, Gramercy Publishing Co., New York.
Weiner, Michael
1972, *Earth Medicine—Earth Foods*, The Macmillan Co., New York.
Wherry, Edgar T.
1948, *Wild Flower Guide: Northeastern and Midland United States*, Doubleday & Co., New York.

Index of Common Names

Index of Scientific Names

pratense, 86, **175**
venosum, 87
Houstonia, spp., 117, **247**
Hybanthus concolor, 31, **8**
Hydrastis canadensis, 31, **9**
Hydrophyllum
  appendiculatum, 52
  canadense, 52
  macrophyllum, 52
  virginianum, 52, **73**
Hypericum perforatum, 84, **164**
Hypoxis hirsuta, 78, **142**

I

Impatiens
  capensis, 76, **136**
  pallida, 76
Inula helenium, 80, **151**
Ipomoea
  hederacea, 124, **266**
  lacunosa, 124
  purpurea, 124
Iris
  cristata, 112
  prismatica, 112
  pseudacorus, 81, **155**
  verna, 114
  versicolor, 112, **233**
  virginica, 112
Isotria
  medeoloides, 68
  verticillata, 68, **109**

J

Jeffersonia diphylla, 36
Justica americana, 121, **259**

K

Kosteletzkya virginica, 102, **214**

L

Lactuca
  biennis, 131
  canadensis, 85, **170**
  floridana, 131, **282**
  puchella, 131
Lathyrus
  japonicus, 118, **250**
  latifolius, 119
  palustris, 118
Leontodon autumnalis, 72

Leonurus cardiaca, 134, **291**
Lespedeza, spp., 133, **289**
Liatris spicata, 101, **209**
Lilium
  canadense, 74, **129**
  grayi, 74
  michauxii, 73
  philadelphicum, 74, **128**
  superbum, 73, **127**
  tigrinum, 74
Linaria
  canadensis, 117, **245**
  vulgaris, 84, **166**
Dinum usitatissimum, 129, **278**
Liparis
  lilifolia, 128, **276**
  loeselii, 44, **46**
Listeria
  australis, 129
  cordata, 129
Lithospermum
  canascens, 70
  croceum, 69, **114**
  incisum, 70
Lobelia
  cardinalis, 101, **210**
  elongata, 127
  inflata, 127
  kalmii, 128
  nuttallii, 128
  puberula, 127, **274**
  siphilitica, 135, **293**
  spicata, 127
Lonicera
  japonica, 36, **21**
  sempervirens, 68, **111**
Lotus corniculatus, 77, **140**
Lupinus perennis, 119, **253**
Lychnis
  alba, 31
  chalcedonica, 105, **222**
  flos-cuculi, 104, **217**
Lycopus virginicus, 47, **57**
Lysimachia
  ciliata, 83
  quadrifolia, 83, **162**
  terrestris, 83
Lythrum
  hyssopifolia, 123
  lineare, 123
  salicaria, 122, **262**
  virgatum, 123

M

Maianthemum canadense, 42, **39**

Malva moschata, 103
Medeola virginiana, 54, **77**
Melilotus
  alba, 40, **34**
  officinalis, 83, **163**
Melanthium virginicum, 44
Mertensia
  maritima, 114
  virginica, 114, **239**
Mimulus
  alatus, 129
  ringens, 129, **277**
Mitchella repens, 54, **78**
Mitella
  diphylla, 34
  nuda, 34
Monarda
  didyma, 104, **218**
  fistulosa, 104, **219**
  punctata, 76, **135**
Monotropa
  hypopithys, 141, **304**
  odorata, 141
  uniflora, 59, **93**
Myosotis
  arvensis, 113
  laxa, 113
  scorpioides, 113, **235**

N

Nepeta cataria, 42, **40**
Nuphar
  advena, 81
  microphyllum, 81
  sagittifolium, 81
  variegatum, 81, **153**
Nymphaea
  odorata, 58, **89**
  tuberosa, 58

O

Obolaria virginica, 34, **17**
Oenothera
  biennis, 85, **169**
  fruticosa, 85
Orchis spectabalis, 99, **202**
Orobanche uniflora, 36, **20**
Orontium aquaticum, 68, **110**
Osmorhiza
  claytoni, 55, **80**
  longstylis, 55
Oxalis
  corniculata, 78
  grandis, 78
  montana, 62, **101**
  stricta, 78, **144**

Stenanthium gramineum, 44, **47**
Strophostyles
  helvola, 106
  umbellata, 106, **225**
Stylophorum diphyllum, 71, **118**
Symplocarpus foetidus, 112, **234**

T

Taenidia interrima, 73
Tanacetum vulgare, 82, **158**
Taraxacum
  erythrospermum, 72
  officinale, 72, **122**
Thalictrum polygamum, 53, **74**
Tiarella cordifolia, 34, **16**
Tradescantia
  ohiensis, 120
  subaspera, 120
  virginiana, 120, **255**
Tragopogon
  porrifolius, 86
  pratensis, 86, **173**
Trichostema dichotomum, 120, **256**
Trientalis borealis, 61, **98**
Trifollium
  arvense, 99, **203**
  hybridiium, 98
  pratense, 98, **199**
  repens, 43, **45**

Trillium
  catesbaei, 29
  cernuum, 29
  cuneatum, 95
  erectum, 94, **189**
  flexipes, 29
  grandiflorum, 29, **2**
  luteum, 95
  nivale, 29
  pusillum, 29
  recurvatum, 95
  sessile, 95
  undulatum, 29, **1**
Triphora trianthophora, 108, **232**
Tussilago farfara, 71, **121**
Typha
  angustifolia, 140, **301**
  latifolia, 140

U

Urtica dioica, 47
Utricularia, spp., 81, **154**
Uvularia
  grandiflora, 70
  perfoliata, 70
  sessilifolia, 70, **116**

V

Veratrum viride, 45, **49**
Verbascum
  blattaria, 85, **168**
  thapsus, 82, **160**

Verbena
  hastata, 121, **260**
  simplex, 122
  stricta, 122
  urticifolia, 122
Vernonia
  altissima, 126
  noveboracensis, 125, **269**
Veronica filiformis, 117, **248**
Veronicastrum virginicum, 39, **30**
Vicia
  americana, 119
  cracca, 119, **251**
  sativa, 119
  villosa, 119
Viola
  conspersa, 118
  lanceolata, 30, **6**
  papilionaceae, 118, **249**
  pedata, 117, **246**
  pensylvanica, 69
  pubescens, 69
  rostrata, 118
  rotundifolia, 69, **112**
  striata, 31
  tripartita, 69

Z

Zizia
  aptera, 73
  aurea, 72, **124**

Credits

All photographs are by John E. Klimas, except where otherwise noted.

1, George Zepko; 2, Les Line; 4, Ken Lewis; 5, Ed Degginger; 6, John Lynch; 7, Harry Boulet; 8, Ellwood Carr; 9, Ken Lewis; 11, Edo Streekmann; 12, Harry Boulet; 13, Shenandoah Nat'l Park; 14, James Cunningham; 16, Harry Boulet; 17, 18, Charles Johnson; 20, Robert McIlvin; 21, Jean Buermeyer; 22, Les Line; 23, James Cunningham; 24, Bernard Horne; 25, Harry Boulet; 26, Les Line; 27, 28, 29, Bernard Horne; 31, Charles Johnson; 32, John Lynch; 34, James Cunningham; 35, Shenandoah Nat'l Park; 36, Edo Streekmann; 37, John Lynch; 39, James Cunningham; 42, Ruth Allen; 45, Edo Streekmann; 46, Bernard Horne; 47, John Lynch; 49, Ken Lewis; 50, 52, 54, John Lynch; 55, 56, 57, Edo Streekmann; 59, George Elbert; 60, Edo Streekmann; 64, Charles Johnson; 71, Les Line; 73, Ken Lewis; 76, Bernard Horne; 77, James Cunningham; 78, 79, Shenandoah Nat'l Park; 80, James Cunningham; 81, Harry Boulet; 83, Edo Streekmann, 84, James Cunningham; 86, Les Line; 87, Charles Johnson; 88, John Lynch; 89, Jack Dermid; 90, Ed Degginger; 91, Elwood Carr; 93, Harry Boulet; 94, Bernard Horne; 95, 96, Harry Boulet; 101, Jean Buermeyer; 102, Edo Streekmann, 103, Harry Boulet; 104, Bernard Horne; 106, Charles Johnson; 108, Jack Dermid; 109, Bernard Horne; 110, Jack Dermid; 113, Bernard Horne; 114, Les Line; 115, Werner Schulz; 116, Shenandoah Nat'l Park; 117, James Cunningham; 118, John Lynch; 119, Jean Buermeyer; 120, George Elbert; 121, Ed Degginger; 122, Jack Dermid; 123, 124, Shenandoah Nat'l Park; 125, James Cunningham; 126, George Elbert; 127, Ed Degginger; 130, Harry Boulet; 131, Jean Buermeyer; 133, 134, Harry Boulet; 135, James Carmichael; 136, Dorothy Richards; 137, Harry Boulet; 138, Werner Schulz; 139, 140, 141, 146, Edo Streekmann; 147, Les Line; 150, Charles Johnson; 151, Bernard Horne; 152, Edo Streekmann, 153, Bernard Horne; 154, Jack Dermid; 155, Bernard Horne; 156, Harry Boulet; 158, James Cunningham; 159, Bernard Horne; 160, Ken Lewis; 161, James Cunningham; 164, Les Line; 165, Bernard Horne; 166, Les Line; 167, Ed Degginger; 168, James Cunningham; 169, Harry Boulet; 171, Dorothy Richards; 172, Bernard Horne; 173, Les Line; 174, John Lynch; 176, Dorothy Richards; 177, Charles Johnson; 178, Herbert Haas; 179, Harry Boulet; 180, Bernard Horne; 181, Charles Johnson; 182, Werner Schulz; 184, Shenandoah Nat'l Park; 185, Harry Boulet; 186, James Cunningham; 187, Harry Boulet; 188, Edo Streekmann; 190, 192, Harry Boulet; 193, Evelyn Appel; 194, John Lynch; 197, Les Line; 199, Edo Streekmann; 200, John Lynch; 201, Harry Boulet; 202, Bernard Horne; 205, Shenandoah Nat'l Park; 206, 207, 208, Les Line; 209, John Lynch; 210, Les Line; 212, Charles Johnson; 213, 214, Ed Degginger; 215, Harry Boulet; 216, Charles Johnson; 217, Jean Buermeyer; 218, Ken Lewis; 219, George Elbert; 220, Shenandoah Nat'l Park; 221, Charles Johnson; 222, Les Line; 224, Robert McIlvin; 225, Charles Johnson; 226, 228, Les Line; 229, Charles Johnson; 230, Ruth Allen; 231, Edo Streekmann; 232, Dorothy Richards; 233, Ellwood Carr; 234, George Zepko; 235, Bernard Horne; 236, Harry Boulet; 237, Shenandoah Nat'l Park; 238, Bernard Horne; 239, Dorothy Richards; 240, Harry Boulet; 241, Les Line; 242, Charles Johnson; 243, George Elbert; 244, 245, Charles Johnson; 246, Shenandoah Nat'l Park; 247, Les Line; 249, James Cunningham; 251, Harry Boulet; 252, John Lynch; 253, Charles Johnson; 254, Bernard

Horne; 255, John Lynch; 256, Vinton Richard; 258, 259, Charles Johnson; 261, Jean Buermeyer; 262, James Cunningham; 264, Ed Degginger; 265, Harry Boulet; 266, Charles Johnson; 267, Les Line; 268, Charles Johnson; 269, Shenandoah Nat'l Park; 270, 272, Les Line; 273, Ed Degginger; 274, Harry Boulet; 275, Charles Johnson; 278, James Cunningham; 279, John Lynch; 281, Jack Dermid; 282, Charles Johnson; 284, John Lynch; 286, Bernard Horne; 287, James Cunningham; 288, Evelyn Appel; 290, James Cunningham; 293, Les Line; 294, Charles Johnson; 295, Ken Lewis; 296, Charles Johnson; 297, Bernard Horne; 298, Harry Boulet; 299, Charles Johnson; 300, Ellwood Carr; 301, Ed Degginger; 302, Dorothy Richards; 303, Ellwood Carr; 304, Harry Boulet.

All drawings of flower parts and types of leaves were supplied by Rachel Speiser, former illustrator for the New York Botanical Garden.

Symbols for chapter openings were drawn by Irva Mandelbaum.

This book was planned and produced by Chanticleer Press, Inc., New York
Publisher: Paul Steiner
Editor: Milton Rugoff
Managing Editor: Gudrun Buettner
Associate Editor: Celeste Targum
Art Director: Carol Nehring
Color Layout: Laurie McBarnette
Production: Helga Lose, Anne Duke
Printed by Kingsport Press, Kingsport, Tennessee